WOMEN TRAVEL
COLONIAL I

WOMEN TRAVELLERS IN COLONIAL INDIA

THE POWER OF THE FEMALE GAZE

Indira Ghose

OXFORD
UNIVERSITY PRESS

OXFORD
UNIVERSITY PRESS

YMCA Library Building, Jai Singh Road, New Delhi 110 001

Oxford University Press is a department of the University of Oxford. It furthers the University's objective of excellence in research, scholarship, and education by publishing worldwide in

Oxford New York

Athens Auckland Bangkok Bogota Buenos Aires Calcutta Cape Town Chennai Dar es Salaam Delhi Florence Hong Kong Istanbul Karachi Kuala Lumpur Madrid Melbourne Mexico City Mumbai Nairobi Paris Sao Paulo Shanghai Singapore Taipei Tokyo Toronto Warsaw

with associated companies in Berlin Ibadan

Oxford is a registered trade mark of Oxford University Press in the UK and in certain other countries

Published in India
By Oxford University Press, New Delhi

First published 1998
Second impression 1999
Oxford India Paperbacks 2000

ISBN 019 565 4552

Typeset by Images, Chennai 600 018
Printed by Wadhwa International, New Delhi 110 020
Published by Manzar Khan, Oxford University Press
YMCA Library Building, Jai Singh Road, New Delhi 110 001

For Walter, without whom

Contents

Acknowledgements

My greatest debt of gratitude goes to Manfred Pfister, whose unfailing interest and enthusiasm has supported this project from the very start. I am grateful for the comments and criticism of John MacKenzie, whose work first introduced me to this exciting field. I am also grateful for the encouragement and advice by Tim Youngs, Nigel Leask, and Reina Lewis, all of whose work I have eagerly drawn upon. Richard Bingle has always been a source of support. I owe a special debt to Sara Mills, not only for her inspirational work but also for the help and hospitality she so generously imparted. I am greatly indebted to the work of Robert Young and am grateful for his helpful hints at a later stage. Lastly, my thanks to my editor, Anita Roy, who has encouraged this project from the the moment we met, and whom I chased around half the world to find. The flaws in this work remain, of course, mine alone.

I am extremely thankful to the Senate of Berlin for supporting my research by means of their women's research grants. I also wish to thank the staffs of the British Library and the India Office Library for their help and cooperation. Last of all, I wish to express my gratitude to Henry and Elli Adler and Alex Purucker for making my stay in London such a warm one.

Introduction

A woman traveller in India in the nineteenth century once asked of another lady what she had seen of the country and its inhabitants since she had been in India. 'Oh, nothing!' the lady answered, 'Thank goodness, I know nothing at all about them, nor do I wish to: really I think the less one sees and knows of them the better!'[1]

To be sure, not all women who travelled to India were like this—on the contrary, the women travellers I set out to describe were quite different, filled with curiosity about the country they visited. Their texts have now been forgotten, gathering dust in some antiquarian bookshop. I hope to rekindle interest in these neglected texts, however, not only to help displace the stereotype of the memsahib, which still enjoys widespread circulation, but to draw attention to the contribution these women travellers have made to the genre of travel writing.

The trope I have chosen to focus on, in my study of women travellers, is that of the female gaze. Did women travellers perceive Indian differently from men? This question is bound up with the vexed issue of whether women are intrinsically different to men and has implications for related fields such as the debate on women's role in colonialism. I hope to contribute to these debates by focusing on the genre of travel writing and on one specific geographical area. Colonial India works, as it were, as a burning glass to bring the larger issues at stake into focus.

This involves a fresh look at women's travel writing. It is surely no accident that gender and genre stem from the same root,[2] for generic conventions have always been inflected by concepts of gender. This is particulary true for travel writing, which remain~d a firmly male-dominated preserve until the nineteenth century. Although women have written accounts of their travels as early as the Middle Ages,[3] the genre as a whole has remained largely in the hands of male writers and has sustained its connotations of male adventure, exploration and escape.

In literary criticism travel writing has been marginalized until very recently, studies focusing mainly on texts produced by famous authors and the implications of their travel writing for their oeuvre. However, as Susan Bassnett has pointed out, 'one of the most significant developments of more recent comparative literary study involves a change in our readings of accounts of journeys, of the diaries, letters, translations and tales told by travellers.' [4] Criticism of travel writing has traditionally fallen prey to the mimetic fallacy: travel writing was seen as a transparent reflection of the reality of other cultures. Michel Foucault's notion of discourse, however, has exploded the opposition between truth and fiction and the rigid categories of genre. The truth claims of travel writing are increasingly being exposed as rhetorical strategy — the 'other' produced by travel writing is increasingly being seen as a textual construction, an interpretation and not a reflection of reality. An important role in these constructs of reality is played by an intertextual exchange between texts. Thus travel writing serves to circulate stereotypes and images of the other and actively participates in the production of knowledge and the dissemination of the effects of power. Finally, recent critics have pointed to the fact that travel writing about the other really serves as a mirror held up to the self.

Travel writings are also often tapped as a source in historiography. In this field, too, the opposition between historical texts and literary texts, between truth and fiction, has been deconstructed by critics like Hayden White.[5] White, who has scrutinized the textuality of historical writings, has pointed out the rhetorical techniques at work in these texts:

> ...no given set of casually recorded historical events in themselves constitute a story, the most that they offer to the historian are story *elements*. The events are *made* into a story by the suppression or subordination of certain of them and the highlighting of others, by characterization, motific repetition, variation of tone and point of view, alternative descriptive strategies, and the like—in short, all of the techniques that we would normally expect to find in the emplotment of a novel or a play.[6]

In other words, historiography draws on the very devices literary texts employ to emplot historical events into meaningful narrative.

But independent of the work of deconstructionist critics, traditional critics of travel writing have long hinted at the brittleness of the truth/fiction opposition. Percy Adams has devoted a study to 'travel liars'[7] and has traced the cross-fertilization between the genres of the novel and of travel literature.[8] He rejects efforts to define travel writing and compartmentalize it: 'The literature of travel is gigantic; it has a thousand forms and faces'.[9] In fact, the very amorphousness of the genre cooperates in the poststructuralist project of dissolving the boundaries of genre.

In recent studies of travel writing, the focus has shifted to the textuality of travel writing as well as its enmeshment in power relations—to the poetics as well as the politics of travel writing. Edward Said's radical critique of Western discourse on the Orient included travel literature in its broad sweep.[10] Other analyses of travel writing such as those by Rana Kabbani,[11] Mary Louise Pratt[12] and Tim Youngs[13] have demonstrated how the 'other' constructed in travel writing has not only played a role in the consolidation of colonialism but has also simultaneously served to stabilize the Western constitution of 'self'.

Criticism on Women Travellers

Unfortunately, research on women travellers remains largely uncontaminated by poststructuralist theory. While women travellers have become the focus of a tremendous upsurge in interest, thanks to the popularity of women's studies, work on women travellers tends to wallow in the anecdotal and to concentrate on constructing a myth of the intrepid, autonomous heroine braving all odds in the wilds. Travel writings are read as adventure tales. While the emancipatory function of travel for women is rightly stressed, in the case of female writers all critical faculties, so acutely deployed in the analysis of men's texts, are, it seems, suspended, and critics obediently read along with the text instead of reading it against the grain. The historical context and the relations of power that the traveller is bound up in, are conveniently elided.

More worrying still, studies of Western women's position in colonialism tend to fall back on a notion of 'the white woman's burden' in their attempts to revalorize women's roles in empire. While an effort to question the stereotype of the memsahib bandied about in masculinist colonial fiction and historiography is wholly justified, surely conclusions like 'They had a duty to do and they did it to the best of their abilities'[14] are not helpful in analysing women's collusion in exploitative structures of power. Instead, what needs to be looked at in more depth is how notions of gender were bound up with hegemonic ideologies, and how women were both made an instrument of, and were complicitous with, the politics of imperialism. Elizabeth Fox-Genovese points to 'the indispensable contributions of women to collective life in society, including class and racial dominance'.[15] If women's long history of oppression has anything to teach us today, 'it must be that we must uncover the history of women in all its tragic complexity'.[16]

An exception in this respect is the path-breaking work of Sara Mills on women travellers. Adopting a Foucauldian framework, Mills uncovers the intersection of a variety of discourses, such as those of colonialism and of femininity, in the construction of the personae of these travellers.[17] In her later work Mills focuses on the way concepts of gender are bound up with colonialist ideology[18] and on the collusion of women travellers in the politics of knowledge-production.[19] It is at the crossroads of feminist theory and colonial discourse theory, where Mills' work is located, that I wish to position my study of nineteenth-century women travellers in India.

For, as post-colonial feminist critics have pointed out, the myth of an independent, individualistic Western heroine is predicated on a construction of other women as a homogeneous and oppressed mass.[20] In her deconstruction of Charlotte Bronte's *Jane Eyre,* an iconic text of Western feminism, Gayatri Chakravorty Spivak displaces the centre-margins dichotomy of the text to focus on the colonial other, the madwoman in the attic (who, as one tends to forget, is a Jamaican Creole):

> In this fictive England, she must play out her role, act out the transformation of her 'self' into that fictive Other, set fire to the house and kill herself, so that Jane Eyre can become the feminist individualist heroine of British fiction. I must read this as an allegory of the general epistemic violence of imperialism, the construction of a self-immolating colonial subject for the glorification of the social mission of the colonizer.[21]

It is my contention that celebratory feminist criticism is ultimately only a variation of traditional, liberal humanist, literary criticism. By focusing on gender to the exclusion of all other determinants of subjectivity, such as race and class, these critics deny the fragmentation of identity and collude in humanism's eternal quest for unity. It is precisely liberal humanism, however, which, by positing a universal subject, has always worked to exclude women (as a form of the other) from its privileged discourses. Travel, in fact, serves as an ideal paradigm to study the intersection of different axes that construct identity: by locating Western women in other parts of the world, it points out the contradictory position of women as colonized by gender, but colonizers by race. By privileging gender and constructing woman as an ahistorical, transcendent category, critics only serve to confirm traditional male notions of woman as inherently different—more intuitive, etc. The interest at stake in this type of criticism is the self-presentation of the white, bourgeois, female individualist. And in an age when tourism has become a central tool of self-definition for the Western subject, the deflation of the myth of the woman traveller is too fraught with unpleasant implications to elicit much interest. It is in this spirit that critic Mary Russell performs the acrobatic feat of defending the women travellers Fanny Bullock Workman and May French Sheldon for thrashing their mutinous coolies, with the remark, 'It is only fair to point out that both these women took large parties of bearers with them—Sheldon had 130 porters—and their organizational problems must have been formidable.'[22]

The Female Gaze

The trope of the female gaze is bound up with the issue of women's writing and its difference from men's writing, one of the main concerns feminist literary criticism centres around. As various critics have made clear, it is in the best interests of feminism to align itself with poststructuralism and relinquish cherished notions of a female essence.[23] For a critic drawing on insights from poststructuralism, there can be, of course, no inherently 'female gaze'. Women are *'multiply organized* across positionalities along several axes and across mutually contradictory discourses'.[24] Further, the category of woman is itself a social and cultural construction. Even the notion of a separate woman's world is now rejected by the very anthropologists who supported this notion in their inquires into other cultures. Admitting that the 'two spheres' ideology shaped the framework of their earlier findings, M.Z.Rosaldo now sees women as always bound up in social relationships.[25] She calls for women to be understood in terms of relationships with men—as participating in creating social formations (that may well oppress women). Women, albeit marginalized, are nevertheless participants in the dominant culture.[26] Donna Haraway comes to a drastic conclusion: 'The feminist dream of a common language, like all dreams for a perfectly true language, of a perfectly faithful naming of the experience, is a totalizing and imperialist one.'[27] Feminist literary critics should not expend their effort in unearthing an authentic women's voice, but instead scrutinize the strategies of subversion of dominant discourses that women writers have employed.[28] Similarly, however seductive the notions of woman's different relationship to vision are—such as French feminist critics' assertions of women privileging the sense of touch over that of vision—these notions are ultimately tied up with an essentialist concept of womanhood that leads women straight back to where we started off—to the idea of woman's inherent difference.

Epistemological Assumptions of the Gaze

The crux of the issue of travel writing seems to me to be the question: how do we constitute the other?[29] Two seemingly contradictory forms of constructing the other are generally seen in operation: the construction of the other as negation of the self, as completely other[30]—or the assimilation of the other as same (but lacking). For, as Wlad Godzich has noted, 'it is ideologically inconceivable that there should exist an otherness of the same ontological status as the same, without there being immediately mounted an effort at its appropriation'.[31] In the colonial context this is described in psychoanalytic terms by Homi Bhabha as either a form of paranoia, linked to aggression, or narcissism, a confirmation of the self through reflection in the other.[32] These reactions to the other are not as clean-cut as would appear, and are often to be found in the same situation—for Bhabha the very anxiety of colonialism is reflected in the oscillation of the imperial subject between both poles. What is common to both constructions of the other, however, is that they are moulded in the image of the self and serve the function of self-definition.[33]

This question of the epistemology of the other is closely bound up with ideas on vision as the fundamental act of cognition. These ideas stem from the Cartesian distinction between the subject and object of knowledge, the *res cogitans* and *res extensa*, and the privileging of vision in Lockean tenets.[34] Rationalist and empiricist thought postulate a transcendent viewer of reality—a concept to which such an enormous prestige has accrued that it has passed into the realm of common sense.[35] Indeed, as Johannes Fabian notes, 'the root metaphor of knowledge remains that of a difference, and a distance, between thing and image, reality and representation. Inevitably, this establishes and reinforces models of cognition stressing difference and distance between a beholder and an object.'[36]

Poststructuralist theories of cognition, on the other hand, postulate that reality is not given but is produced in discourses. These discourses shape perception. This would imply that reality is not reflected but is produced by modes of perception. And the texts produced by travellers do not simply reflect a pre-given reality, but create the world they purport to describe. Knowledge is not produced from a transcendent position at all, but is a product of social and 'sensuous interaction'.[37]

In addition, the politics of knowledge implies that the gaze is linked to a specific political agenda: it effaces itself from the situation of perception. This enables it both to distance itself from the object of observation and, as a 'technology of power', to monitor and thus control the other.[38] As Peter Mason points out, 'The innocent eye has never existed.'[39]

Marxist critics (such as the Frankfurt School) and poststructuralist critics have pointed to the implication of humanism in colonialism — the universalizing claims of the Enlightenment were linked to the political hegemony of the West. The philosophical self-creation of Europe was thus dependent on the constitution of the other: 'the European has only been able to become a man through creating monsters and slaves.'[40] In his Preface to Frantz Fanon's *The Wretched of the Earth* (1961) Sartre writes of Fanon's demolition of humanism: 'There you can see it, quite naked, and it's not a pretty sight. It was nothing but an ideology of lies, a perfect justification for pillage; its honeyed words, its affectation of sensibility were only alibis for our aggressions.'[41]

It was the end of colonialism that put Western concepts of knowledge most radically into question. Robert Young stresses the importance of practices such as deconstruction and colonial discourse analysis in this connexion:

> The politics of poststructuralism forces the recognition that all knowledge may be variously contaminated, implicated in its very formal or 'objective' structures. This means in particular colonial discourse analysis is not merely a marginal adjunct to

> more mainstream studies, a specialized activity only for minorities or for historians of imperialism and colonialism, but itself forms the point of questioning Western knowledge's categories and assumptions.[42]

THE GAZE AND SUBJECTIVITY

Not only the epistemological assumptions of the gaze, but its other ideological implications as well, make it productive trope to deploy in an analysis of women's travel writing. The notion of a transcendent viewer of reality is closely linked to the concept of a unified, autonomous subject. Women's autobiographical writings are one site where this notion of subjectivity is produced.[43] In fact, women's travel writings radically assert a female identity in the public sphere in a two-fold way: by producing a public self in print and by locating the traveller's persona in the public world of travel. Thus their writings simultaneously reflect the bourgeois/humanist ideology of identity and disrupt it — by resisting the dominant constructions of gender. In effect, however, the production of gender identity is contained within the ideological assumptions of this notion of subjectivity, posited as it is on an illusion of control over one's own identity. The constitution of self also always hinges on the setting up of a 'self-consolidating Other',[44] which in the case of women travellers was particlarly represented by the 'other' woman—less 'free' than the Western woman. Further, the idealized status of a transcendent self produced a subject located outside of specific historical conditions.Lastly, the search for a unified, non-fragmented and static self, caged women in an essentialist definition of womanhood and functioned as a 'technology of self-regulation'. The interesting thing about the female gaze is the way it is refracted by other, controlling gazes. This is particularly evident in the case of women travellers, who were by no means always as celebrated as now and were often the focus of critical scrutiny. The traveller was also, of course, the object of observance by the observed — a fact either effaced or registered with various emotions, ranging from detached amusement to rage and fear.

THE GAZE AND WOMEN'S POSITION IN COLONIALISM

This brings me to my last point: the trope of the gaze seems to me peculiarly suited as a metaphor for Western women's location in colonialism.

While women's travel writing contested a form of gender power for women, the distancing effect produced by humanist/empiricist principles of vision situated women as spectators of empire and effaced their implication in the specificity of colonial power. The gaze constructs itself as absent from the site of observation while simultaneously serving the function of surveillance over the other. Epistemic mastery is, in our case, directly linked to political hegemony. By producing knowledge about the other and circulating colonial stereotypes, travel writing is implicated in the reproduction of colonialism. As Fabian points out, 'there is no knowledge of the Other which is not also a temporal, historical, a political act.'[45] By constructing themselves as busy collecting picturesque scenes or curios or flowers (as in the case of the naturalist-traveller Marianne North), looking on while men managed the dirty business of politics, women travellers epitomize the stance of British women in empire—as located outside of historical and material conditions. Paradoxically, feminist critics have been only too prepared to take this self-presentation of women as spectators of empire at face value. By colluding in the myth of women's non-involvement in colonialism, we are denying precisely those women agency who rightly earn our admiration by actively shaping their own lives by travelling! If we wish to restore women as subjects of their own history, we cannot restrict their responsibility to the aspects that suit us.[46] In addition, by constructing women as perennial victims in all spheres of life, we support the very male myths that fashion women as perennially passive.[47] Similarly, by constructing women as not involved in empire we support masculinist historiography that marginalizes women.

The question that begs to be asked in the case of all assertions of woman's inherent difference such as a specific female gaze is: whose gaze? An essentialist notion of womanhood necessarily entails the exclusion of some. What needs to be scrutinized is the site from which women gaze, that is the positions of power in which they are located.

In effect, what I am arguing is that the transcendent traveller's gaze is the colonial gaze. The opposition between self and other set up in travel writing is, like all binary oppositions, grounded on an implicit (and sometimes explicit) hierarchy. And the Hegelian model of knowledge-constitution that the gaze is premised on, is in itself grounded on an epistemic appropriation of the other.

Organization of the Study

In this study I am using the gaze as an organizing trope for the production of knowledge and its enmeshment in relations of power. Other related issues that I will be looking at are questions of subjectivity and women's collusion in—and subversion of—colonialism.

In my research on women's travel writing I have come to the conclusion that women's perception of the other as constructed (not reflected) in their writings is certainly different from that of men. This difference is not grounded in an instinctive empathy with the other, as is often asserted/wished. Instead, if we posit the observing ego to be situated *in* reality and not transcending it, we will readily admit that perception is constrained and produced by dominant discourses. Thus perception was informed by gender ideology: what it was possible to *see* as a woman was determined by the discourses of feminity in circulation at a specific moment in history. Although there are many aspects in common, texts by women travellers focus on different aspects as compared to texts by male travellers. These different foci are not a result of naturally or socially produced spheres of interest (domestic life for women travellers, for example), but are constrained by the web of conditions of production and reception for these texts.[48] In fact, women travellers to India were not particularly interested in the domestic life of Indians (partly because access was difficult). What these women travellers were particularly interested in was producing eyewitness accounts of the harem or zenana, a no-entry zone for male travellers that met with keen interest on the part of publishers and readers. Similarly, as they were denied access to male preserves like the Great Game of imperial politics, women were confined to aesthetic appropriation of the country though the strategy of the picturesque.

What I hope to present is a plurality of gazes. There was not *the* woman traveller in India, but a variety of different women—there is no overarching story to be told. Similarly, different discourses are always co-present at the same point in time and intersect to produce these texts—colonialism was at all times an ambivalent and not a monolithic project. My approach will be selective, not exhaustive, and will focus on published travel accounts. What emerges from the travel accounts is how the other is constituted ambivalently, but always serves the function of self-definition.

In the case of early women travellers, the influence of Orientalist discourses are clearly perceptible in the travellers' fascination with ancient Indian culture. Women Orientalist travellers contest for gender power by producing Orientalist knowledge in their texts. Nevertheless, they remain excluded from the field of scholarly Orientalist research. At the same time their texts are informed by the discourses of Evangelicalism and Utilitarianism, which evinced a deep contempt towards everything Indian and laid the foundations for the ideology of the 'white man's burden' and mission to carry civilization to the empire. These ideological contradictions are to be found located within the texts.

The aesthetics of the picturesque offers women travellers a mode of perception ideally suited to women's self-image in colonialism. Originally a movement in landscape art, the picturesque is increasingly deployed as a rhetorical strategy in travel literature, evoked in the service of simultaneous imaginative appropriation of the other and detachment from the other. While not by any means restricted to women, it serves to epitomize women's position in empire. In these texts, occasionally colonial reality breaks in to disturb the smooth facade of the picturesque.

The one field of research for women travellers taken seriously by male scholars was—the production of knowledge about the harem (or in the case of India, the zenana, the women's quarters). At the same time, it provided the site for the projection of (male and female) fantasies. Nowhere is the range of travellers' gazes more clearly shown than in the descriptions of visits to the zenana. In the course of the century the voyeuristic, erotic gaze of traveller Fanny Parks (influenced by the discourses of Romanticism) gives way to a rigid perception of the Indian woman as backward. Repressed truths about women's disenfranchisement in their own society were rigorously deflected and projected onto the other. With the emergence of the New Woman in Britain, another shift in the perception of Indian women in the zenana is discernible in the texts of conservative-minded travellers: the 'feminine' qualities of Indian women are increasingly lauded by conservative travellers and the zenana is transmuted from a prison to an ordinary domestic sphere. Early feminists, on the other hand, were also busy setting up an image of the Indian woman that served their own political purposes, as we shall see. The Indian woman has consistently served as the refractory foil for the self-constitution of the Western woman.

An entire chapter is devoted to Emily Eden, the best-known woman traveller in India. I argue that her text at certain moments evinces an awareness that the traveller-observer is involved in the viewing process and comes closest to a refusal of the transcendent viewer position. Her ironic gaze debunks colonial myths (such as the civilizing mission) and operates as a distancing strategy toward the ideological norms of her own society. Nevertheless, the silence on colonial reality in her text works to contain its subversive implications. The supreme irony remains the fact that Eden's account has become the most popular of women's travel accounts of India, celebrated for its image of a timeless India of princes, palaces and pageants!

Mutiny accounts by British women represent the experiential mode of travel writing—most of them were produced in conditions of siege. Their perception of India is accordingly shaped by the predicament they find themselves in. Their writings reveal colonial anxieties about the fragility of power. In addition, they tell us about woman's role in empire. Interestingly enough, their texts remain silent on one of the main myths of colonialism for which the signifier woman (white) was instrumentalized: the rape myth. The attack on the colonial body politic was recoded into an attack on British women's bodies. This myth—grounded on no evidence—was deployed in the service of colonial punitive measures and gained authoritative status in colonial historiography. By contrast, mutiny accounts by women are centered on women's survival strategies and thus contain subversive implications for the colonialist construction of women as passive victims.

Early feminists recruit the image of the Indian woman for their own purposes: by calling for a 'white woman's burden' in the empire with the goal of uplifting the degraded Indian woman, they staked a claim to a place for women in imperial politics. Mary Carpenter was one woman traveller whose voyage to India was solely devoted to the cause of women's education. Informed by the tradition of women's philanthropy in the early nineteenth century, the gaze embodied in her text is the gaze of social surveillance.

Finally, I look at questions of travel and power. In analysing the meaning of travel for women, I argue that the very act of travel constituted a form of gender power for women. By entering the public world of travel, women transgressed gender norms that relegated them to the home. In addition, their autobiographical writings gave them further access to the public sphere and helped them shape an autonomous female identity. Women travellers in the empire were, however, also implicated in colonial power structures. The knowledge they produced was both a form of epistemic power and served to further the ends of colonial power. Lastly, in their personal interactions with the colonized, women travellers also exercised a considerable power.

As a coda, I wish to present some examples of other gazes/gazes of the other. As Homi Bhabha has shown, the power to gaze is by no means solely in the hands of the colonizer: 'In the objectification of the scopic drive there is always the threatened return of the look.'[49] Within (and against) these colonial texts, a host of gazes are crowding in on the margins, ranging from colonial mimicry to a direct (and penetrating) stare.

OTHER WOMEN

Finally, it needs to be pointed out that travellers and memsahibs were not the only British women in India. Occasionally other women wander into these texts—English nannies or soldiers' wives who are emphatically *not* ladies. What is interesting to observe is the mechanisms at work to construct the lower-class woman as other. Mrs King muses 'if it is true that the lower orders have the same feelings as we have'[50] and goes on to describe how soldiers' wives are engaged 'two and three deep' as a precautionary measure against their husbands falling while in active service (they received no pensions). She concludes: 'Feelings, no doubt, they have; but we cannot gauge them truly by our own.' (51) Emma Roberts pronounces soldiers' wives to be lazy, insolent and overbearing[51] and deplores the unaccustomed life of luxury these women now enjoy. She trains a voyeuristic gaze on the other woman: '... curious scenes are displayed to view through the open doors. Some fat and unshapeable lady, attired in a loose white gown, indulging in a siesta in an elbow-chair, with a native attendant, ragged and in wretched case, who, fan in hand, agitates the air around her' (3: 49-50).

What this passage expresses is above all a sense of outrage at the other woman's violation of class boundaries.

This life in the lap of luxury appears in a slightly different light in Marianne Postans' text. Admitting that the women are immoral, quarrelsome and generally drunk,[52] she explains:

> In remarking on the irregularities and vices of soldiers' wives in India, it is only just to notice the temptations, restraints, and miseries, to which this class of women are subject, in a country

> so little calculated to cherish their better feelings, or to provide them with necessary occupation, or common comfort. Unable, from extreme heat, to move out of the little room allotted to them in the 'married men's quarters', during the day, and provided, for two rupees a month, with a Portuguese 'cook boy', who relieves them from the toil of domestic duties, the only resource of the soldiers' wives is in mischievous associations, discontented murmurings, and habits of dissipated indulgence. (165-66)

The narrator evinces a certain sympathy for the constraints under which these women live as well as the uprootedness from their familiar surroundings that haunts their lives in the colonies.

Most travellers, however, efface the presence of these other women, a silence critics collude in.

WHY WOMEN?

Why another study on women travellers, focusing on Western women and seemingly unable to 'wrench [itself] away from the mesmerizing focus of the 'subject-constitution' of the female individualist'?[53] I admit that one selfish reason lies simply in the pleasure of salvaging forgotten texts, in mapping largely uncharted territory. Despite the large circulations that they achieved among readers, these women's voices were marginalized within colonial discourse and largely erased within masculinist historiography. With historians like Elizabeth Fox-Genovese and Joan Scott, I believe that it is necessary both to reinstate women as agents of their own history and simultaneously to challenge a reductionist approach that privileges gender to the exclusion of all other factors that construct identity. As Scott says, 'The realization of the radical potential of women's history comes in the writing of histories that focus on women's experience *and* analyse the ways in which politics construct gender and gender constructs politics.'[54] It was feminists, after all, who were to challenge the paradigms of the objective (male) gaze and argue how it reflected relations of gender power. It is in this tradition that I wish to locate my work. I hope the extensive quotations from these accounts incorporated into my own text will help to convey a hint of the flavour of these women's writings.

The India presented in these travel accounts is not the 'real' India, but India in the colonial female imaginary. This study will concentrate on identifying the discourses traversing the texts and uncovering the textual disturbances within the web of the text. It is these fissures that reveal the anxiety and desire colonial power is always bound up with.[55] Anthropologist Nicholas Thomas observes:

> ... colonial rule was frequently haunted by a sense of insecurity, terrified by the obscurity of 'the native mentality' and overwhelmed by indigenous societies' apparent intractibility in the face of government; even if colonial knowledge often took the form of a panoptical, encyclopaedic appropriation of indigenous customs, histories, relics and statistics, such displays of intellectual rapacity were frequently accompanied by a kind of despair, which found the space and social entity of the colony to be intangible, imperceptible and constantly untrue to the representations that might be fashioned of it.[56]

By revealing these anxieties, travel accounts by women demonstrate the limits of their own overarching project, namely that of transcending colonialism. One truth these texts expose is the truth about colonialism and women's ambivalent role in colonialism, caught between subversion and affirmation. The gaze at the other is, in effect, a gaze into the mirror.

Notes

1 Julia Charlotte Maitland, *Letters from Madras, during the years 1836-39, by a Lady* (London: 1843) 53.

2 See The Marxist-Feminist Literature Collective, 'Women's Writing: Jane Eyre, Shirley, Villette, Aurora Leigh', *Ideology and Consciousness* 3 (1978): 31

3 For example, the fourth-century pilgrimage account written by Egeria. See Mary B. Campbell, *The Witness and the Other World: Exotic European Travel Writing, 400-160* (Ithaca: Cornell University Press, 1988) 15-46.

4 Susan Bassnett, 'Constructing Cultures: The Politics of Travellers' Tales', *Comparative Literature: A Critical Introduction* (Oxford: Blackwell, 1993) 92.

5 See Hayden White, *Metahistory: The Historical Imagination in Nineteenth-Century Europe* (Baltimore: Johns Hopkins University Press, 1973).

6 Hayden White, 'The Historical Text as Literary Artefact', *Clio* 3.3 (1974): 281.

7 See Percy G. Adams, *Traveler and Travel Liar: 1660-1800* (Berkeley: University of California Press, 1962).

8 See Adams, *Travel Literature and the Evolution of the Novel* (Lexington: University of Kentucky Press, 1983).

9 Adams, *Travel Literature* 281.

10 Edward Said, *Orientalism* (London: Routledge & Kegan Paul, 1978).

11 Rana Kabbani, *Europe's Myths of Orient* (London: Pandora, 1986).

12 Mary Louise Pratt, *Imperial Eyes: Travel Writing and Transculturation* (London: Routledge, 1992).

13 Tim Youngs, *Travellers in Africa: British Travelogues 1850-1900* (Manchester: Manchester University Press, 1994).

14 Margaret MacMillan, *Women of the Raj* (London: Thames & Hudson, 1988) 236.

15 Elizabeth Fox-Genovese, 'Placing Women's History in History', *New Left Review* 133 (1982): 7.

16 Fox-Genovese 29.

17 See Sara Mills, *Discourses of Difference: An Analysis of Women's Travel Writing and Colonialism* (London: Routledge, 1991).

18 See Mills, 'Gender and Colonialism: Discourses of Difference' paper given at Gender and Colonialism conference, UCG, Galway, Ireland, 1992.

19 See Mills, 'Knowledge, Gender and Empire', *Writing, Women and Space: Colonial and Postcolonial Geographies*, eds. Alison Blunt and Gillian Rose (New York: Guildford, 1994) 29-51.

20 See in particular Chandra Talpade Mohanty, 'Under Western Eyes: Feminist Scholarship and Colonial Discourses', *Third World Women and the Politics of Feminism*, eds. Chandra Talpade Mohanty, Ann Russo, and Lourdes Torres (Bloomington: Indiana University Press 1991) 51-80.

21 Gayatri Chakravorty Spivak, 'Three Women's Texts and a Critique of Imperialism', *'Race', Writing and Difference*, ed. Henry Louis Gates, Jr. (Chicago: University of Chicago Press, 1985) 270.

22 Mary Russell, *The Blessings of a Good Thick Skirt: Women Travellers and their World* (London: Collins, 1986) 207.

23 See, for instance, the collection of essays in Linda J. Nicholson, ed. *Feminism/ Postmodernism* (London: Routledge, 1990).

24 Teresa de Lauretis, 'Displacing Hegemonic Discourses: Reflections on Feminist Theory in the 1980s', *Inscriptions* 3/4 (1988): 136.

25 See M.Z. Rosaldo, 'The Use and Abuse of Anthropology: Reflections on Feminism and Cross-Cultural Understanding', *Signs* 5 (1980): 389-417.

26 Also see Sigrid Weigel, 'Der schielende Blick: Thesen zur Geschichte weiblicher Schreibpraxis', *Die verborgene Frau: Sechs Beiträge zu einer feministischen Literaturwissenschaft*, eds. Sigrid Weigel and Inge Stephan (Berlin: Argument, 1983) 83-137.

27 Donna Haraway, 'A Manifesto for Cyborgs: Science, Technology and Socialist Feminism in the 1980s', Nicholson (1990) 215.

28 See Weigel.

29 In the following I am particulary indebted to Robert Young's *White Mythologies: Writing History and the West* (London: Routledge, 1990). Also see Wlad Godzich, 'Foreword: The Further Possibility of Knowledge', *Heterologies: Discourse on the Other* by Michel de Certeau, trans. Brian Massumi (Minneapolis: University of Minnesota Press, 1988) vii-xxi.

30 This can include an idealization of the other, as has, for instance, been the case with Western travel writing on the South Seas.

31 Godzich xiii.

32 See Homi K. Bhabha, 'The Other Question: Difference, Discrimination and the Discourse of Colonialism', *The Politics of Theory*, ed. Francis Barker *et al.* (Colchester; University of Essex, 1983) 148-72.

33 Ortfried Schäffter defines self-constitution through the other as a third category. This seems to me to overlook the function that both other modes of defining the other serve in constituting the self. See Ortfried Schäffter, 'Modi des Fremderlebens: Deutungsmuster im Umgang mit Fremdheit', *Das Fremde: Erfahrungsmöglichkeiten zwischen Faszination und Bedrohung*, ed. Schäffter (Opladen: Westdt, Verlag, 1991) 11-42.

34 See Johannes Fabian, *Time and the Other: How Anthropology Makes Its Object* (New York: Columbia University Press, 1983) 105-142.

35 Common sense is, as Stuart Hall reminds us, the most highly ideological structure of all. See Stuart Hall, 'Signification, Representation, Ideology: Althusser and the Post-Structuralist Debates', *Critical Studies in Mass Communication* 2.2 (1985) 105.

36 Fabian 160.

37 Fabian 163.

38 See Michel Foucault, *Power/Knowledge: Selected Interviews and Other Writings 1972–1977*, ed. Colin Gordon, trans. Colin Gordon, Leo Marshall, John Mepham, Kate Soper (Brighton: Harvester, 1980).

39 Peter Mason, *The Deconstruction of America*, Diss., University of Utrecht, 1990, 29.

40 Jean-Paul Sartre, Preface, *The Wretched of the Earth*, by Frantz Fanon, trans. Constance Farrington (Harmondsworth: Penguin, 1967) 22.

41 Sartre 21.

42 Young 11.

43 See Felicity A. Nussbaum, *The Autobiographical Subject: Gender and Ideology in Eighteenth-Century England* (Baltimore: Johns Hopkins University Press, 1989).

44 Gayatri Chakravorty Spivak, *In Other Worlds: Essays in Cultural Studies* (New York: Methuen, 1987) 209.

45 Fabian 1.

46 Restoring agency to women in history does not necessarily imply reinstating a humanist perception of subjectivity. S. P. Mohanty calls for a post-humanist concept of subjectivity that would impute agency—responsibility for their own actions—to both the self and the other while rejecting the humanist notion of subjectivity based on a hierarchy between these binary oppositions. See S.P. Mohanty's perceptive 'Us and Them: On the Philosophical Bases of Political Criticism', *New Formations* 8 (1989): 55-80. See also Roland Barthes' definition of 'progressive Humanism' in contrast to classical Humanism in his *Mythologies*, trans. Annette Lavers (New York: Hill & Wang, 1981) 101.

47 I am not arguing that women were not victims of the notoriously misogynist colonial structures. What I hope to show is that women were *both* victims *and* actors on the stage of empire.
48 See especially Mills, *Discourses* 67-124.
49 Bhabha, 'The Other Question', 169.
50 Mrs Robert Moss King, *The Diary of a Civilian's Wife in India 1877-1882*, 2 vols. (London, 1884) 2: 51. All further references to be given in parentheses in the text.
51 Emma Roberts, *Scenes and Characteristics of Hindustan, with Sketches of Anglo-Indian Society*, 3 vols. (London, 1835) 3: 49. All further references to be given in parentheses in the text.
52 Marianne Postans, *Western Indian in 1838*, 2 vols. (London, 1839) 1: 161. All further references to be given in parentheses in the text.
53 Spivak, 'Three Women's Texts' 264.
54 Joan Wallach Scott, *Gender and the Politics of History* (New York: Columbia University Press, 1988) 27.
55 See Bhabha, 'The Other Question'.
56 Nicholas Thomas, *Colonialism's Culture: Anthropology, Travel and Government* (Oxford: Polity, 1994) 15-16.

Chapter 1

Women Travellers and Orientalism

There is a remarkable passage in Marianne Postans' travel narrative:

> The festivals of the East, are curious to the researcher into the manners of the ancient nations; . . . at these seasons of national mirth, the oft seemingly timid, and gentle Hindoo, gives license to his genuine disposition, and laughs, sings, and adorns himself with garlands, as if he still inherited his native soil, in a happy state of constitutional freedom; it is at these periods, that his character may perhaps be best discerned. . . .
>
> The native population of India, are peculiarly reserved in their intercourse with us . . . Their prejudices of caste, prevent our having any intercourse with them of a social nature; and their religious ceremonies are less known from personal observation, than from the communications of intelligent natives, which, after all we can acquire, little informs us on the real character, manners, and feelings of the people, when removed from the restraint of foreign espionage. (1: 191-2)

The text uncannily sets up an equation between the 'researcher into the manners of the ancient nations' (in other words, the Orientalist traveller) and the foreign spy. Like the spy, the Orientalist traveller, it would seem, compiles information for a political purpose. Both are the vanguard of a political appropriation of the other. A century and a half later Edward Said would come to a similar conclusion regarding the implication of Orientalist researchers in relations of power.[1] The position of the spy is, of course, the ultimate reification of the disembodied gaze paradigm: it offers visual pleasure and power without involvement. The Oriental other in the text, however, frustrates this pleasure. He (or she) baffles the attempt to observe him, to record, catalogue and classify him, and only when he is outside the scope of the Orientalist gaze does he reveal his 'genuine disposition'. And the Orientalist traveller-narrator of the text? Her position seems to oscillate between awareness of the role she plays and exasperation at the recalcitrant object of observation, the inscrutable native.

This chapter is the tale of three travellers—women travellers in India in the early years of the nineteenth century. All three women are remarkable for pursuing a career in writing after the publication of their travel narratives. Maria Graham (later Lady Callcott) travelled to India in 1809 with her father and married her first husband there. After a stay of two years, mainly in the coastal centres of Bombay, Calcutta and Madras, she returned to England with her husband in 1811. She was destined to lead an adventurous life as a traveller and spent a couple of years in Chile where she became involved in the movement for independence. She gained fame particularly for her *Essays towards the History of Painting* (1836) and her history book for children, *Little Arthur's History of England* (1835)—a list of its reprints fills two entire pages in the British Library Catalogue. The second, Anne Katherine Elwood, accompanied her husband, Lieutenant-Colonel Elwood, to India in 1825 and stayed there for three years. She stakes out a claim to fame for being the first woman traveller to take the overland route to India via Egypt and the Red Sea. We know little about her except that she later published two volumes of *Memoirs of the Literary Ladies of England from the Commencement of the Last Century* (1843).[2] Finally, Marianne Postans (later Young) is known for various books of which the well known *Western India in 1838* was the second travel account on India that she had published, the first being *Cutch; or Random Sketches, taken during a Residence in one of the Northern Provinces of Western India; interspersed with Legends and Traditions* (London, 1839). Later, she was to write a book on *The Moslem Noble* (1857) as well as publish three volumes of *Facts and Fictions, Illustrative of Oriental Character* (1844).

What these three women travellers in India have in common is the fact that their travel accounts are informed by the discourses of Orientalism in circulation at the beginning of the nineteenth century. The term 'Orientalists' in the Indian context refers to the small group of scholars who uncovered the heritage of classical India to the West for the first time. Sir William ('Asiatic') Jones, who founded the Asiatick Society of Bengal in 1784, is generally credited with being the founder of Indology. He was the first to claim that Sanskrit and European languages were related to one another and dismantle the theory that the latter were derived from Hebrew. Other scholars painstakingly translated ancient Indian texts or undertook archaeological research, often publishing their results in the *Asiatick Researches*. Their findings swiftly spread to Europe and had a great impact on the intellectual scene there, leaving their mark on both the German and English Romantic movements.

These were no disinterested scholars, however, but were actively involved in the administration of the East India Company's Indian colonies. They were virulently opposed by certain Utilitarian thinkers, who later came to be known as the 'Anglicists'.[3] Foremost amongst these was James Mill, whose *The History of British India* (1817) was largely a refutation of Jones' ideas. Mill and the Utilitarians had nothing but scorn for a culture based on a respect for tradition and set up an ambitious agenda of remodelling Indian culture in their own image. In this they were supported by the Evangelicals, who though opposed to political radicalism formed an unholy alliance with the Benthamites in the field of Indian policy, fired by the thought of millions of heathens waiting to be converted. It was the discourses of Evangelicalism and Utilitarianism that laid the foundation for the notion of 'the white man's burden' to bring enlightenment to the East. A milestone in the formulation of Utilitarian policy with regard to India was Macaulay's 'Minute on Education' (1835), (in)famous for programmatic statements such as 'a single shelf of a good European library was worth the whole native literature of India and Arabia.'[4] In this momentous policy statement Macaulay voiced the British plan to implement a sweeping programme of Anglicization, based on education in English language and values, with the aim of creating a class of native informants or mimic Englishmen, 'a class who may be interpreters between us and the millions whom we govern—a class of persons Indian in blood and colour, but English in tastes, in opinions, in morals and in intellect.'[5] Nigel Leask sees this as the liberal fantasy of the Oriental peoples colonizing themselves in the name of Western values.[6]

As various historians have pointed out, the conflict between the Orientalists and the Anglicists was basically a British one and reflected the interests of the two main forces in British politics— the conservative forces with their power base in the aristocracy, and the rising middle classes with their disdain for tradition and their call for change in every sphere.[7] As Eric Stokes notes, 'it is remarkable how many of the movements of English life tested their strength and fought their early battles upon the Indian question.'[8] Thus Burke, for instance, defended the traditional society of India in the same terms as he defended the French *ancien regime* in his *Reflections on the Revolution in France* (1790).[9] It was the middle classes who carried the day, just as did the Anglicists in the government of India.

To return to our three travellers: they are all deeply influenced by the Orientalist excavation of ancient Indian culture and prove themselves to be extremely well-read on the subject. Maria Graham presents herself as the friend of well-known Orientalist scholars, such as Dr Leyden. She produces one of the earliest descriptions of the cave temples at Elephanta and Karle, rich in descriptive detail and embellished by her own sketches. She incorporates a poem translated from Sanskrit in her text and adds further translated sources on Zoroastrian and Hindu mythology to her journal in an appendix. Anne Katherine Elwood, who is fond of striking a Romantic attitude, presents her readers with a detailed introduction to Indian mythology, declaring:

> In spite of Southey's declaration of the anti-picturesque and unpoetical nature of the mythological personages of the Brahmins, I must be presumptuous enough to say, that there appear to me to be more boldly sublime, and magnificently grand ideas frequently to be met with in their sacred writings, then are to be found in any other place but the Bible. . . . [10]

In the tradition of Jones, she draws continual analogies between Indian and Greek mythology.

Marianne Postans, writing at a time when the Anglicist programme for transforming India was in full swing, displays a deep respect for the Brahmin tradition of learning and of 'arts and wisdom, such as in ancient days illuminated the archives of this long neglected land' (1: 52). Of a Jain temple she remarks:

> The columns are peculiarly beautiful, from the fineness of their proportions, which gives them a lightness and elegance of effect, I have never seen surpassed, even by the finest specimens of Grecian art. The same remark may be made of the figures, which prove a correct knowledge of the rules of art, and of the characteristic graces of the male and female figure, which awakens the highest admiration. (2: 59)

For Postans, Indian art is on par with the highly valorized art of classical Greece. To grasp the implications of this remark one need only compare it to that of a traveller to India in the latter part of the century. Mary Carpenter, for instance, deplores the 'most remarkable deficiency in the drawing or sculpturing of the human figure' in Indian art and calls for the establishment of a school of art to train young Indian art students. However, one great obstacle lies 'in the deficiency of any good works of art, ancient or modern, to guide the studies of learners.'[11] Only a few decades after the Orientalist travellers the scale of civilization has been reversed with the Indians requiring tuition from their superior Western counterparts.

Aware of dwindling official interest in Orientalist research at the time she writes her book (published in 1838), Postans launches an appeal to the British in India to devote their time to uncovering the treasures of India, instead of frittering away their stay yearning for the comforts of home. For: 'The mythology of the Hindoos . . . the costly temples . . . the stores of learning yet encased in the casket of Sanskrit literature, offer a high reward to the industrious researcher into the history of an ancient people' (2: 235). With enthusiasm she reports on the recent deciphering of ancient Buddhist rock inscriptions — ironically, this scholarly feat is destined to be one of the last coups of the British Orientalists.

The Politics of Orientalism

Until recently historians have tended to idealize the school of 'Orientalists' in contrast to their grim Anglicist counterparts and to commend their interest in, and respect for, Indian culture and tradition. While their scholarly achievement remains impressive even today, post-colonial critics have begun to scrutinize the ideological assumptions that are inscribed into Orientalist discourse. In the wake of Said, Ronald Inden has undertaken a deconstruction of Orientalist discourse on India and has applied the Foucauldian paradigm of the collusion of knowledge in power relations to the Indian context.[12] He has pointed to the hierarchical relationship between the knowledge of the Orientalist scholar and his object of knowledge, the Oriental. The Oriental is consistently denied the power to know and represent him or herself. This implies that the Oriental other is also denied the power to produce and transform his or her own world, not just to adapt to it. By denying agency to the Oriental object of knowledge, the Western Orientalist subject appropriates it for him or herself — it is he (or she) who has the power to produce the Orient through his/her production of knowledge. The Orientalist gaze of the traveller reinforces this relationship of power/knowledge by transcending reality rather than being situated in it. And the image of India constructed in Orientalist discourse is one of mythical, dreamlike irrationality. Thus the Orient serves as a 'self-consolidating other'[13] which reinforces the European self-image of rationality.

Lata Mani has taken a closer look at the Orientalist discourse on sati (widow-burning) and has come to the conclusion that for all its apparent respect for Indian religious tradition, the discourse is a colonial discourse, i.e. the material power relations of the time are inscribed into it.[14] By privileging textual sources over religious practice, British Orientalist officials tended to valorize Brahmanical interpretations of scripture as irrefutable. In actual fact sati was a social practice that was neither explicitly condoned nor encouraged in Hindu scriptures — themselves a highly heterogeneous body of texts.[15] By supporting Brahmanical discourse, the British helped stabilize and strengthen the power of this elite — which conversely bolstered the Orientalist image of India as deeply religious, traditional and unchanging, and the reformist view of India as priest-ridden. As historian Chris Bayly points out:

> Traditional India was not a rigid society. It was British rule which made it so, codifying many localised and pragmatic customs into a unified and Brahminised 'Hindoo Law' and classing people into immutable castes through the operation of the courts and ethnographic surveys. Colonial society was seeing a mirror image of itself when it understood Indian society as rigid and stultified.[16]

The Orientalism of early British rule in India was imbued with a deeply conservative impulse which sought to consolidate a traditional hierarchical society in India to legitimize their own position at the top of the hierarchy. Their rejection of radical change was a reflection of their anxiety about the French Revolution. Mani calls the traditional historians' opposition of Orientalists and Anglicists into question and raises the issue 'of the extent to which the Anglicist program for social engineering was determined by Orientalist analysis of Indian society.'[17]

Mani points to other assumptions that also underlie Orientalist discourse on India, such as the conviction that Hindu society had declined from a Golden Age and that the once-glorious culture had fallen into disarray. These assumptions are supported by the travel writing of the period. Johannes Fabian has looked at the politics of time in travel accounts and calls the discrepancy in time between the West and other cultures enacted in these texts 'the denial of coevalness.'[18] As its corollary, moral and cultural superiority were now attributed to the West. We find these ideas reflected particularly in Graham's text, which, for all its interest in ancient India, evinces a sharp sense of disillusion with India. In her preface she laments that she did not get an opportunity to meet with 'any of those remnants of the age of gold—any of those combinations of innocence, benevolence, and voluptuous simplicity, with which the imaginations of some ingenious authors have peopled the cottages of the Hindoos.'[19] In an excursion to one of these cottages, she strikes up a conversation with the couple living there. She concludes:

> Before I left the cottage, its inhabitants dressed themselves in their finest jewels, for the purpose of attending a marriage. I accompanied them a little way to join the procession, which at a distance looked like the groupes we see on antique bas-reliefs; in short, I every day find some traces of the manners and simplicity of the antique ages; but the arts and virtues that adorned them are sunk in the years of slavery under which the devoted Hindoos have bent; these people, if they have the virtues of slaves, patience, meekness, forbearance, and gentleness, have their vices also. They are cunning, and incapable of truth; they disregard the imputations of lying and perjury, and would consider it folly not to practise them for their own interest. (27)

A shadow of a different set of discourses altogether falls across her account — that of a construction of the native as inherently devious and in need of control. This is reinforced by her repeated conviction of Western superiority: 'the most agreeable speculations are always those that point homeward to that Europe, where the mind of man seems to flourish in preference to any other land.' She continues: 'If we look around us, the passive submission, the apathy, and the degrading superstition of the Hindoos; the more active fanaticism of the Mussulmans; the avarice, the prodigality, the ignorance, and the vulgarity of most of the white people, seem to place them all on a level, infinitely below that of the least refined nations of Europe' (134).

Interestingly enough, at this stage the category of class still has precedence over that of race — Graham pours her scorn equally on Indians and the Anglo-Indian[20] society of India, which she pronounces to be 'under-bred and over-dressed, and with the exception of one or two, very ignorant and very grossière' (28).

An illuminating and entertaining insight into the political realities at work in the production of Orientalist discourse is afforded by the following example. Elwood recounts at length startling parallels between Hindu mythology and Biblical history, such as a Sanskrit version of the story of Noah and his three sons. Another legend she narrates is that of the King Vikramaditya, who hears a prophecy that he is to be deposed by 'a divine child, who was to be born of a virgin, and whose reputed father was to be a carpenter' (2: 33). Vikramaditya attempts to destroy this child but finally meets the end he deserves. 'It must surely be admitted that these are singular and striking facts and anecdotes, and they would almost lead one to imagine the Hindoos had been acquainted with our holy Scriptures at an early period', she concludes (2: 33).

Elwood derives these extravagant tales from research essays published in the *Asiatick Researches*. Nigel Leask has recently excavated the series of articles in which these sensational theories were aired.[21] Between 1799 and 1810 a certain Francis Wilford published a series of articles on ancient Hindu mythography, which had an enormous impact at the time, especially on the Romantic movement.[22] In his essays Wilford's theories escalate from the curious to the exorbitant, culminating in the implicit claim that the Brahmins of India were descended from the druids of ancient Britain. The ideological implications involved are clear: the authenticity of Biblical narrative is reaffirmed — an urgent project at a time when French philosophers were increasingly putting Christian tenets into question — and the hierarchy of cultures comfortably reinstated.

Wilford's theories are allegedly all corroborated by Sanskrit texts. The irony of this tale lies in Wilford's discovery that the Brahmin pundit he employed to help him sift through the mass of ancient texts had been merrily forging sources to comply with his employer's demand for these myths. Leask reads this as a parable of the colonial power-relations that informed the agenda of Orientalist research: 'The discrepancy lies between Wilford's notion of his pundit as "pure" channel for the trans-mission of timeless 'scriptural' truth, and the pundit's subaltern position within the apparatus of British colonial power.'[23]

The interesting question that remains for us to speculate on is why Mrs Elwood expends so much energy and paper in recounting these speculations. As she expressly bases her knowledge on a perusal of the *Asiatick Researches*, Wilford's confession (published in 1805) and the scandal surrounding it will barely have escaped her attention. Could it be that Elwood turns these theories to her own ends by using them to air her own contribution to speculative Orientalism? During her travels in India, Elwood learns of the existence of a colony of Jews who settled in South India centuries ago. It is from these Jews, she claims, that the Brahmins borrowed the ideas for their distortions of Biblical stories (1: 27). This thesis, apart from giving renewed credibility to Wilford's ideas, also securely reinforces the idea of Biblical superiority and smoothes over the subversive implications lurking in them — who could guarantee, after all, that it was not the prophets of the Old Testament who had copied the myths from the Brahmins?[24]

Women's Stake in Orientalism

This brings us to the crux of the issue as regards women 'Orientalist' travellers: the question of what the women's stake was in contributing to the discourses of Orientalism. I would argue that women travellers sought access to Orientalism as a strategy to negotiate a form of gender power and to contest male dominance in scientific and scholarly modes of writing. This is most apparent in Maria Graham's text, where she claims credit for producing the first manners-and-customs account of the community of the Parsis (or Guebres), who emigrated to India from Persia and still follow the precepts of their prophet Zoroaster:

> The fragments of the ancient books of Zoroaster or Zerdusht, still extant, have been introduced in Europe by M. Anquetil, under the name of the Zendavesta; and there is a good deal of interesting matter concerning the establishment of Pyrolatry in Persia, in the Chevalier D'Ohsson's *Tableau Historique de L'Orient,* chiefly on the authority of the Shah Nameh of Firdousi. But I do not know that there is any account of the present state of such of the Guebres as are settled in India; and as these people form the richest class of inhabitants in Bombay, I have undertaken some pains to collect what information I could concerning them, both from Moola Firoze and other individuals of the nation (37).

This passage is revealing as to Graham's scholarly ambitions. The language used is the scientific mode: it bristles with erudition and scholarly references which spill over into two footnotes (which I have omitted) for this passage alone. For fire-worship, for instance, she uses the term 'pyrolatry'. The narrator produces herself as conversant with the most recent Orientalist research, and implies a mastery of the French language not merely as a fashionable medium for conversation but in its scholarly variant. No feminine disavowal is to be found in these lines — instead, the narrator informs us that her informant is none other than the chief priest of the community, Moola Firoze. The rhetorical device of autopsy — implicit in all travel writing — is foregrounded as an authorizing strategy in her text.

Graham's description of the cave temple of Karle corroborates this impression:

> When at length we looked round, we almost fancied ourselves in a Gothic cathedral. Instead of the low flat roof of the cave of Elephanta, this rises to an astonishing height, with a highly coved roof, supported by twenty-one pillars on each side, and terminating in a semicircle. Opposite to the entrance is a large temple (if I may call it so), not hollowed, with a dome, on which is fixed a huge teak umbrella, as a mark of respect. Without the pillars there is a kind of aisle on each side of about six feet wide; the length of the cave is forty paces, and its breadth is fourteen.

> Here are no sculptures within the cavern except on the capitals of the pillars. The columns are mostly hexagons, though the number of the angles varies; the bases are formed like compressed cushions; the capitals resemble an inverted flower, or a bell, on the top of which are two elephants, with two riders on each; and on several of the columns there are inscriptions in a character not hitherto decyphered (64).

There is very little of the sublime here — Graham does not expand on her introductory remark in which she draws an analogy to a Gothic cathedral. One might suppose that to a traveller in the early nineteenth century a cave temple might well conjure up Burke's notion of the sublime, associated with qualities such as terror, obscurity and vastness.[25] However, Burke himself claims, 'It is our ignorance of things that causes all our admiration, and chiefly excites our passions. Knowledge and acquaintance make the most striking causes affect but little.'[26]

Faced with the choice between adopting a rhetoric of the sublime with its celebration of a lack of control, or taking up the detached subject position of the knowing, sovereign subject implied in scientific discourse, Graham opts for the latter. Her sights are set much higher:

> When we had tired ourselves with examining the various wonders of the cavern of Elephanta, I sat down to make a sketch of the great compartments opposite to the entrance, and on our return to Bombay, comparing the drawing with those in Niebuhr, we were satisfied that its resemblance to the original is the most correct (57).

Niebuhr, whose work forms the basis of comparison, was a member of a Danish scientific expedition to the East in the eighteenth century. His sketches of the Elephanta cave sculptures gained authoritative status in Orientalist circles.[27] Graham, an amateur artist, attempts nothing less than a bid to usurp his position.

Though Postans is more modest in her pretensions, she too defines her aim in the programmatic 'Introduction' to her work as that of presenting 'a valuable addition to our present knowledge of India' (viii). In fact, she defines this as the duty of every traveller, irrespective of his or her literary pretensions:

> Of the great and varied beauties of the natural scenery of India, some vague ideas may have been formed; but of its social

> condition, of its agricultural capabilities, of its vegetable productions, of its geological formations, of its necessities as an empire, or of its value as a colony, little indeed is generally understood; . . . it is, I think to be regretted, that so few among us chronicle our experiences of Indian life. Every individual who visits India, whether his sojourn is for a brief, or a lengthened period; whether he possess the pen of an accomplished writer, or a more humble talent, that of careful observation, may yet afford some valuable information, if he but faithfully describe all that may have interested or attracted his attention. . . (Introduction, vii).

What counts is not a graceful or elegant style but the production of knowledge or 'valuable information'. Accordingly, Postans' book is structured more like a guide book than a travel narrative, devoting a chapter each to different aspects such as the Parsis, the Moslems, the peasantry, festivals, etc. While neither Graham nor Postans efface the narrator-author fully,[28] they foreground the descriptive mode in their texts.

Despite their efforts, however, women travellers remain amateurs in the increasingly professionalized field of Orientalism. As yet they are not able to excavate ancient caves, decipher inscriptions or employ fraudulent Brahmins to help them in their research, all of which remains a monopoly of male practitioners in the field. There is, however, one domain in which they are endowed with exclusive rights — in the production of accounts from the harem. All three women travellers sallied forth into a harem, and all of them presented the results of their investigations in their texts. This aspect of women's travel writing shall be dealt with in a separate chapter.

Anne Elwood differs from the other two women travellers in one significant way, however. While the other two Orientalist travellers employ a quasi-scientific, neutered mode in their texts, she clearly draws on gendered conventions. Where Graham explicitly locates herself in the tradition of male travel adventurers ('my great predecessor Sindbad the sailor') (120), Elwood produces herself as a latter-day Lalla Rookh. While she, too, displays her learning in ancient Indian culture, and, as we have seen, actively intervenes in Orientalist discussions, she is equally interested in playing the Romantic heroine. Her text is informed by the Romantic dicourses in vogue in Europe at the time — which were themselves influenced by the Orientalist discovery of ancient India.[29] Observe, for instance, her presentation of herself travelling:

> First of all, several heavy carts, drawn by bullocks, preceded us, in which were such things as were absolutely necessary for our accommodation on the road — tents and tent furniture, couches, chairs, tables, working utensils, and other articles, — then followed our retinue, and their numerous families, — C-'s horses and grooms, — and lastly ourselves, as we remained till everything was fairly off, at the tent of a friend, with whom we dined. C- rode on horseback, — and some of our attendants on camels, — and others were on foot, — and I travelled in my palanquin, which was carried and attended by an extra number of Hamauls, — and we were escorted by some Russulda horse, and by a Haveldar, Naig, and twelve Sepoys; so that though my first Indian march might not quite equal the celebrated expedition of Lalla Rookh in splendour and magnificence, we formed a tolerably large party; and the wildness of the country, the half-savage look of the natives, and the reports of, and the apprehensions of meeting with the marauding Meyannas, all tended to give an air of novelty and originality to the journey (2: 178).

The text conjures up an image of Oriental grandeur as well as its obverse, barbaric lawlessness. Despite her disavowal, the analogy to Lalla Rookh is explicitly foregrounded.

Unlike Graham or Postans, Elwood explicitly addresses an implied female reader, holding out a promise of vicarious pleasure and adventure for the reader:

> . . . since, if she may judge from her own feelings, women naturally take a lively interest in what concerns their own sex, she flatters herself, that the following account of the adventures of the first and only female who has hitherto ventured overland from England to India, may at least prove not wholly unacceptable to the fair part of the reading community (Preface, vi).

Unlike the other two lady travellers her preface is all feminine disavowal, fears of seeming presumptuous in publishing her letters, and little of an Orientalist agenda to produce knowledge. Yet in her very first letter a highly self-conscious persona emerges, that of an intrepid lady traveller, one whose bid for a public subject position is based on her claim to having broken through gender boundaries:

> I may safely say, that I am the only Lady who ever travelled thither overland, by this,or perhaps by any other route; and probably mine was the first Journal ever kept by an Englishwoman in the Desert of Thebais, and on the shores of the Red Sea. When we first started our idea of travelling to India by way of Egypt, our project was treated as visionary by several, and numbers considered it impracticable *for a Lady*... but though we were fully aware this was a route hitherto but little frequented even by gentlemen, and that *no* lady had ever attempted the *outward* overland journey to Bombay, we were not to be deterred by imaginary difficulties. We resolved, at least, to *try* whether our plans were feasible . . . (1: 3).

Here we see how travel serves as a medium for the construction of a self-confident female subjectivity. Elwood performs the feat of exploiting Romantic discourse to serve her own ends, that of reclaiming a sense of agency for her own life:

> Instead of the Popes and Cardinals who grace the Diaries of other migratory damsels, you will meet with Agas and Cacheffs, and hear of Pashas and Rajahs; and for the ceremonies of the Holy Week, you will have the initiatory rites of the Mahometan Hadje, the Mohurrum, and the Hindoo Hoolie. You must ascend the Pyramids, and descend into Joseph's well, penetrate into the tomb of King Sesotris, and explore the caves of Elephanta. You will be exposed to Camseens and Siroccos; to Monsoons and tropical heats; you will sail in Egyptian Cangias, Arab Dows, and Indian Pattemars; travel in a Tacktrouan and Palanquin; take up your abode in tents, Caravanseras, and Durrumsallahs; hear of places seldom or perhaps never before visited by any of our countrywomen; and I shall have the pleasure of introducing you to a Turkish Divan at Djidda, an Arab Haram at Hodeida, a Jahrejah's Zenana at Bhooj, and a Brahmin's Pinjrapole at Broach (1: 2).

The glamour of the East and the lure of adventure, it is all there in the text. An Eastern pageant unfolds majestically before our eyes, enhanced by the string of exotic words deployed for their onomatopoeic effect,

More of a Childe Harold than a Lalla Rookh here, Elwood writes herself as a cicerone on the reader's journey into a land of Orientalist fantasy. One tends to overlook the fact that she travels as an 'incorporated wife'[30] whose life was intimately bound up in her husband's duties and not merely for pleasure as an independent lady traveller.

THE POLITICS OF THE SELF

Thus women travellers appropriate both scientific and Romantic conventions of travel writing to serve their own ends in constructing subjectivity and agency for the authors. However, the self is not a transhistorical category but the construct of a specific historical formation. The ideological interests at stake in the constitution of self have been scrutinized by critics such as Felicity Nussbaum.[31] She points out that the construction of the self as coherent, rational and in possession of a free will fulfills an ideological requirement of the emerging market economy. By locating the self at the centre of meaning the bourgeois pursuit of self-interest is legitimized. The ideology of self is thus a middle-class invention that had its corollary in the Enclosure Acts and the usurpation of the traditional rights of the working class. The bourgeois concept of self also informs and interacts with the discourses of Orientalism, where the uniqueness of the Western individual as opposed to the faceless masses of the Orient legitimizes the traveller's mission to know and represent the other.

The implications of this concept of self for a gendered subjectivity are ambivalent. For the bourgeois concept of self does not only produce the subject as the centre of the world — it is also a regulatory 'technology of the middle-class self', a term Nussbaum adopts from Foucault. While the mythology of self enables women to achieve a sense of identity and agency, it does so through the means of producing an illusion of control over one's own identity. The subject is posited as a transcendent category instead of seen as produced within discourses. Writing is one site for the production of subjectivity. Autobiographical genres such as the diary, the journal, the letter, and often, the travel narrative produce a sense of subjectivity for women. This sense of self is supplemented by the production of a public self in print. Thus women's texts contain subversive implications for the very notions of gender that the ideology of the bourgeois self is based on. Simultaneously, however, this ideology works to contain them within gender norms and boundaries.

We find the same mechanisms at work in women's Orientalist travel writings. The authors intervene in Orientalist discourses to contest male hegemony in the production of knowledge. This enables them to articulate a sense of female identity. The notion of self that they hereby confirm, however, is premised on the sovereign subject of knowledge, detached from the object of knowledge. In this empiricist model of self, subjectivity is always constituted by the definition of an other. Ironically, one of the others constituted into an object of knowledge— particularly in the eighteenth and nineteenth centuries in the field of medicine— is woman. The gaze of knowledge/power deployed by the Orientalist woman traveller is trained on her, too: for the universal subject of liberal humanism is implicitly male.

Anglicist Discourse

In view of their avid interest in ancient Indian culture, all three women travellers are to be classified as Orientalist. Nevertheless, the influence of Anglicist discourses are perceptible in their texts too. Thus in her programmatic 'Introduction', Maria Graham voices the hope that with respect to 'this singular people' (the Indians) she might contribute 'to the means of improving their moral and intellectual condition' (vii). Paradoxically, her interest and admiration for Hinduism is restricted to its manifestations of past glory — when she encounters Hindu worship in a temple she wishes to inspect, she is filled with revulsion: 'I returned to our tents, filled with reflections not very favourable to the dignity of human nature, after witnessing such a degrading instance of superstitious folly' (72). In fact, the text hints that part of her confusion is caused by a phallic sculpture that she 'was desired not to approach', so that she was unable to gratify her curiosity. In repressed rage and frustration she announces:

> If I could be assured that the communication with Europe would in ever so remote a period free the natives of India from their moral and religious degradation, I could even be almost reconciled to the methods by which the Europeans have acquired possession of the country (72).

Here a classic Anglicist stance is exemplified, for both Evangelicals and Utilitarians were vocal in their critique of the rapaciousness of the early adventurer-soldiers (Robert Clive and his ilk) and their methods in gaining possession of India. Although the hesitant rhetoric reveals the narrator as unwilling to endorse the Anglicist position wholeheartedly, the pious hope voiced in the text — the conversion of the Hindus to Christianity — is one of the main tenets of Anglicist policy.

Marianne Postans, too, is clearly influenced by Anglicist discourse — in addition to increasing the knowledge of India she pledges to contribute towards 'the means by which her condition may be efficiently improved' (viii). Despite her interest in Indian festivals, for instance, she notes severely that 'Hindoo holidays interfere sadly with the labours of the working classes' (2: 207). However poor the people may be, they still insist on celebrating their festivals with a carnevalesque abandon and disregard for the Puritan work ethos and the value of sobriety. (In this respect the working classes in India and England appear remarkably similar.) She waxes eloquent about a native school she visits and exhorts her countrymen to fulfill their sacred obligation to introduce enlightenment into India (1: 68). Postans' text is infused with the Macaulayan belief in the reformable native, the black Englishman eventually groomed and ready to take up the reins of his own government. Precisely this notion exposes an internal contradiction in Anglicist thought: as Eric Stokes notes, 'It was India which most clearly exposed the paradox in utilitarianism between the principle of liberty and the principle of authority'.[32] The Anglicists were caught between the urge to produce mimic men in their own image and, on the other hand, the need to justify continued rule and postpone the transfer of power (not yet, not here). Thus colonial mimicry 'is the desire for a reformed, recognizable Other, as *a subject of a difference that is almost the same, but not quite*', as Homi Bhabha puts it.[33] The figure of the educated native confronts the colonial rulers with the ambivalence at the heart of colonial discourse. The disturbance caused to the British by the educated native stems in part from a sense of prescience — it is precisely these mimic Englishmen who are later to overturn British rule.

As we have seen, Marianne Postans' text at times evinces a grasp of realities that escapes the controlling plot of her story. In the political analysis she presents at the end of her text, the reader is confronted with the following passage:

> . . . while we move onwards, flushed with success, repelling encroachment, and securing territory; in tracts which we leave slightly guarded, the people of India are thinking for themselves,

> are overcoming prejudice, and are gaining knowledge. This progress is dangerous to our supremacy . . . (2: 285).

Despite her endorsement of the project of native reform, her text articulates the threat posed by the educated native. What it conveys is a sense of the precariousness of power.

Notes

1 See Edward Said, *Orientalism*.

2 Biographical information is given in Jane Robinson, *Wayward Women: A Guide to Women Travellers* (Oxford: Oxford University Press, 1990) and K. K. Dyson, *A Various Universe: A Study of the Journals and Memoirs of British Men and Women in the Indian Subcontinent, 1765-1856* (Oxford: OUP, 1978).

3 For an overview of this conflict see especially Francis Hutchins, *The Illusion of Permanence: British Imperialism in India* (Princeton: Princeton University Press, 1967) 3-20, and George D. Bearce, *British Attitudes Towards India, 1784-1858* (London: OUP, 1961).

4 Thomas Babington Macaulay 'On Education for India', *Imperialism*, ed. Philip D. Curtin (London: Macmillan, 1971) 182.

5 Macaulay 190.

6 Nigel Leask, *British Romantic Writers and the East: Anxieties of Empire* (Cambridge: CUP, 1992) 78.

7 See especially Javed Majeed, *Ungoverned Imaginings: James Mill's* The History of British India *and Orientalism* (Oxford: Clarendon Press, 1992).

8 Eric Stokes, *The English Utilitarians and India* (Oxford: Clarendon Press, 1959) xii.

9 Majeed 9.

10 Anne Katherine Elwood, *Narrative of a Journey overland from England, by the Continent of Europe, Egypt, and the Red Sea, to India; including a Residence there, and Voyage home, in the years 1825, 26, 27, and 28*, 2 vols. (London, 1830) 2: 27. All further references to be included in parentheses in the text.

11 Mary Carpenter, *Six Months in India* (London, 1868) 2: 135. All further references to be given in parentheses in the text.

12 Ronald Inden, 'Orientalist Constructions of India,' *Modern Asian Studies* 20.3 (1986): 401-46.

13 Gayatri Spivak, *In other Worlds* 209.

14 Lata Mani, 'The Production of an Official Discourse on Sati', *Europe and Its Others*, 2 vols., ed. Francis Barker *et al.* (Colchester: University of Essex, 1985) 1:107-27.

15 In fact, Anand Yang has classified sati as an 'invented tradition'. See Anand A. Yang, 'Whose Sati? Widow Burning in Early 19th Century India', *Journal of Women's History* 1.2 (1989): 14-17.

16 C. A. Bayly, *Indian Society and the Making of the British Empire* (Cambridge: Cambridge University Press, 1988) 156.

17 Mani 127.

18 Fabian 37-70.

19 Maria Graham, *Journal of a Residence in India* (Edinburgh, 1812) Preface, vi. All further references to be given in parentheses in the text.

20 In the context of colonial India the term Anglo-Indian referred to the society of British residents in India.

21 I am extremely grateful to Nigel Leask for making his paper on 'Francis Wilford and the Colonial Construction of Hindu Geography 1799-1822', given at the 'Romantic Geographies' Conference at Glasgow University, 27 September 1994, available to me.

22 Leask points out that Wilford's article on a Sanskrit version of the story of Noah is quoted in Southey's *The Curse of Kehama* (1810).

23 Leask, 'Francis Wilford' 20.

24 See Leask 4.

25 See Frances Ferguson, 'The Sublime of Edmund Burke, or the Bathos of Experience', *Glyph* 8 (1981): 70.

26 Edmund Burke, *A Philosophical Enquiry into the Origin of Our Ideas of the Sublime and Beautiful* (1757), 61, quoted in Ferguson 71.

27 Partha Mitter, *Much Maligned Monsters: History of European Reactions to Indian Art* (Oxford: OUP, 1977) 108.

28 Mary Louise Pratt sees this as one of the characteristics of the informational form of travel writing, which she contrasts to the experiential or sentimental mode. See her 'Scratches on the Face of the Country; or, What Mr. Barrow Saw in the Land of the Bushmen', Gates 138-62.

29 As Mitter points out, Southey's *The Curse of Kehama* (1810) had been inspired by descriptions of Indian rock-temples. See Mitter 136. Also see Leask, *British Romantic Writers and the East.*

30 See Hillary Callan and Shirley Ardener, eds, *The Incorporated Wife* (London: Croom Helm, 1984).

31 Felicity A. Nussbaum, *The Autobiographical Subject. Gender and Ideology in Eighteenth-Century England* (Baltimore: John Hopkins University Press, 1989).

32 Stokes viii.

33 Homi Bhabha, 'Of Mimicry and Man: The Ambivalence of Colonial Discourse', *October* 28 (1984): 126.

Chapter 2

In Search of the Picturesque

> How much I enjoy the quietude of floating down the river, and admiring the picturesque ghats and temples on its banks! This is the country of the picturesque. . . .[1]

The aesthetics of the picturesque were enormously influential in moulding nineteenth-century travellers' perceptions of India. Particularly texts by women travellers were shaped by the conventions of the picturesque.

The aesthetic movement known as the picturesque began to emerge around the middle of the eighteenth century and evolved from Edmund Burke's discussion of the sublime and the beautiful. In his treatise *A Philosophical Enquiry into the Origin of Our Ideas of the Sublime and Beautiful* (1757), Burke had challenged classical norms of beauty by establishing the aesthetic category of the sublime, founded on the sensations of awe and terror. The aesthetics of the picturesque were a further rejection of classical categories. In his influential study Christopher Hussey locates the picturesque movement at the point of transition from Classicism to Romanticism—when art 'shifted its appeal from the reason to the imagination'.[2] Due to the enormous popularity of the seventeenth-century French and Italian landscape painters Claude Lorrain, Nicholas Poussin and Salvator Rosa on the continent, collecting landscape painting came into fashion with the British wealthy classes in the late eighteenth century. This led to a displacement of both history painting and portraits by landscape painting as the most highly valorized mode of art. At the same time classical literature was being challenged In the field of poetry, where a shift towards a celebration of national rather than classical scenery reflected the project of cultural and national self-definition.[3]

Several stages may be traced within the development of the picturesque. The first consisted in arranging a landscape, manipulating a view so as to render it more suitable for a painting.[4] The first theorist of the picturesque, William Gilpin, stressed the fact that nature was not inherently picturesque. While beautiful objects in nature were characterized by smoothness, the picturesque called for the introduction of a rugged element into the scene, rendering it more fit for pictorial representation. Gilpin illustrated this idea in a series of uninspiring landscape sketches which he juxtaposed to scenes enhanced by the addition of irregularized lines.[5] A later theorist, Uvedale Price, developed Gilpin's notions by definining the picturesque as a distinct third category to be set against Burke's sublime and the beautiful. He produced a list of items suitable for the picturesque—they included ruins, cottages, dilapidated mills, hovels, shaggy goats, the worn-out cart-horse, but also gypsies, beggars, in fact the entire gamut of rural poor.[6] With Richard Payne Knight the move towards a romantic sensibility became even more perceptible. He claimed that impressions of beauty, sublimity, as well as picturesqueness, were directly linked to the modes of viewing of the spectators, thus stressing the role of the perceiving subject in the act of perception and distancing himself from mechanical notions of sensation.[7]

In her perceptive study of the politics of the picturesque, Ann Bermingham points out that the cult of an irregular landscape coincided with the hitherto most massive interference in the agricultural landscape of Britain—the large-scale enclosure of the English countryside. It 'idealized a landscape that was in fact rapidly vanishing.'[8] In its harking back to a golden age of pastoral bliss, it sentimentalized the old order of rural paternalism. She identifies a denial of the realities of enclosure and the agricultural revolution in the cult of the picturesque, which mystified the agency of social change, so that it appeared inevitable. The aestheticization of rural poverty was linked to a clearly defined sense of social snobbery and elitism—Knight names the ownership of property as a precondition for an aesthetic sensibility.[9] The picturesque flaunts its anti-utilitarianism: in a notorious passage Gilpin wrote, 'In a moral view, the industrious mechanic is a more pleasing object than the loitering peasant. But in the picturesque light, it is otherwise. The arts of industry are rejected; and even idleness... adds dignity to a character.'[10] However, as Bermingham points out, despite its celebration of the old order and its rejection of industrialism, at a deeper level the picturesque embodied the values and worldview of the wealthy landowning classes whose economic decisions had introduced the changes to the landscape.

Though originally imported from Italy to England and soon linked to a celebration of the native English countryside, the picturesque soon spilt over the borders of Britain. The first picturesque artist to arrive in India was William Hodges. Hodges, who gained fame for his sketches of the South Seas while accompanying Captain Cook on his voyages, published a series of aquatints entitled *Select Views in India* in 1786. The genre of the picturesque travel-book emerged and became a passion in Britain from the 1790s.[11] From a movement in landscape art the picturesque evolved into a broadly defined aesthetics. The most famous contribution to the Indian picturesque was undoubtedly that by the Daniells (uncle and nephew), whose aquatints were enormously influential in defining the early nineteenth-century view of India.[12] Their Arcadian construction of India coincided with the high-water mark of the school of Orientalism focusing on classical Indian culture, and their influence was felt in fields as diverse as architecture and fashion. As Mitter points out, the original design of the Brighton pavilion drew heavily on a classical Indian style of architecture.[13]

For the wave of travellers to India who followed in the wake of the Daniells a sketch-book was a *sine qua non* of their (cultural) baggage. The genre of travel writing was permeated by the aesthetics of the picturesque. Recent critics have interrogated 'the extent to which the Picturesque...can be seen to shape British (or wider European) accounts of colonial landscapes and cultures.'[14]

The search for the Indian picturesque was a part of the project of Orientalism. Just as the picturesque movement in Britain preserved the English countryside in an eternal Arcadian age, Orientalism constructed the Orient as timeless and immutable. Similarly, the Orientalist concern with the glorious past of the East was reflected in the picturesque nostalgia for ruins and tombs. Traditionally, historians have tended to acclaim the school of 'Orientalists', led by Sir William Jones, who shaped British policy in India at the turn of the eighteenth to the nineteenth century. Fascinated by Indian culture, they set about creating a vast store of knowledge about India and unlocking the treasures of Indian arts and philosophy for the West. However, as Said has shown, Orientalism, too, was a hegemonic strategy which produced a construct of India in accordance with Orientalist ideas of an ideal classical past. Accordingly, the social reality of India is effaced in order to freeze the scene depicted in an aesthetic tableau.[15] As Stephen Copley and Peter Garside put it, 'the Picturesque translates the political and the social into the decorative.'[16] An extract from an exemplary text of the picturesque by the traveller Fanny Parks will serve to illustrate this point:

> The river is very picturesque; high cliffs, well covered with wood, rising abruptly from the water: here and there a Hindoo temple, with a great peepul-tree spreading its fine branches around it: a ruined native fort: clusters of native huts: beautiful stone ghats jutting into the river: the effect greatly increased by the native women, in their picturesque drapery, carrying their vessels for water up and down the cliffs, poised on their heads. ... But the most picturesque of all are the different sorts of native vessels; I am quite charmed with the boats. Oh that I were a painter, who could do justice to the scenery! (1: 333)

All the ingredients of the Indian picturesque are to be found here: an Arcadian landscape, Hindu temples and ruins, and statuesque Oriental women. The literary mode corresponding to the picturesque is the mode of sensibility.

Stephen Greenblatt has analysed early travelogues on America and has pointed to the deployment of the marvellous as a rhetorical strategy in the service of a process of appropriation.[17] Similarly, the organizing trope of the picturesque was evoked in colonial travelogues in the service of an imaginative appropriation of the other world. The process of aesthetic possession is accompanied by the scientific appropriation of India in the form of land surveys and the rise of anthropological studies of the natives. As S. P. Mohanty points out, 'the nineteenth century was the period when colonial rule consolidated itself through a phenomenal increase in its 'scientific' knowledge of the various populations of India as well as the land itself.'[18] Despite the differences between the scientific mode and the mode of sensibility, both projects are variations of the same quest—the colonial urge to 'know' the other. Interestingly enough, the woman traveller Fanny Parks presents herself to the reader as an 'amateur ethnographer',[19] complete with pocket-book.

The acquisitive connotations of the search for the picturesque were not hidden from its contemporaries and occasionally surface in texts. William Marshall, in his 1795 history of landscape painting, sees 'something of the big-game hunter in these tourists, boasting of their encounters with savage landscapes, 'capturing' wild scenes, and 'fixing' them as pictorial trophies in order to sell them or hang them up in frames on their drawing-room walls'.[20] While Fanny Parks casts herself as a pilgrim ('a poor haji in search of the picturesque') (1: 240) in the programmatic title of her book (*Wanderings of a Pilgrim in Search of the Picturesque*), the impression created by her vast compendium of information is that of insatiable collection rather than tranquil recollection. Parks' voracious appetite for the picturesque is by no means limited to eye-witness accounts of Indian scenes. She boasts a large collection of idols and artifacts, and during a trip home she writes,

> Visited the British Museum; the new rooms that have been added are handsome, and well filled with Egyptian curiosities; mummies in crowds, and very fine ones. The Elgin marbles, in a handsome hall, are also shown to great advantage. My collection of Hindoo idols is far superior to any in the Museum; and as for Ganesh, they never beheld such an one as mine, even in a dream! (2: 334)

The project of cultural mastery is epitomized in the obsessive accumulation of exotic artifacts. These curios present the Orient as a commodity for consumption by the Western traveller. James Clifford has analysed the collecting of souvenirs as as 'one of the crucial processes of Western identity formation' in the capitalist order.[21] As Parks herself points out, within the project of colonial appropriation she finds herself in the best of company.

Nowhere does Parks present herself more elaborately as a pilgrim to the East than in the introduction of her book, preceded by a wordy invocation to the Hindu god Ganesh, patron of learning:

> Moon-crowned! Triple-eyed!
> Thou who in all affairs claimest precedence in adoration!
> Calamity-averting Ganesh!
> Salam!!

> Thou who art invoked on the commencement of a journey,
> the writing of a book,
> Salam!!

It is precisely while describing the image of the god depicted in the frontispiece that the text is disrupted by a rhetoric of possession:

> This idol is made of solid white marble, and weighs three hundred weight and a quarter. It is painted and gilt, as in the Frontispiece. It was brought down from Jeypur to the sacred junction of the triple rivers at Prag, at which place it came into my possession. There he sits before me in all his Hindu state and peculiar style of beauty—my inspiration—my penates. (xxv)

The excessive veneration displayed so far suddenly gives way to a calm computation of material attributes and an assertion of ownership: as Sara Suleri points out, during this passage the god invoked mutates from deity to artifact.[22] Like the Oriental words liberally sprinkled in the text, the enumeration of exotic curios serves as a rhetorical strategy to underline the authenticity of the traveller/narrator. In Fanny Parks' travel book we have a paradigmatic text of the Indian picturesque. In her work of a thousand pages she remorselessly piles episode on episode, copious excerpts from scholarly works and Indian myths and garnishes the finished product with (inappropriate) Oriental proverbs. In forays into the zenana she adopts a voyeuristic gaze and assiduously adds her bit to the production of knowledge about the Oriental woman.

The picturesque programme of these texts is at times undermined by internal contradictions, which expose colonial anxieties. Even in the travel book of the Daniells, *A Picturesque Voyage to India* (1810), the violence of colonial appropriation and the complicity of the picturesque in this project is hinted at in the author's paradoxical desire to take part in 'guiltless spoliation' in the interests of knowledge and to 'transport back picturesque beauties of those favoured regions'.[23] Parks, too, generally employs an idiom more reminiscent of plundering invaders than of peaceful pilgrims when she speaks of artifacts that catch her eye ('A great many Hindoo idols...I shall carry some off should I return this way.') (2: 30). Nevertheless, she does evince a sense of guilt at a headless figure of a sati (commemorating a widow-burning) she carries off which is an object of veneration. An ominous note in the text is struck when the ship carrying the artifact is wrecked. However, she displaces responsibility for the theft onto the master of the ship over-eager to please her:

> Alas! my beautiful Seagull; she has folded her wings for ever, and has sunk to rest! ... The headless image of the sati, that had graced the cabin, had brought rather too much wind. When the sarang[24] lamented her loss, I could only repeat, as on the day he carried off the lady, ... ill deeds never thrive. (2: 59)

Her own complicity in this act of spoilation is conveniently effaced.

THE GENDER POLITICS OF THE PICTURESQUE

Recent criticism has discussed the implications of the notion of the picturesque in terms of gender and has argued that the picturesque 'has been, from its inception, a practice culturally coded 'male'.'[25] In a conflation of aesthetics and erotics, nature as an object of desire has traditionally been encoded as feminine. Vivien Jones has analysed the structure of the picturesque in terms of 'a voyeuristic consumption of the landscape',[26] while Gillian Rose in her scrutiny of the gender relations implicit in the discipline of geography makes the point that 'visual pleasure in landscape is specifically sexual.'[27] I would like to shift the discussion away from an exclusive focus on gender to the elision of other categories informing perception—without, however, denying the masculinist assumptions of the gaze. Instead, I would like to point to the power relations inherent in the picturesque—of which gender relations are only one dimension. The picturesque gaze, like the voyeuristic gaze (discussed in chapter three) and the gaze of surveillance (discussed in chapter six) are all variants of the transcendent observer paradigm. The aesthetic pleasure offered from the site of the disembodied viewer is always linked to a sense of power and control over the image. It seems to me reductionist to argue that in the colonial context women travellers take up a male position towards the other. Instead, the complex field of force informing specific relations of power needs to be taken into account. In colonial India, for example, the aesthetics of the picturesque played a particular role in shaping the image of India in travelogues by women travellers. ('What bits to sketch! what effects here! what colouring here!' exclaims Lady Falkland.)[28] In 1822, a School of Art for Ladies specializing in the picturesque was opened in Bombay.[29] While the mode of the picturesque was by no means the preserve of women travel writers, they tended to disport themselves in this field as so few other avenues were open to them. During the twenty-four years that Fanny Parks spent in India (from 1822 to 1846), breathlessly pursuing one picturesque scene after the other, other Orientalist authors were writing learned disquisitions on the antiquities of India—such as Colonel Tod, from whose authoritative *Annals and Antiquities of Rajasthan* (1829-32) she quotes at length. Alternatively, like William Sleeman, they were travelling in a region on a political mission—Sleeman was sent for reconnaissance to Oudh, one of the last independent kingdoms on the East India Company's borders, in order to assess whether an invasion and incorporation of the kingdom into British territory would be advisable.[30] I argue that the aestheticizing stance displayed in the texts of the picturesque is symptomatic both of women's marginalized position in British India as well as of women's self-image as spectators of empire.

For aesthetic appropriation of the other is premised on a denial of implication in colonial reality.[31] The stance of the disinterested, aesthetic viewer obscures relations of power in the scene being viewed. An example from a text by an Englishwoman in India should serve to illustrate this point:

> The common sights along an Indian road, too, are always picturesque—the wide plains, with great herds of smoke-coloured, delicate-limbed cattle being driven slowly home for the night.... Then gangs of wayfarers clad in every colour and degree of costume, from the simple suit of ashes of the Fakir, to the gorgeous combination of white and coloured raiment of some rich man who has just dismounted hurriedly from his carriage, drawn by a pair of white humped oxen, to salaam to R. Some of the men we met had rather a fiendish look, their whole bodies as well as their scanty garments being of a dark hideous blue colour; they were men employed in indigo-making, which at this time of the year is in full swing. (King 1: 124-5)

The narrator is, she informs us, the wife of a Collector, a high administrative post in colonial India. The natives that heighten the charm of the Arcadian scene unfolding before the readers are merely paying tribute to the political realities underlying the scene—a law obliged Indians to cede the right of way to the British on all occasions.

The picturesque if slightly threatening figures ('fiendish') the narrator encounters are labourers on indigo plantations—a form of labour commonly referred to as 'indigo slavery' and whose employers, the plantation owners, are notorious for abusing labour. These unsavoury historical realities are safely deflected from King's text by the imposition of a picturesque frame. Similarly, she insists on producing the Orient as a timeless set piece on every occasion. Workaday life is represented as follows:

> . . . we enjoyed driving through the bazaars, and seeing all the artisans at work—hammering iron, embroidering shawls, engraving brass, setting jewels, fashioning trinkets, coats, baskets—everything, in short, that is made being made [sic] in the open air before your eyes. It is such a cheerful, busy scene, and no one looks hardworked or worn with care as they do in Europe: life is not lived here at such a pace. (2: 236)

This passage could come straight out of a glossy tourist brochure on the Orient today, where the discursive economy of the picturesque is still very much in circulation.

In another passage, King is more explicit about the political agenda informing her variety of the picturesque. When describing children employed in carpet making, she gushes:

> . . . six little boys, varying in age from eight to eleven, were working it, while one of them read out the pattern from a slip of paper. Their small brown fingers worked so nimbly, knotting on the various coloured wools and cutting off the ends with a knife, that one could hardly see what they were doing. It seemed amazing that such young boys could have attained such dexterity. Their pay is from four to six rupees a month—*i.e.* eight to twelve shillings a *month*; think of that, ye discontented operatives of England! (2: 114)

Child labour is sentimentalized and romanticized in order to castigate labour agitation in England. A standard ploy in travelogues: the Orient is set up as a contrastive foil—to be either idealized or denigrated—to the traveller's own culture.

THE PICTURESQUE AND THE OTHER

This brings me to a further aspect of the picturesque: it serves as a distancing device towards the other. It had an insulating function for the traveller and operated as a strategy to domesticate the threat posed by the radically other. In the colonial world, where women were relegated to the margins of society yet burdened with the responsibility of upholding the home culture, the picturesque offered women a secure position from which to deal with the reality of India. It served to intercept a frame between the other and oneself. 'For the female as colonizer, the picturesque assumes an ideological urgency through which all subcontinental threats could be temporarily converted into watercolours and thereby domesticated into a less disturbing system of belonging.'[32] Thus Fanny Parks pronounces a sinister religious mendicant, whom she describes as having held one arm erect for so long that the nails of the clenched hand had pierced the palm in the form of a claw, to be 'remarkably picturesque' (1: 256). At other times, the aesthetic gloss applied to life in India cracks, and heat, dust and disease—the British neuroses in India—come pouring through. At such a moment Parks exclaims, 'Woe is me that I sojourn in this land of pestilence, that I dwell afar from the home of my fathers!' (1: 303). As both Leask and Suleri have shown, colonial anxieties were often displaced onto the fear of infectious disease.[33]

In a provocative essay, Hayden White calls for a reintroduction of the politics of the sublime in historiography.[34] For him, the disinterested observer stance taken up by positivist historians is responsible for the exorcizing of a visionary politics in historiography. Instead, he calls for a reading of history as vertiginous, incomprehensible, and confusion. Ironically, Burke himself banishes the sublime from history in favour of the beautiful in order to insist on the virtues of the English constitution in contrast to the French Revolution. What interests us here is the extent to which the concept of the sublime offers an epistemological alternative to that of the picturesque.

David Punter, too, points up the difference between the picturesque and the sublime in their approaches to the other.[35] The picturesque, he points out, is concerned with framing the other, filtering it through an aestheticizing lens (literally in the case of the Claude glass, an accessory of the picturesque traveller which served to manipulate a landscape). The picturesque worked to detach the traveller from the scene and to contain the threat posed by the other by arranging it into an aesthetic frame. In contrast, 'the Sublime has to do with being overwhelmed, surprised, being taken out of one's frame by a scene which, in a parallel way, threatens its boundaries as well as our own.'[36] This is the kind of vertiginous experience undergone by the fictitious travellers in *A Passage to India* in Homi Bhabha's reading of what happens in the cave, which he sees as a symbol for 'cultural anarchy' and 'unreadability.'[37] But none of the women travellers discussed so far are willing to let the tight narrative control of their texts slip. At certain moments, however, colonial reality breaks in to disturb the smooth facade of the picturesque. In the following instance, Parks is once again to be found busy sketching a ruin that appeals to her:

> I returned to the ancient Hindu building that had so much interested me, to sketch it at leisure, and was thus employed, when I was surrounded by numbers of the starved and wretched villagers. I performed my task as quickly as possible, and whatever errors there may be in the performance must be attributed to the painful scene by which I was surrounded. ... I picked up a curious piece of ancient sculpture, Mahadeo, with Parvati in the centre, and a devi on each side, which I brought to my tent on the elephant. Considering it too heavy to carry about on the march, we buried it at night under a peepul tree, and shall take it away on our return home, if it will please to remain there. (2: 145)

The narrative of the picturesque exerts itself visibly to regain control and returns to the haven of the picturesque as quickly as possible—unwilling or unable to draw an analogy between the narrator's rapacious quest for the aesthetic and colonial rapaciousness (the famine in question was exacerbated by Governor-General Lord Auckland's exorbitant march through the Indian countryside accompanied by a train of 12,000 camp attendants and their animals, all requiring sustenance). Nevertheless, the text cannot repress a hint of guilt in its elaboration of the stealth required for the further accumulation of the picturesque East.

The elitist element in the English picturesque with its denial of aesthetic sensibility to the lower classes is transferred to the native in the colonial context. A recurrent lament in the texts of the travellers is the native's lack of appreciation for the aesthetic: 'The natives very rarely have an eye for the picturesque, or any admiration for nature', Lady

Falkland complains (1: 283). Mrs Colin Mackenzie offers a graphic example of the cultural philistinism of the native:

> The Hindustanis are very apathetic to scenery. I have never known one to stop to admire anything. My husband cross-questioned a chaprassi[38] (from Delhi I think) to find if he had any appreciation for the beauties which surrounded him. Not in the least. He said the pain in his legs in running up and down hill with messages was not to be expressed, and that if it were not for the wants of his stomach he would not stay here a day.[39]

The irony that strikes the contemporary reader seems to be unintentional in Mackenzie's case, for she goes on to elaborate on the further inadequacies of the natives. ('There is such a wide distinction between the conquering and the subject race...') (164). Like so many other superior attributes, an eye for the picturesque remains firmly the prerogative of the colonial rulers. Aestheticization, it seems, always proceeds from a position of privilege.

Notes

1 Fanny Parks, *Wanderings of a Pilgrim in Search of the Picturesque, during Four-and Twenty Years in the East; with Revelations of Life in the Zenana* (1850; Karachi: OUP, 1975) 1: 197. All further references to be given in parentheses in the text.

2 Christopher Hussey, *The Picturesque: Studies in a Point of View* (London: Putnam, 1927) 4.

3 Malcolm Andrews, *The Search for the Picturesque: Landscape Aesthetics and Tourism in Britain, 1760-1800* (Aldershot: Scolar Press, 1989) 3-23.

4 See John Barrell, *The Idea of Landscape and the Sense of Place, 1730-1840* (Cambridge: CUP, 1972).

5 See Andrews 31.

6 Andrews 59; see also Ann Bermingham, *Landscape and Ideology: The English Rustic Tradition, 1740-1860* (Berkeley: University of California, 1986) 69.

7 Bermingham 71.

8 Bermingham 68.

9 Bermingham 71.

10 Quoted in Bermingham 80.

11 Mildred Archer and Ronald Lightbrown, *India Observed: India as viewed by British Artists 1760-1860* (London: Victoria and Albert Museum, 1982) 80.

12 Partha Mitter, *Much Maligned Monsters* 126-29; see also G. H. R. Tillotson, 'The Indian Picturesque: Images of India in Landscape Painting, 1780-1880', *The Raj: India and the British, 1600-1947,* C. A. Bayly *et al.*, eds. (London: National Portrait Gallery, 1990) 144-47.

13 Mitter 29.

14 Stephen Copley and Peter Garside, eds., *The Politics of the Picturesque: Literature, Landscape and Aesthetics since 1770* (Cambridge: CUP, 1994), Introduction 2.

15 Also see Nicholas Thomas, *Colonialism's Culture* 54-5.

16 Copley and Garside 6.

17 See Stephen J. Greenblatt, *Marvellous Possessions: The Wonder of the New World* (Oxford: OUP, 1991).

18 S. P. Mohanty, 'Kipling's Children and the Colour Line', *Race & Class* 21 (1989): 33.

19 Sara Suleri, 'The Feminine Picturesque', *The Rhetoric of English India* (Chicago: University of Chicago Press, 1992) 75.

20 Quoted in Andrews 67.

21 James Clifford, 'On Collecting Art and Culture', *The Predicament of Culture, Twentieth-Century Ethnography, Literature, and Art* (Cambridge, Mass.: Harvard University Press, 1988) 220.

22 Suleri 84.

23 Quoted in Mitter 127.

24 Master of the ship.

25 James Buzard, *The Beaten Track: European Tourism, Literature, and the Ways to 'Culture' 1800-1918* (Oxford: Clarendon Press, 1993) 16.

26 Vivien Jones, '"The Coquetry of Nature': Politics and the Picturesque in Women's Fictions', Copley and Garside 129.

27 Gillian Rose, 'Geography as a Science of Observation: The Landscape, the Gaze and Masculinity', *Nature and Science: Essays in the History of Geographical Knowledge*, eds. Felix Driver and Gillian Rose (London: Historical Geographical Research Group, 1992) 16.

28 Viscountess Amelia Cary Falkland, *Chow-Chow; Being Selections from a Journal Kept in India, Egypt and Syria*, 2 vols. (London, 1857) 1: 9. All further references to be given in parentheses in the text.

29 Mary Ann Lind, *The Compassionate Memsahib: Welfare Activities of British Women in India, 1900-1947* (New York: Greenwood Press, 1988) 26.

30 See William Sleeman, *A Journey Through the Kingdom of Oude in 1849-1850*, 2 vols. (London, 1858).

31 See Suleri 86.

32 Suleri 75-6.

33 Leask 6-8; Suleri 89-91.

34 Hayden White, 'The Politics of Historical Interpretation: Discipline and De-Sublimation', *Critical Inquiry* 9 (1982): 113-37.

35 David Punter, 'The Picturesque and the Sublime: Two Worldscapes', Copley and Garside 220-39.

36 Punter 223.

37 The terms are Suleri's, 104. See Bhabha's essay, 'Articulating the Archaic: Notes on Colonial Nonsense', *Literary Theory Today*, eds Peter Collier and Helga Geyer-Ryan (Cambridge: Polity, 1990) 203-18.

38 Messenger.

39 Mrs Colin Mackenzie, *Six Years in India* (London, 1857) 173. All further references to be incorporated in parentheses in the text.

Chapter 3

The Female Gaze: Encounters in the Zenana

The first question that travellers to the East were confronted with on their return, according to Richard Burton, was: 'What are the women like?'[1] Unfortunately, the gentlemen in question were unable to oblige in one important respect—it was virtually impossible for them to gain access to a harem or seraglio. Even Burton's disguises and contortions were of little use in this connection. This was no impediment to their fantasies, however. In 1598 Thomas Dallam claimed to have caught a glimpse of the Turkish Sultan's concubines playing ball in the royal gardens, and in the seventeenth century Sir George Courthope deftly conjured up a scene of royal sport with concubines in a pond in the same gardens (they were empty when he saw them). Alexander Pope fantasized about eunuchs and even cucumbers only being served cut in the harem; Burton's own account was both more drastic and more explicit.[2] And the painter Thomas Daniell's *A Zenana Scene* (1804) with its Oriental beauty draped in gauzy veils was purely the product of his fantasy. It was only with the posthumous publication of Lady Montagu's *Letters* from Turkey in 1763 that an eyewitness account of life in the harem was made available to readerships in the West.

The issue of female spectatorship and the related questions of female desire and subjectivity as well as enmeshment in relations of power/knowledge are brought into particularly sharp focus in the case of eyewitness accounts of the harem by Western women. I wish to look specifically at accounts by Englishwomen and their encounters of the other kind in the

Indian zenana.[3] Despite the fact that zenanas were only to be found in upper-class households in the North and East of India, they attracted an inordinately large portion of curiosity among women travellers.[4] Paradoxically, however, the travellers themselves—as women—were the focus of the male gaze in their own patriarchal home culture. The question to be probed is, what does it mean to look at the other woman from a woman's point of view? This issue is inextricably bound up with recent discussions on the female gaze.

Laura Mulvey's analysis of the position of female viewers of Hollywood films has emerged as a key text in discussions of the female gaze.[5] Originally Mulvey looks at the question of how spectators gain pleasure from mainstream films that are premised on the image of women as sexual commodities whose main *raison d'être* is to cater to male fantasies and desires. She concludes that in Hollywood films the location of the spectator is constructed as masculine, offering him the pleasures of voyeurism and/or the comforts of fetishism and identification with the (invariably male) hero. In other words: the gaze is male. In her later work Mulvey turns to the female spectator and identifies two possible viewing positions for her *vis-à-vis* Hollywood cinema's sexualized and fetishised female star—that of a vicarious identification with a male perspective or that of a narcissistic identification with the woman protagonist in the film, linked to the desire to be as sexually desirable as the film character. In fact, Mulvey posits the female spectator as continually oscillating between these two positions.[6] Thus women have a choice only between objectifying the other woman in an adoption of the male perspective or identifying with the female character in her role as sex object of the male gaze.

These arguments have been further developed (and contradicted) by feminist critics in a variety of fields, who argue in favour of an autonomous female gaze. Thus Rosemary Betterton has examined the female nude in the oeuvre of the painter Suzanne Valadon and has come to the conclusion that the gender of the artist has left its trace in the images of women produced by her.[7] In these paintings Betterton discerns a critical distance to the representation of the woman's body as an eroticized site. Reina Lewis has looked at women Orientalist painters' representations of the harem and detects a palpable difference to male Orientalist art and a latent threat to male Orientalist fantasies.[8] The harem is depicted as a social space rather than an eroticized space, with interactive relationships between the Oriental women focused on rather than the women being represented as merely awaiting the male gaze. Billie Melman, in her scrutiny of women travellers' accounts of their trips to Oriental (Middle Eastern) harems, observes a progressive domestication of the harem in Western women's writings.[9] Lady Montagu's famous claim of the greater (sexual) freedom of veiled women as contrasted to their Western sisters is gradually transmuted in later accounts to the depiction of the harem as a domesticated, bourgeois home, the women assiduously occupying themselves with needlework.

Many of the analyses of the female gaze draw on feminist psychoanalytic theory. However, in recent works on the female gaze the concept itself has come under fire. Feminist psychoanalytic theory is seen to unduly privilege gender.[10] An analysis drawing on discourse theory, on the other hand, would begin by dismantling the very notion of a female gaze: there is, of course, no 'female gaze'. A concept of identity as precarious and overdetermined by a plurality of factors makes it imperative to take coordinates other than gender into account. As Mary Eagleton points out,

> the notion of a 'female imagination' can confirm the belief in a deep, basic, and inevitable difference between male and female ways of perceiving the world. Such 'essentialist' or 'biologistic' beliefs imply that there is something intrinsic in the experience of being female and thus render gender biological rather than cultural; they tend to privilege gender at the expense of class or race; and they can too easily become ahistorical and apolitical, presuming an unproblematic unity among women across culture, class and history.[11]

Gisela Ecker reiterates this point from a different perspective. She points out that women, however marginalized in the patriarchal order, are nevertheless co-opted into the dominant culture and not located outside it.[12] The concept of a female gaze (and, by analogy, that of a women's language) is illusory. As she argues in her 'Introduction' to *Feminist Aesthetics,* it is probably more useful to talk about a consciously feminist than an inherently feminine aesthetics.[13]

In addition, determinants such as race and gender are themselves not characterized by an inherent essence, but are unstable and differential terms. Mulvey's spectator is predicated on a notion of gender as a fixed subject position of binary opposites. For a woman spectator to take up a masculinized viewing position involves, as it were, an act of transvestism. But recent feminist critics have shown gender to be a sophisticated political and social construction and gender identification to rather be a shifting and contradictory process. As Judith Butler explains, 'Gender is the repeated stylization of the body, a set of repeated acts within a highly regulatory frame that congeal over time to produce the appearance of substance, of a natural sort of being.'[14] 'Woman', in other words, is only a myth.[15]

As pointed out in my 'Introduction', the question to be asked is: whose gaze is it anyway?[16] It is the power relations inscripted into the gaze that call for closer scrutiny, as discourse theory has shown. As various critics of Western feminism have pointed out, notions of universal womanhood re-enact the strategies of liberal humanism by setting up the yardstick by which to define the other and ultimately recolonize her.[17] These critics too have demolished the notion of 'woman' and have pointed to the diversity of womanhood. In my analysis of Englishwomen's encounters with the Indian other, I wish to point to the historical dimensions of the gaze—instead of a universal 'female gaze' I wish to look at specific political and historical configurations and how they have informed the gaze. Even within a circumscribed historical constellation, however, a plurality of gazes is discernible.

Finally, the notion of 'the gaze' needs to be interrogated as well. The term 'the gaze' assumes an autonomous viewing subject whose perception gives access to truth. In mimetic theories of art, texts are presumed to transparently reproduce this visual experience. In post-structuralist theory, however, experience is seen as culturally mediated and as historically produced and constructed within discourses. A reductive and homogeneous concept of the gaze needs to be replaced by a historicized notion of perception. As Betterton points out, 'looking, and the psychic mechanisms which structure it, are themselves historically produced.'[18] As regards the travel narratives of women travellers, for example, their encounters with the other woman were structured by the cultural norms and the ideological forces at work at the time. From their accounts we learn more about the fantasies of the viewers than about the material realities of the zenana.

The Erotic Gaze

Meyda Yegenoglu attacks the notion of a female gaze by deconstructing the harem account of Lady Montagu, one of the icons of feminist criticism.[19] She draws an analogy between women travellers' descriptions of the harem and Derrida's concept of the supplement: their accounts, while serving to complement male Orientalist accounts, were simultaneously disavowed as of minor significance. Nevertheless, for European women, barred admittance to scientific discourses, harem literature provided an opportunity to contribute to the discourses of Orientalism and thus gain in prestige. In Montagu's text she identifies a pleasure at being the first to penetrate the space of the other and thus add to the production of knowledge about the other. Yegenoglu attributes the Western subject's voyeuristic desire to 'know' the Oriental woman to the fact that women were seen as the essence of the East, associated as it was with femininity, sensuality and irrationality in the discourses of Orientalism.[20] Yegenoglu sees Lady Montagu and her successors as implicated in Orientalism as they too constitute the other into an object of knowledge and contribute to the unequal power/knowledge nexus. With respect to Montagu's famous description of naked Turkish ladies in the bath she maintains, 'When she looks at the woman as Other, that is to say, as belonging to the Other culture, Montagu's look then turns into a masculine gaze. She takes up the masculine, phallic position . . . the unavoidable masculinity of the subject position the female travellers occupy *vis-à-vis* the Orient and its women' (70).

We are thus faced with two irreconcilable readings of Western women travellers' accounts of the harem: critics such as Billie Melman see a sense of cross-cultural women's solidarity at work here, subverting patriarchal voyeuristic representations of the harem;[21] colonial discourse critics like Janaki Nair[22] and Yegenoglu see these accounts as an example of Western women's complicity in Orientalism and their assumption of a male gaze. There might, however, be another dimension to women's representations of the other hitherto insufficiently theorized. This is addressed in one of the most exciting essays on the female gaze to have appeared recently—'Desperately Seeking Difference' by Jackie Stacey.[23] Stacey looks at the phenomenon of fascination between women, which she considers hardly surprising 'in a culture where the circulation of idealized and desirable images of femininity constantly surrounds us' (114). In particular, she takes a closer look at the pleasures produced for the female spectator by the film *Desperately Seeking Susan* (dir. Susan Seidelman, 1984) which virtually launched the Madonna cult. In this film the main protagonist, a bored and insecure American housewife, is drawn into a series of adventures through her fascination with the seductively anarchic Madonna, representing everything the housewife is not. This fascination, which the spectator is invited to share, 'is neither purely identification with the other woman, nor desire for her in the strictly erotic sense of the word. It is a desire to see, to know and to become more like an idealised feminine other, in a context where the difference between the two women is repeatedly re-established' (115).

Stacey's rejection of the rigid division between objectification (as accomplice of the male voyeuristic look) and identification by pointing to an interplay of both elements offers one way of approaching the accounts of women travellers by focusing on issues of pleasure and fantasy. How else are we to read the following passage in Fanny Parks' *Wanderings of a Pilgrim* (1850):

> The building that most interested me was the Royal Zenana Ghar. At certain times the Emperor of Delhi used to retire to this spot with all his ladies; . . . his amusement was to watch the sports of the ladies of the zenana, as they jumped from the roof of a verandah into the water below, and then came up to jump in again. On the other side is another tank, with a sloping bank of masonry; on this slope the ladies used to sit, and slide down into the tank. In the water, amidst the trees, the graceful drapery of the Musulmani and Hindu ladies clinging to their well-formed persons must have had a beautiful effect. During these sports, guards were stationed around, to prevent the intrusion of any profane eye on the sacredness of the zenana. (2: 208)

The buildings Parks mentions are all ruins—the sport she so lovingly describes are all products of her fantasy (187).

'The perusal of Lady Mary Wortley Montague's [sic] work has rendered me very anxious to visit a zenana, and to become acquainted with the ladies of the East', Parks announces (1: 59). In her text Parks produces herself as Montagu's successor and is applauded by reviewers accordingly.[24] When she receives an invitation to pay a visit to a real zenana, she exults, 'Was this not delightful? All my dreams . . . were to be turned into reality. I was to have an opportunity of viewing life in the zenana, of seeing the native ladies of the East, women of high rank, in the seclusion of their own apartments, in private life' (1: 378).

A juxtaposing of Montagu's text with that of Parks is revealing for the insights it produces of an intertextual dialogue at work. Montagu's encounter with the fair Fatima is described in the following passage:

> I have seen all that has been called lovely either in England or Germany, and must own that I never saw anything so gloriously beautiful . . . I confess, though the Greek lady had before given me a great opinion of her beauty I was so struck with admiration that I could not for some time speak to her, being wholly taken up with gazing. That surprising harmony of features! that charming result of the whole! that exact proportion of body! that lovely bloom of complexion unsullied by art! the unutterable enchantment of her smile! But her eyes! large and black with all the soft languishment of the bleu! every turn of her face discovering some new charm![25]

In Parks' text Fatima has mutated to Mulka:

> How beautiful she looked! how very beautiful! Her animated countenance was constantly varying, and her dark eyes struck fire when a joyous thought crossed her mind. . . . I felt no surprise when I remembered the wondrous tales told by the men of the beauty of an Eastern woman. . . .
>
> I had heard of Mulka's beauty long ere I beheld her, and she was described to me as the loveliest creature in existence. Her eyes, which are very long, large, and dark, are remarkably fine, and appeared still larger from being darkened on the edges of the eyelids with soorma: natives compare the shape of a fine eye to a mango when cut open. Her forehead is very fine; her nose delicate, and remarkably beautiful. . . . Her figure is tall and commanding; her hair jet black, very long and straight; her hands and arms are lovely, very lovely. (1: 383-4)

When Parks retires to bed that night, her dreams are 'haunted by the beautiful Begum' with whom she has spent the evening (1: 388).

While the pleasure in gazing is presented in a similar way, Montagu's textualized gaze is far more self-reflexive, however. In one instance, the famous anecdote in the Turkish bath where she describes how the Oriental women marvel at the corset she is wearing, she produces herself as the object of the other's gaze and locates herself firmly in the viewing process. Here, for once, it is not only the corporeality of the Eastern woman that is under scrutiny by the disembodied viewer. The narrator is highly aware of the social and cultural implications of the voyeuristic gaze—at one point, her eye caught by some seductive slave girls, she notes, 'I was sorry that decency did not permit me to stop and consider them nearer' (129). Her defense of the voyeuristic gaze attempts to de-eroticize the gaze, instead locating it within pseudo-religious and learned discourses as a legitimizing strategy and aestheticizing the object of the gaze:

> I think I have read somewhere that women always speak in rapture when they speak of beauty, but I can't imagine why they should not be allowed to do so. I rather think it virtue to be able to admire without any mixture of desire or envy. The gravest writers have spoken with great warmth of some celebrated pictures and statues. The workmanship of heaven certainly excels all our weak imitations, and I think has a much better claim to our praise. For me, I am not ashamed to own I took more pleasure in looking on the beauteous Fatima than the finest piece of sculpture could have given me. (130)

In Parks' text the sense of unease articulated by Montagu has quite disappeared. The narrator complacently reminds the reader that 'so few persons ever have an opportunity of seeing native ladies' (1: 458).

In both these travel accounts there is an undeniable sense of excitement, a frisson, in the descriptions of the Oriental other, which might, but not entirely, be attributable to homoerotic attraction. Stacey's development of the notion of the erotics of difference offers a useful analytical tool here, especially in the light of a culture where eroticized images of Oriental women were continually circulated. An escapist element might well play a role here as well: in the projection of women's repressed sexual fantasies onto the other. Stacey does not seek to deny homoerotic desire—she sees purely erotic desire as only one element that informs a fascination with otherness between women. Above all, she points the way to a more active model of spectatorship for women, one that regains a space for women viewers to control the meaning of an image.[26]

Similarly, what I am arguing here is for a more ambivalent reading of female spectatorship in the harem—one that accounts for women's own voyeuristic pleasure in gazing at other women. Contrary to Mulvey's concept of fixed, pre-determined subjectivity, a notion of subjectivity as shifting and contradictory would take these women travellers' fractured gaze into account. To be sure, travellers like Montagu and Parks employ their privileged eyewitness status in the service of the voyeuristic male gaze. Women were, after all, both observer and observed—they themselves were particularly subject to the regulatory gazes of their own patriarchal society and their viewpoint is refracted accordingly. But not only do Parks and Montagu look vicariously from a male point of view, but they also derive their own pleasure from the sight—a pleasure that may well be inflected by homoerotic desire and that is, above all, attributable to the erotics of difference. This fascination with otherness is familiar to us from other travel narratives as well. Similarly, the reader constructed by their texts is not necessarily male—their texts cater to both male and female curiosity and voyeuristic fantasy.

The gaze is never innocent, however, but is located in specific relations of power. The voyeuristic gaze, whether male or female, is always linked to a sense of mastery over the image. The main difference between Madonna and Mulka/Fatima lies in the different political and historical formations they are located in. The texts of both travel writers put their own pleasure at the service of Orientalism in their production and dissemination of knowledge about the other. By the nineteenth century, moreover, the world equation of power had shifted significantly. Parks' gaze serves the colonial policy of 'knowing' the other, a strategy to implement an improved surveillance of the colonized. Her text quickly recuperates the threat articulated to hegemonic discourses in its fascination with the other and showers the reader with a wealth of stereotypical information such as, 'never was any place so full of intrigue, scandal, and chit-chat as a zenana' (1: 450); 'Science has not yet entered the confines of the zenana; nature and superstition reign supreme; nevertheless, native women suffer less on the birth of a child than the women of Europe' (1: 453).

The Compassionate Gaze

The image produced of the zenana in most other women travellers' texts is quite different from that created by Parks. Many travellers to India never manage to visit a zenana and openly admit that their descriptions are based on second-hand knowledge. The globe-trotter Constance

Gordon Cumming, for instance, spends a year travelling in India without catching more than a glimpse of a native woman (servants and peasant women excluded).[27] By the middle of the nineteenth century the policy of racial segregation had been well-established, with the inter-dining and mutual visits of the previous century confined to a minimum. By analogy with the textual strategies which—as Billie Melman has shown—increasingly domesticize the harem in the texts of women travellers to the Middle East, the zenana, too, is produced less and less as a site of sensual pleasures and increasingly constructed as a bourgeois home. Any sense of fascination with otherness is repressed in these later texts. Instead, the image presented of the Indian woman is that of a Victim.[28]

This correlated with the increase of reforming zeal concerning Indian society fuelled by the Evangelical revival in England in the early part of the nineteenth century.[29] The position of women in a society was seen as an index of its level of civilization. For the Evangelicals as well as the Utilitarians who gained political control of Indian government policy in the 1830s, Indian civilization was degenerate and decadent. The 'Indian women's question' became a political issue, with reformers clamouring for a radical transformation of Indian society. Large numbers of missionaries travelled to India filled with a crusading spirit to help uplift the downtrodden Indian woman. When Utilitarian influence on Indian politics ebbed, the banner for the reform of the condition of Indian women was taken up by the early feminists.[30] Women travellers' accounts of Indian women contributed to this image of Indian womanhood and thus served a further function—namely that of self-definition for the Western woman. By defining the other as backward, English women were able to define themselves as emancipated, civilized and rational creatures. The battles of feminism were also fought on the battleground of the zenana. And here the Indian woman fulfilled the function of the 'self-consolidating other'[31].

In Frances Duberly's account of her visit to a zenana in 1858, we see these discourses at work.[32] First her account reveals a sense of fascination and bewilderment at the other, which is transmuted into a synecdochical obsession with ornamentation, perhaps not untinged with material envy:

> The ladies, who received us in the durbar room, were seated on chairs in a row. . . . The eldest lady conversed: the rest sat in silence. I never saw such a profusion of jewellery in my life. The forehead of each was hidden by a circular ornament of precious stones, and even their eyelids were fringed with diamonds; nose jewels, the size and weight of which distorted the nostril, completed the decorations of the face. Several necklaces, some apparently of solid gold, others of strings of pearls, covered the neck and bosom; while massive bracelets, blazing with rubies and emeralds, encircled their arms from elbow to wrist. One bracelet I particularly remember; it was a thick and heavy circlet of gold, studded with about thirty emeralds the size of peas. On their ankles they wore three or four chains and anklets of different patterns, and each toe was covered with an ornament resembling enamelled leaves. The Ranee who conversed appeared to be an unusually intelligent woman. . . . Her information was, I believe, acquired from a Persian newspaper, which she receives once a week (39).

It is perhaps not wholly misplaced to read a hint of class envy in the encounters between Englishwomen and Indian women, for most Englishwomen in India were from a middle-class background while the women they met were usually from the native aristocracy. Nevertheless, the narrator is convinced that the Indian woman envies her. After confirming, in answer to a query, that she had actually been present at a battle, the princess 'fell back in her chair and sighed. A whole lifetime of suppressed emotion, of crushed ambition, of helplessness, and weariness, seemed to be comprehended in that short sigh' (41). No doubt personal motives predisposed the 'heroine of the Crimea' (Duberly was the only woman to have accompanied the British troops during the Crimean War) to identify the Indian princess as unfortunate—including a portion of personal vanity. What is recurrent in Englishwomen's descriptions of Indian women, however, is the fact that they serve the project of self-presentation for the Western woman as more free than her Eastern counterpart.

Another celebrated traveller, Isabella Bird, is quoted on the same theme in the following way:

> I have lived in Zenanas, and have seen the daily life of the secluded women, and I can speak from bitter experience of what their lives are—the intellect dwarfed, so that a woman of twenty or thirty years of age is more like a child of eight, intellectually; while all the worst passions of human nature are stimulated and developed in a fearful degree: jealousy, envy, murderous hate, intrigue, running to such an extent that in some countries I have hardly ever been in a woman's house without being asked for drugs with which to disfigure the favourite wife, or to take away the life of the favourite wife's infant son. This request has been made of me nearly one hundred times. This is only an indication of the daily life of whose miseries we think so little, and which is a natural product of the systems we ought to have subverted long ago.[33]

In this horror scenario, rife with mutilation and murder, it is striking how Bird rhetorically aligns herself with the powers that be in the name of the higher cause—defined by Gayatri Spivak as that of 'white men saving brown women from brown men.'[34] The accounts of Englishwomen from the zenana served an ideological function, of course, namely that of supporting British colonial policy with regard to social reform. It was in the interests of the colonial power to define the Indian women as oppressed and Indian men as domestic oppressors to legitimize continued colonial rule over a people so obviously unfit to take up responsibility for itself.[35] Thus women travellers' accounts served both as an alibi for colonial policy and as a deflection of critique from their own oppression in Western society.

Despite the efforts to defuse the eroticism of Indian women, a sense of unease at the zenana as an uncolonized space remains: 'This was the unreasonable, illogical space that resisted colonization and, thus, civilization.'[36] Rumours about Indian women's obsession with sexuality remain in circulation. Paradoxically, the oppressed Indian women are constructed as immensely powerful in controlling their men and seen as a site of resistance to social reform instigated by the colonial power. As the social reformer Mary Carpenter remarks, 'It is everywhere felt among the enlightened, that the stronghold of idolatry, and all its attendant evils, is in the home' (2: 75).

The types of gazes looked at so far all reflect the two main modes of perceiving the other that dominate Western discourses. The other is presented as wholly other—the object of either fascination or repulsion (as in the voyeuristic harem accounts of Montagu and Parks). Conversely, the other is reduced to the same—but is presented as inferior to the self (as in the accounts of the backward Indian woman). In both cases the other serves as a foil for the fantasies and/or self-definition of the self.

The Conservative Gaze

With the emergence of the 'New Woman' in England at the end of the nineteenth century, a further variation in the image of the Indian woman is to be observed. For conservative-minded travellers such as the journalist Mary Billington or the Anglo-Indian writers Maud Diver and Flora Annie Steel, the Indian woman now embodies all the feminine qualities that are under threat in England. Billington undertakes a lengthy journey to India for the *Daily Graphic* in order to investigate the hidden lives of Indian women. The conclusion she comes to is that 'Indian women are not altogether in such pitiful plight as some of their so-called friends come and tell us.'[37] Billington emphatically denies the reports of the immorality of Indian women and claims they are as moral as Englishwomen: 'I am quite certain that if all present zenana restrictions were withdrawn, the Indian female population would stand woman for woman upon quite as high a platform as ourselves in this direction' (123). She stresses her high respect for 'the gentle fortitude that . . . is one of the most admirable traits in the native female character' (4). In her account we gain a wealth of background information on what women's lives in the zenana are really like—among other facts she records 'the wit of the zenana', the games girls play, as well as the regional variation in jewellery.[38]

Her benevolence towards Indian women is startling only if one overlooks the political agenda informing her text—written, after all, for the home market. Her text is haunted by the 'noisy and assertive' femininsts at home (20), either riding bicycles or 'uncompromising trousers' (25), who become increasingly threatening figures as the text progresses (on page 176 they are 'in a frenzy' at the thought of their Eastern sisters' contentment with their more womanly lives). Similarly, she makes a visit to various communities of workers and denies reports of labour agitation, describing them instead as a 'happy community' (152) kept busy with interesting and gainful employment. At one point she compares Indian women mine workers to English women workers: 'Remembering, as one does, the terrible descriptions of the swearing, drunken, degraded disgraces to their sex that the north-country women workers underground used to be, the most remarkable point about them was their perfect gentleness and modesty' (155). A variation on this theme is given in the following key passage, where the narrator cannot suppress a passing vitriolic dig at an insolent working-class at home getting above its place :

> According to modern 'emancipated' lights, the answer of a poor Mohammedan woman in Calcutta to my question as to what she regarded as the chief happiness she would desire for herself might seem a contracted one. 'To see my husband happy, and to know that what I have cooked and done for him has helped to make him so; to see my sons grow up as men, honest and strong, and to know that my daughters are well married'—is, in my view, a praiseworthy domestic ideal, enough even when set beside the possibilities of a bank holiday on Hampstead Heath. (173)

The gentle and docile Indian woman is conflated with the obedient worker. This conflation of race and class is a marker of colonial discourse, and finds its most absurd expression in the remark Lord Curzon is reported to having made on seeing British soldiers in India bathing—how strange it was that the poor should have such white skins.[39]

The conservative backlash against both the worker's movement and the women's movement in Britain represented by Billington and her ilk correlated to what historians have identified as the resurgence of Orientalism in colonial policy in India.[40] Francis Hutchins points out that with the waning of reformist fervour—in part due to the fact that a wholesale conversion of the teeming millions of India to Christianity was nowhere in sight—India became the preserve of conservative-minded officials who insisted it was in the best interests of Britain to conserve the traditional society of India—naturally with the British at the top of the hierarchy. They claimed to know the requirements of the Oriental mind and repulsed any attempt at reform that would destabilize the status quo.[41] A frequent lament is the decline of traditional Indian values under British reformist influence. Billington, for instance, lays the blame for the deterioration of traditional arts and crafts on missionaries: 'drawn, as so large a percentage of their teachers are, from the lower middle classes, and imbued with the worst philistinism of their order' (189), they are unable to appreciate the true wonders of the East. As in (the equally conservative) politics of the picturesque, there is an implicit elitist element at work here. Maud Diver reproves missionaries for trying to break down social barriers by mingling with natives by reminding them that 'the Oriental is a profound respector . . . of all outward and visible signs of power',[42] and Flora Annie Steel emphasizes 'the absolute necessity for high-handed dignity in dealing with those who for thousands of years have been accustomed to it—they love it.'[43]

Of course, the 'thousands of years' of history that these imperial voices fall back on is a constructed history of India, just as the Oriental traditions of pomp and pageantry adopted by the rulers of India were, in the term employed by Eric Hobsbawm, an 'invented tradition'.[44] The late nineteenth-century imperialists in India were determined to freeze the country in a timeless Oriental tableau which denied any possibility of social and political change. The image of the meek and docile Indian woman produced in Billington's text fits seamlessly into this frame. At the same time—in the wake of a long tradition of travelogues that idealize the other as a critique of their own culture—her text holds up an admonitory mirror to the society at home.

A Different Gaze

Finally, I wish to look at the image of zenana women produced in the text of the Orientalist traveller, Marianne Postans. Her image transgresses the conventions generally employed in the description of Indian women and challenges reader expectations. While visiting a Muslim prince she is introduced to his four wives. Her descriptions of these beautiful and playful creatures draws heavily on discourses of Orientalism: in the royal gardens these birds of paradise disport themselves wreathing blossoms in their hair and adorning the narrator with their jewels, then inhale the smoke of 'richly-adorned hookahs, whose delicately-scented goracco was tempered by the finest rose water' (2: 107). Nevertheless, a more complex image of these women emerges in the course of her text. Her description of their chambers, though equally luxurious, sets a different note: 'There was an air of privacy and quietness, about this little Mohammedan boudoir, particularly inviting; and while its arrangement promised an unusual degree of comfort, a free circulation of air was insured by its height. Numerous windows of wrought stonework which surrounded it, afforded the fair inmate a charming view' (2: 92).

Most descriptions of the zenana, on the contrary, stress the lack of elements like privacy, freedom, air, or a view. Postans discovers that the wives all have separate apartments, and learns to read the intricate jewelry (so often remarked upon) as a code for rank. She goes on to present an image of gender solidarity in the zenana—quite in contrast to the usual stereotype of female intrigue. When court intrigues are directed at the prince's concubine, who also inhabits the zenana, the four wives unite to support her cause. The most radical disruption of conventional constructions of the zenana is to be found in the following passage, when the narrator confesses herself to be 'a little anxious on the matter of Mohammedan husbands' generosity, and the weighty affair of pin money.' The Rahit Buckté (the principal wife) she is talking to, sets her mind quite at ease by explaining that she has her own financial resources at her disposal: 'The Rahit Buckté proved herself during our conversation, to be a good woman of business, quite *au fait* on the subject of grain, ploughs, mangoe trees, et cetera, from which her revenue is derived; large ledgers, written in the Guzzeratee character, were produced, and particular pages readily referred to, in explanation of the subject' (2: 94-5).

The downtrodden Indian woman as a hard-headed businesswoman, at a time when Englishwomen were still unable to own property in their own right after marriage—quite a morsel to swallow for her readers in England.

It is only appropriate to end this chapter based on eyewitness accounts from the zenana with a further eyewitness account—without, however, according it a greater degree of authenticity than the other accounts. In her *Indian Tales of the Raj* Zareer Masani quotes Tara Ali Baig, who grew up in a conservative Bengali family, on Indian women's reactions to visits by Englishwomen:

> The Indian women would say: 'What sort of people are these? . . . Look at those white arms; they look as if they haven't been cooked. And why do they wear those peculiar things on their heads?' And the British women would leave the place saying: 'Really, isn't it shocking, these women are so backward. . . .'[45]

This alternative account hints at more things going on in the zenana than are dreamt of in the travellers' tales. The traveller's transcendent gaze fails to penetrate the darkest recesses of the other's mind—the other eludes the epistemic grasp of the traveller.

Notes

1 Richard Francis Burton, *Personal Narrative of a Pilgrimage to Al-Madinah and Meccah*, 2 vols. (London, 1856) 2: 85.

2 For early accounts of the harem see Rana Kabbani, *Europe's Myths of Orient* 14-36.

3 Women's quarters, where the women lived in seclusion.

4 By contrast, the matriarchal society of the Nairs in South India is virtually ignored in these accounts.

5 Laura Mulvey, 'Visual Pleasure and Narrative Cinema', *Screen* 16.3 (1975): 6-18.

6 Mulvey, 'Afterthoughts on 'Visual Pleasure and Narrative Cinema' inspired by *Duel in the Sun*', *Feminism and Film Theory*, ed. Constance Penley (New York: Routledge, 1988) 69-79.

7 Rosemary Betterton, 'How Do Women Look? The Female Nude in the Work of Suzanne Valadon', *Looking On: Images of Femininity in the Visual Arts and Media*, ed. Rosemary Betterton (London: Pandora, 1987) 217-34.

8 Reina Lewis, ''Only Women should go to Turkey': Henriette Browne and Women's Orientalism', *Third Text* 22 (1993): 53-64.

9 Billie Melman, *Women's Orients: English Women and the Middle East, 1718-1918: sexuality, religion and work* (Basingstoke: Macmillan, 1992).

10 See Lorraine Gamman and Margaret Marshment, eds, *The Female Gaze. Women as Viewers of Popular Culture* (London: Women's Press, 1988) Introduction 1-7.

11 Mary Eagleton, ed., *Feminist Literary Theory. A Reader* (Oxford: Blackwell, 1986) Introduction 2.

12 Gisela Ecker, 'Blicke auf den weiblichen Körper: Erica Pedretti, Ferdinand Hodler und die Kunstgeschichte', *Differenzen: Essays zur Weiblichkeit und Kultur*, ed. Gisela Ecker (Dünen-Hiddingsel: Tende, 1994) 323-48.

13 Gisela Ecker, ed., *Feminist Aesthetics* (Boston: Beacon, 1986) Introduction 21.

14 Judith Butler, *Gender Trouble: Feminism and the Subversion of Identity* (New York: Routledge, 1990) 33.

15 A point Simone de Beauvior made more than forty years ago in *The Second Sex* (Harmondsworth: Penguin, 1972). Also see Monique Wittig, 'One is Not Born A Woman', *Feminist Issues* 1.2 (1981): 47-54.

16 Also see Shelagh Young, 'Feminism and the Politics of Power. Whose Gaze is it Anyway?' Gamman and Marshment, 173-88.

17 See, for instance, Gayatri Spivak, 'Three Women's Texts'; and Chandra Talpade Mohanty, 'Under Western Eyes.'

18 Betterton, Introduction 12.

19 Meyda Yegenoglu, 'Supplementing the Orientalist Lack: European Ladies in the Harem', *Inscriptions* 6 (1992): 45-81.

20 See Said, *Orientalism*.

21 A similar argument is to be found in Lisa Lowe's *Critical Terrains: French and British Orientalisms* (Ithaca: Cornell University Press, 1991).

22 Janaki Nair, 'Uncovering the Zenana: Visions of Indian Womanhood in Englishwomen's Writings, 1813-1940', *Journal of Women's History* 2.1 (1990): 8-34.

23 Gamman and Marshment 112-29.

24 The reviewer of *The Court Journal*: 'To the authoress of the twenty-four years' 'Wanderings' has been reserved the honour of superseding the vivacious correspondent of Alexander Pope, and of taking the first rank as the chronicler of the scenes of the Zenana.' Quoted on the dust-jacket of Fanny Parks, *Asiatic Gallery, Baker Str. Bazar, Portman Square Grand Moving Diorama of Hindostan, displaying the Scenery of the Hoogly, the Bhagirathi, and the Ganges, etc.* (London, 1851).

25 Lady Mary Wortley Montagu, Letter to Lady Mar, Adrianople, 18 April 1717, reprinted in Christopher Pick, ed., *Embassy to Constantinople: The Travels of Lady Mary Wortley Montagu*, (London: Century, 1988) 129-30. Subsequent references in parentheses in the text.

26 Stacey develops her concept of active female spectatorship and the interplay of desire and identification in women's fascination with other women in her recent *Star Gazing: Hollywood Cinema and Female Spectatorship* (London: Routledge, 1994).

27 Constance Gordon Cumming, *In the Himalayas and on the Indian Plain* (Edinburgh, 1884) 14. All further references to be given in parentheses in the text.

28 See especially Janaki Nair, 'Uncovering the Zenana'.

29 For further historical background information see Hutchins, *The Illusion of Permanence* 3-19.

30 See especially Antoinette M. Burton, 'The White Woman's Burden: British Feminists and 'The Indian Woman', 1865-1915', *Western Women and Imperialism*, eds, Nupur Chaudhuri and Margaret Strobel (Bloomington: Indiana University Press, 1990) 137-57.

31 Gayatri Spivak, *In Other Worlds* 209.

32 Frances Isabella Duberly, *Campaigning Experiences in Rajpootana and Central India, during the Suppression of the Mutiny, 1857-1858* (London, 1890). All further references to be given in parentheses in the text.

33 Quoted from an address at Exeter Hall on 1 Nov.1893, in Irene H. Barnes, *Behind the Pardah. The Story of the Church of England Zenana Missionary Society Work in India* (London, 1897) 51.

34 Gayatri Chakravorty Spivak, 'Can the Subaltern Speak?' *Marxism and the Interpretation of Culture*, eds, Cary Nelson and Lawrence Grossberg (Urbana: University of Illinois Press, 1988) 296.

35 See also Rosemary Hennessey and Rajeswari Mohan, 'The construction of woman in three popular texts of empire: towards a critique of materialist feminism', *Textual Practice* 3.3 (1989): 323-59.

36 Nair 21.

37 Mary Frances Billington, *Woman in India* (1895; New Delhi: Amarko Book Agency, 1975) xiii. All further references to be given in parentheses in the text.

38 Indeed, as Leila Ahmed has pointed out, women living in seclusion have often developed an elaborate social world of their own. 'Here, women share living time and living space, exchange experience and information, and critically analyse—often through jokes, stories, or plays—the world of men.' Leila Ahmed, 'Western Ethnocentrism and Perceptions of the Harem', *Feminist Studies* 8 (1982): 529.

39 Philip Mason, *Prospero's Magic: Some Thoughts on Class and Race* (London: OUP, 1962) 1.

40 See Hutchins 153-85; and Bearce 180-212.

41 In fact, a constant source of tension in colonial India was the friction between the government of India and its moderate attempts at reform and the official 'man on the spot', who rejected these whole-heartedly—a motif that threads Kipling's fiction, for example.

42 Maud Diver, *The Englishwoman in India* (London: Blackwood, 1909) 133-4. All further references to be given in parentheses in the text.

43 Flora Annie Steel, *The Garden of Fidelity* (London: Macmillan, 1929) 133. All further references to be given in parentheses in the text.

44 Eric Hobsbawm and Terence Ranger, *The Invention of Tradition* (Cambridge: CUP, 1984).

45 Zareer Masani, *Indian Tales of the Raj* (London: BBC, 1987) 58.

Chapter 4

The Ironic Traveller: Emily Eden

There is striking paradox about Emily Eden: the best-known and most widely-read travel account by a woman traveller in India, Emily Eden's *Up the Country* (1866), was written by a traveller who not only had not the slightest ambition to travel, but actually loathed every minute of it. When she hears rumours of the impending promotion of her brother George, Lord Auckland, to the post of Governor-General of India, she writes in characteristically ironic style:

> There was a great *sough* of India for about a fortnight, but I always said it was too bad to be true, which is a dangerous assertion to make in most cases, it only hastens the catastrophe. But this was such an extreme case, such a horrible supposition, that there was nothing for it but to bully it; and the danger is over now. Botany Bay would be a joke to it. There is a decent climate to begin with, and the fun of a little felony first. But to be sent to Calcutta for no cause at all! [1]

Exactly a year later, in October 1835, she set sail for India to accompany her bachelor brother George and assist him in his social and ceremonial duties. They were accompanied by her sister Fanny and her nephew William Osbourne, who was to become Lord Auckland's Military Secretary. Their sojourn in India was to last a long six years, during which time Emily Eden never ceased to lament over life in India and reiterate her sense of home-sickness.

Emily Eden was different from most of the other women travellers in India in several significant ways. Born into a distinguished Whig family, she grew up in an atmosphere of Regency tolerance and escaped the most restrictive gender bonds by which her middle-class compatriots were bound. Throughout her life she remained her brother's political adviser and was a lively participant in Whig political circles, her advice eagerly sought by eminent statesmen, including the later prime ministers Lord Melbourne and Lord Palmerston.[2] In addition, although courted by Lord Melbourne, friend and patron of her brother's, she was wise enough to avoid the restrictions of marriage: 'I am more and more confirmed in the idea that a life of single blessedness is the wisest', she wrote to her friend Theresa when she was twenty-nine.[3] What Emily Eden missed in India was the stimulation of the London society she moved in, the polished wit, the discussion of new books, plays, operas, political scandals. Anglo-Indian society in India, a society composed of a preponderance of middle-class aspirants to an illusion of aristocracy in India,[4] bored and disgusted her with its triviality, gossip and philistinism.

The narrative of *Up the Country* describes a tour made by Governor-General Auckland between 1838 and 1840 from Calcutta to Simla, paying extended visits to princely states on the way. It was a political journey, urged on him by his advisers to display British presence, consolidate allegiances to native rulers and above all, to reaffirm the treaty of friendship his predecessor Lord Bentinck had signed in 1831 with the 'Lion of the Punjab', Maharaja Ranjit Singh—Britain's most important ally in India. The march itself was a lavish affair, designed to impress the Orientals with an 'Oriental' style. The previous decade (1828-38) had been one of reform in the rule of India, beginning with Bentinck's abolition of sati in 1829 and finding its culmination in Macaulay's *Minute* of 1835, implementing a vast educational policy designed to produce 'mimic' Englishmen[5] of the Indians. The aim was to produce a reservoir of cheap educated labour—in the main clerks and petty officials — to facilitate the smooth running of the machinery of empire. With Auckland, however, a period of what historian George Bearce terms 'a resurgence of imperialism' began, taking up the threads of imperial expansionism pursued by the generation of Governor-Generals preceding the reformers.[6] This was marked by an Orientalization of Indian policy, a firm belief that Oriental pageantry and splendour were an indispensable part of rule to appeal to and suitably impress 'the Oriental mind'.[7] And whereas the reforming party had firmly believed (or rather, expressed their belief) in an eventual devolution of power from the British to the Indians, in the later age the 'illusion of permanence' increasingly took hold of the rulers' minds and the idea of Indian self-rule receded more and more into the shade of good intentions.[8]

Accordingly, a vast imperial machinery was cranked into action for the tour, with a cavalcade ten miles long led by the Governor-General and his sisters on elephant and on horse-back, followed by armies of elephants, camels and horses and their grooms; next, the British members of the party, on horse-back, in carriages or in palanquins; then came bullock-carts loaded with household goods; eight thousand soldiers in all, and trailing at the end, crowds of camp followers, including fakirs and robbers.

'They say there are about eleven thousand people with the camp, and elephants and camels innumerable, which, added to the Bodyguard, Artillery, and Infantry, form an immense multitude. It is said his Lordship's marching about the country costs the Government 70,000 rupees a month....', notes Fanny Parks, who joins the cavalcade for a while (2:183).

The enormous machinery is set into motion for only two hours a day, between six o'clock and eight o'clock in the morning, after which the heat makes further progress impossible. 'It seems wicked to move 12,000 people with their tents, elephants, camels, horses, trunks, &c., for so little, but there is no help for it', Eden observes drily.[9] Camp is struck, while an advance party of servants moves ahead, ensuring that a camp is prepared at the next site and breakfast steaming when the travellers arrive. Eden hates the dusty life of a march, and dubs her luxurious tents (consisting of three carpeted and furnished rooms) 'Misery Palace' (37).

The Reluctant Traveller

From the very start, Eden assumes the stance of a reluctant traveller: '... I do say, that for a person who required nothing but allowed the undisturbed enjoyment of that small Greenwich house and garden, with all its little Cockney pleasures and pursuits, I have been very hardly treated and rather overworked.' (1)

The sub-genre her text employs, that of the letter, fits this purpose admirably, with its emphasis on the personal rather than the panoramic. Instead of a strategy of self-authentication through a display of knowledge, so frequently to be found in travel narrative, Eden flatly announces, 'I never ask questions, I hate information' (62). The text seems to take a perverse pleasure in deflating the expectations of its readers—at the outset of her journey across the greater part of Northern India she declares of the scenery: 'they say, we shall see nothing prettier, or rather less hideous, between this and Simla, except at Raj Mahl' (4). And early on in the narrative she announces that their plans do not include the otherwise obligatory trip to the Taj Mahal— 'the only thing that, all Indians say, is worth looking at' (40).[10] The text appears to refuse to participate in the power/knowledge relations Mary Louise Pratt sees most travel writing implicated in, be they written in the scientific or experiential mode.[11]

Ironically enough, the travel account she produces was to become a classic of colonial literature and fuel the myth of an India of barbaric splendour, ablaze with gold and glittering with diamonds. Here is a sample from her text:

> We rode about till it was quite dark, and then the rajah proposed we should return; and when we came to the turn of the road, the whole of the village and his castle, which is an enormous building, was illuminated. Wherever there was a straight line, or a window, or an arch, there was a row of little bright lamps; every cross of the lattices in every window had its little lamp. It was the *largest* illumination I ever saw. We went on the elephants through the great gateway, in a Timour the Tartar fashion, into the court. Such torches and spearmen and drums and crowds,... We got off at the door of an immense hall, a sort of court, and the rajah's servants spread a path of scarlet and gold kincob from the door to the seat at the farthest end, for us to walk on. Considering that it is a pound a yard, and that I have been bargaining for a week for enough for a wadded *douillette*, and was beat out of it, it was a pity to trample on it... (27-8).

It is through her vivid depiction of the party's reception by the princes of India, as in the scene depicted above, that she produced an image of India which, despite her ironic idiom, confirmed a view of India as a fairy land overflowing with riches to the generation of readers conditioned by works such as Thomas Moore's *Lalla Rookh* (a bestseller in its day) and Robert Southey's *The Curse of the Kehama.* Eden herself ironically confirms this impression, in a rare display of enthusiasm:

> In the afternoon we went to see the king's yacht, which he had decked out for us, and then his garden. Such a place! the only residence I have coveted in India. Don't you remember where in the 'Arabian Nights', Zobeide bets her 'garden of delights' against the Caliph's 'palace of pictures?' I am sure this was 'the garden of delights!' (62)

In her forced encounter with a strange world, the pleasures of discovery slowly grow on her, so that she is ready to enthuse of the Kutub Minar, a tower in Delhi built by a member of the Delhi Sultanate:

> Well, of all things I ever saw, I think this is the finest. Did we know about it in England? I mean, did you and I, in our old ancient Briton state, know? Do you know now, without my telling you, what the Kootub is? Don't be ashamed, there is no harm in not knowing, only I do say it is rather a pity we were so ill taught. ... I expected the Kootub would have been rather inferior to the Monument. One has those little prejudices. It happens to be the Monument put at the top of the column in the Place Vendrome, and that again placed on a still grander base (99).

Eden has travelled a long way since declaring there was nothing to see in India apart from the Taj Mahal. Unlike most travellers of either gender, who are anxious to demonstrate their superior knowledge to their readers, Eden ridicules her own (and general British) ignorance and superiority towards other nations — quite a feat for an aristocratic Whig priding herself on her intellectuality.

The epistolary mode she employs is ideally suited to her ironic style. This private, conventionally feminine sub-genre not only provides the writer with the freedom to deviate from the conventional duties of a travel writer (producing a description of the land being visited), but also establishes a close bond with the readers through its more direct form of address. The personal form of address enables the writer to give free rein to a sardonic, irreverent style that might call for a tighter control in a more public form of text. The addressee also informs the style in another way, however. In a form of text addressed openly to social equals the writer need make no bones about her sense of class superiority — as we shall see in Emily Eden's case.

IRONY AS A RHETORICAL DEVICE

The greatest difference between Eden's travel account and those of other travellers is not merely her reluctant traveller stance, nor her privileged access to the crème de la crème of Indian society, but as will have been amply noted by now, her Austen-like mordant wit. Her book is a study in irony. She employs irony as a strategy to serve different purposes: to subvert reader expectations, to parody her own anxieties and fears, to cope with the strangeness of the situation she finds herself in, and, as we shall see, to puncture colonial self-importance. It is the saving grace that prevents her narrative persona from drowning in petulance or self-pity. And it is a sharp weapon against those who earn her disdain.

It is her ironic gaze that enables her to create a sense of distance to the narrative persona— an awareness that she is as much an object of analysis by the other as vice versa. Her self-conscious narratorial position implies involvement in the viewing process and not a transcendent observer position. One scene she depicts is that of sketching, surrounded by a crowd of natives:

> It is not an uncivil crowd, all things considered — we merely threw them one and all into genuine fits of laughter, but X., who understands their language, says they did not say anything meant for impertinence, only they had never seen a European woman before, and 'what an odd thing it was to be so white!' And then my leghorn bonnet was a great subject of wonder and dispute (229).

The sense of self-mockery conveyed by the text contrasts refreshingly with the pompous delineation of similar scenes in other travel narratives, where the narrator constructs him or herself as an object of admiration and wonder for the natives, stressing the European traveller's individuality vs. the faceless mass of Orientals. Eden manages to convey this sense of reciprocity even in the depiction of a visit to the zenana, so often the occasion for women travellers to present themselves as vastly superior to the victimized Oriental woman: 'they laughed at our bonnets,and we rather *jeered* at their nose-rings,' she remarks (233).One of the few times Eden admits to the burden of her political status is when she remarks rather wistfully: 'I should like to see some of these high-caste ladies several times, without all this nonsense of presents, &c., but so as to hear their story, and their way of life, and their thoughts' (237).

If her irreverent wit is often a tool for self-mockery — of her relief at the cool climate of the hill-station of Simla, she remarks, 'like meat, we *keep* better here' (129) — it is a merciless implement to excoriate the (largely middle-class) Anglo-British society she holds in contempt: 'Mrs T. wears long thick thread mittens, with black velvet bracelets over them. She may have great genius, and many good qualities, but, you know, it is impossible to look for them under those mittens'(87).

Eden has little patience with the racial prejudice rampant in this society,[12] and uses her status to push through corrective measures:

> We had a meeting of ladies to settle about the fancy sale, which was easily done, as before they came I wrote a paper of proposals and they all read it, and said it would do very well;... The only novelty I suggested was to ask the wives of the uncovenanted service (the clerks in public offices) to send contributions. This was rather a shock to the aristocracy of Simla, and they did suggest that some of the wives were very black. That I met by the argument that the black would not come off on their work,... (159).

The clerks she is referring to are to a great extent Eurasians, who are by this time vigorously despised by the British. (The time when East India Company Officials were exhorted to take Indian wives, and the creation of a Eurasian class of collaborators with the British rulers was considered indispensable, are long forgotten.)[13] In an age of rising racial prejudice characterized, according to Peter Mudford, by 'the birth of the nigger,'[14] Eden records the following episode:

> He [General E.] cannot, of course, speak a word of Hindoostanee, neither can his aide-de-camp. 'My groom is the best of us, but somehow we never can make the bearers understand us. I have a *negro* who speaks English, but I could not bring him dak.'[15] I suppose he means a native, but that is being what the 'artful dodger' in 'Oliver Twist' would have called 'jolly green'. He can hardly have picked up a woolly black negro who speaks Hindoostanee. I wish I knew (389-90).

Francis Hutchins sees this passage as the first appearance of the term 'nigger' for Indians in colonial literature and reads it as an elegantly coded articulation of Eden's disapproval.[16]

Subjectivity, produced by an interaction of different coordinates, among which race, class and gender are salient, is not inflected by these factors to an equal extent. Within certain historical and social constellations certain of these factors might exert a greater influence than others. In the case of Emily Eden it is clear that gender and race play a subordinate role to a sense of class affiliation. Thus racial barriers do not hinder her from feeling a sense of shared class superiority with the elite of Indian society. This is something that distinguishes her from her mainly middle-class fellow women travellers, whose sense of class envy at times informs their descriptions of native aristocratic women in a zenana, as we have seen.[17] There is a hint of seriousness in her facetious remark about a handsome prince she meets, 'if the rajah fancied an English ranee, I know somebody who would be very happy to listen to his proposal' (119).

The climax of the journey (and her narrative) is undoubtedly the state visit to Ranjeet Singh. The atmosphere is lavish enough to impress even the Governor-General's party:

> The first show of the day was Runjeet's private stud. I suppose fifty horses were led past us. The first had on its emerald trappings, necklaces arranged on its neck and between its ears, and in front of the saddle two enormous emeralds, nearly two inches square, carved all over, and set in gold frames, like little looking-glasses. The crupper was emeralds, and there were stud-ropes of gold put on somethings like a martingale. … The next horse was simply attired in diamonds and turquoises, another in pearls, and there was one with trappings of coral and pearl that was very pretty. Their saddle-cloths have stones woven into them. It reduces European magnificence to a very low pitch (227).

Despite her flippant tone—she finds the legendary ruler 'exactly like an old mouse, with grey whiskers and one eye' (198)—Eden cannot deny that she is impressed by him: 'I think the Maharaj sees through me,' she writes. (225) She sums up with a certain humility:

> He is a drunken old profligate, neither more nor less. Still he has made himself a great king; he has conquered a great and many powerful enemies, he is remarkably just in his government; he has disciplined a large army; he hardly ever takes away life, which is wonderful in a despot; and he is excessively beloved by his people.

> I certainly should not guess any part of this from looking at him (209).

It is apparent that the ruler of the Punjab is regarded as an equal; no sense of racial superiority intrudes here. (In fact, Eden is to grow quite sentimental on hearing of his death.) This attitude of the British is to change in the course of the century as British power spreads—the Punjab itself, which disintegrated after the death of Ranjeet Singh, was to fall to the British after the Sikh War of 1848-9. In the course of the century British policy towards the native princes changes perceptibly. While their rule is carefully preserved in a conservative impulse to conserve traditional India as a prop for British rule, the native princes are increasingly felt to be a threat to the government policy of social and racial distance. Of a superior pedigree than most government officials, they are feted accordingly by British aristocratic circles on their trips to Britain—the same circles that were closed to most Anglo-Indians when they went home.[18]

Emily Eden in the Judgement of Critics

One of the most interesting points about Emily Eden is the judgement passed on her by later generations of historians and critics. While quoted copiously for her vivacious style and privileged eye-witness participation in historical events, the verdict delivered on her ranges from the scathing to the celebratory. In the opinion of John Riddick, 'This collection of witty and opinionated letters might win for Miss Eden the sobriquet, 'The Ugly Victorian'. ... Her letters represent a period piece reflecting deep prejudices towards the natives and their 'savage and heathen' practices.'[19]

It remains unclear how Riddick arrives at his absurd verdict. At the other end of the scale we find the desperate attempt to incorporate Eden into a canon of heroic women travellers.[20] Marian Fowler finds a more 'feminine' reason than adventure for the travels of Eden and her fellow 'first ladies of the Raj': 'All of them went willingly, motivated by duty and love. They went to India not to govern, but to give, looking not for power and a place in history but for praise from their beloved, and a place in his heart.'[21]

In case anyone should be wondering, the man in Eden's life Fowler is referring to is her brother.

Far more revealing is the irritation displayed by J.K. Stanford in his conclusion:

> When all is said, *Up the Country* is a strange, confusing, rather inconsequent document. To read some entries you would think that the European community had half its mind engrossed with its mails from home and its chances of a good posting, and half on the chances of a few days' gaiety in a big station on a night of 'quadrilles and English country dances and waltzing' or picnics or theatricals or charade. You get very little impression of work being done. And yet between times many were unquestioningly overworked, living nearly always in loneliness and often on the edge of sudden death or despair.[22]

Finally a critic has put his finger on the subversive implications of this text—what is missing in Eden's work is a sense of the White Man's Burden. What has consistently been employed to legitimize European encroachment on other parts of the earth is the myth of work being done, something the inhabitants of these lands seem incapable of doing themselves. The British are not in India to make a fortune, but to bear the torch of civilization. And they are heroically ready to pay the price for their noble actions—loneliness, sudden death and despair, as Stanford reminds us. There is no sense of fun at being in India in most colonial texts—as Alan Greenberger points out, 'One element lacking from the image of India at all times is humour.'[23] This is one difference about Emily Eden's text.

But there have been no lack of attempts to recuperate her for this tradition—as revealed by the characteristic remark of Sir Henry Lawrence: 'She tried to do her duty.'[24] The Lawrence brothers (Henry and John) were classic exponents of the so-called 'Punjab school', a set of men who embodied the cult of duty in its sternest form, carrying it to the frontiers of the empire. Hutchins sees the cult of duty as a surrogate for religion in the Victorian Age, an age characterized by a loss of faith and a search for alternative creeds.[25] Informed by the Evangelical revival of the early part of the century, the cult of duty laid the foundation of the civilizing mission. Characteristic of this attitude was a belief in pain and discomfort as character-building, whereas pleasure was frowned upon. This in his opinion explained why the British in India in the nineteenth century were desperately unhappy—quite different from the earlier generation of nabobs, whose life was a whirl of riotous gaiety and greed. While Eden's textual self-construction undoubtedly fuels the cult of exile—a further charactistic of nineteenth-century British society[26]—she herself admits at one point, 'I really should not mind India if you and three or four others were here. The discontent with it arises a great deal from want of the old familiar friends' (107-8). She is simply homesick.

Ironically, contemporary women's accounts of Western women in the empire often pick up the theme of the White Man's Burden only to refashion it into the White Woman's Burden. Both Fowler and Barr are flagrant examples of this category—Fowler asserts, 'Surely the greater burden was the women's',[27] while Barr comes to the conclusion, 'And yet, when all is said, the burden of the white woman in nineteenth-century India was seldom light, and she received scant praise for taking it up.'[28] The goal is to stake a claim for women in what Barr calls 'a great human adventure'[29]—colonialism. This serves to underline my point that celebratory criticism of women travellers in the empire consciously or unconsciously fuels a revival of empire nostalgia in the name of feminism—a feminism that serves above all as a tool for the self-presentation of the Western bourgeois individualistic subject.

Emily Eden and the Subversion of Colonial Discourse

Emily Eden's text, however, displays no sense of a civilizing mission to bring light unto the darkness. In fact, the rhetorical device she employs most—irony—serves to transgress the ideological values of the society she represents. Observe her delineation of the 'shoe controversy', a policy issue of no mean dimension at this period,[30] revolving around the question whether a British ruler would lose prestige when removing his shoes (as a mark of respect) in native places of worship:

> After all the plans were settled, a grand schism sprang up in our camp about G.'s [George] taking off his shoes, and parties ran very high; however, I believe it was settled that it was impossible he could ever take off his shoes, except for the purpose of going to bed; but then it was equally impossible to rebut Runjeet's great civility in letting us go to this temple at all, and it was not a question of state. Runjeet takes off his shoes and stoops down, and puts some of the dust on his forehead; it amounts to taking off a hat, and only answers to the same respect that we should wish anybody to pay on entering one of our own churches. So

> it ended in G.'s drawing a pair of dark stockings on over his boots, and the Sikhs made no objections. F. and I went in white shoes, and pretended to take off our dressing slippers from over them. All they really care about is, that their sacred marble should not be defiled by shoes that have trod the common streets. I am glad we went, and would have given up my shoes, and stockings too, for it (215).

In Eden's text the absurdity of colonial ritual is glaringly exposed. To grasp the subversive implications of her representation a digression is necessary here—to the text by another nineteenth-century Englishwoman in India, the author and educational reformer Flora Annie Steel. Steel too fashions a parable of colonialism from the material of the 'shoe controversy'—but with quite a different message:

> I think this story shows indubitably the value of etiquette in dealing with high-class Indians. We all know the story of Mutiny Nicholson at Jullundhur, the youngest of three generals who were holding a durbar [court] of native notables to test, if they could, their possible loyalty or disloyalty. How the first of the chiefs came in with his shoes on and two generals said nothing, but Nicholson thundered, 'Back to the door and take the shoes off your fellows.'
>
> It was enough. The ruler had spoken.[31]

Nicolson was an authoritarian, fanatical figure who played a leading role in the British punitive expeditions to quell the Mutiny of 1857. His historical contribution includes the recommendation of the flaying alive, impalement and burning of mutineers. Nicolson was idealized by a certain type of Englishman (and woman) in India.

In another, justly famous passage, Eden describes the gaiety of a ball in the hills, to swerve off and write:

> Twenty years ago no European band had ever been here, and there we were, with the band playing the 'Puritani' and 'Masaniello', and eating salmon from Scotland, and sardines from the Mediterranean, and observing that St. Cloup's potage à la Julienne was perhaps better than his other soups, and that some of the ladies' sleeves were too tight according to the overland fashions for March, & c.; and all this in the face of those high hills, some of which have remained untrodden since the

> creation, and we, 105 Europeans, being surrounded by at least 3,000 mountaineers, who, wrapped up in their hill blankets, looked on at what we call our polite amusements, and bowed to the ground if a European came near them. I sometimes wonder they do not cut all our heads off, and say nothing more about it (293-4).

After a masterly build-up of tension in its long enumeration of trivialities, the text abruptly switches its point of perspective (as in a zoom reverse shot in film) to show the scene from the outside. It culminates in a chilling scenario—all the more chilling for the casual tone adopted here. While Eden's observation has gained fame in historian circles for its apparent prescience (less than a decade later the natives were really to rise up and cut off the rulers' heads) I read a sense of the absurdity of Western civilization ('our polite amusements') in it as well. There is no sense of a superior culture (bands and tinned food and soups and tight sleeves) spreading the light to the natives here. At the same time, the passage is an epitome of colonial irrelevance and anxiety. While debunking the colonial experience here, in another passage Eden trains her ironic gaze on her own persona as a colonial traveller:

> An odd world certainly! Perhaps two thousand years hence, when the art of steam has been forgotten, and nobody can exactly make out the meaning of the old English word 'mail-coach', some black Governor-General of England will go and look at some ruins, and doubt whether London ever was a large town, and will feed some white-looking skeletons, and say what distress the poor creatures must be in; they will really eat rice and curry; and his sister will write to her Mary D. at New Delhi, and complain of the cold, and explain to her with great care what snow is, and how the natives wear bonnets, and then, of course, mention that she wants to go home. (66-7)

In what might be termed a deconstructive move, the text exposes the epistemological assumptions of the colonial traveller's persona: the concept of a unique travelling I/eye located outside history and within a natural scale of cultural superiority to the inhabitants of the land he/she travels in, and whose gaze gives access to the true state of things. Instead, what we get is an awareness of the contingency of the travelling self and its location within a given historical context. Neither the innate superiority of the achievements of Western civilization ('when the art of steam has been forgotten') nor that of the British race ('some black Governor-General ... will feed some white-looking skeletons') are assured. While travellers are fond of musing on the transitoriness of civilization, the moral they usually deliver is that the glory of Oriental civilizations is past ('it's our turn now'). In the ironic distance from her own culture that the text enacts, lurks a suspicion of the absurdity and transience of British colonial rule. And finally, what Eden's text sets up for mockery most of all is her own persona: that of a letter-writing, perspiring, bonnet-wearing, homesick traveller.

The Silence in Eden's Text

Despite these virtuoso feats of irony that cause so much enjoyment to the reader, however, Eden's travel narrative as a whole remains caught in the trap of colonial ideology. The reason is to be found in the one great silence in the text that the narrator is unwilling or unable to fill in—that of the catastrophe in Afghanistan. One of the ironies of history is that Lord Auckland, a 'reluctant imperialist' if ever there was one,[32] was nevertheless responsible for one of the most disastrous and futile of imperialist ventures in the history of British India.[33] Urged by his advisers and the President of the Board of Control of the East India Company, Lord Ellenborough, who elaborated an ambitious imperialist agenda for the British in India, Auckland was prevailed upon to send an army to intervene in the independent kingdom of Afghanistan in 1838 to forestall the danger of Russian influence (the bugbear of imperialist policy in India). The popular and able ruler Dost Mohammed was deposed and a puppet inserted in his place. At first all seemed to go well for the invading British army, and triumphant celebrations are recorded in Eden's journal. However, at the end of 1841 the catastrophe unfolds: Afghan rebels stage an uprising, murdering the British envoys and forcing the ignominious and disastrous retreat of the glorious British army in freezing conditions, harassed by guerilla fighters—one officer alone survived the corpse-strewn retreat to tell the tale. The ignominy of this defeat was to be linked to Lord Auckland's name by future generations of historians. In addition, a murky light was cast on him by the revelation that despatches by an envoy opposed to the intervention, Alexander Burnes (also murdered in the uprising), had been tampered with. The motion for an inquiry in Parliament was, however, defeated by the government of his friend Lord Palmerston.

For Emily Eden the outcome of the First Afghan War hastened the end of her sojourn in India. Her letters are strangely reticent on the events in Afghanistan. It remains a matter of speculation as to what extent she influenced her brother, who valued her advice on political matters. It also remains unclear whether it is an evasion of colonial realities or loyalty to her brother that is responsible for her silence. While her discretion is understandable from the viewpoint of the constraints she was under, historian Edward Thompson's vitriolic critique is surely not without justification, either. In his notes to the 1930 re-edition of her letters, he accuses her of a flippant dismissal and defamation of the historical characters involved.[34] In addition, he criticizes her for a general sense of naivety, as in her delineation of the state visit to Runjeet Singh of the Punjab:

> There are few things in literature more poignantly ironical than Miss Eden's record of the gaieties of these days, which were to be so swiftly followed by seven years of anarchy and agony and terrific shock of war, shattering the Sikh power. She had no suspicion of the sordidness that underlay the exciting splendour; she could see the physical beauty of Hira Singh, the 'very handsome boy, Runjeet's favourite,' the only person allowed to sit in his presence, but did not for a moment guess at the nature of the boy's intimacy with his ruler.[35]

In Eden's defence one can only reply to this piece of speculation that there is no evidence that she did *not* suspect the true nature of things. Thompson, a critic of British rule in India and a friend of Nehru's, has a point, though: Eden's text tends to gloss over historical realities and take refuge in the folds of the picturesque. (A gifted amateur artist, Eden's first publication in 1844 is a portfolio of sketches entitled *Portraits of the Princes and People of India.*) While Eden's text rejects the usual pitfalls of 'femine' writing in this age, a moralistic tone, it does revert to a gendered mode in its celebration of the picturesque (a style particularly prevalent in women's colonial travel writing).

What remains is a further tragic paradox about Emily Eden: the most self-deconstructive and witty text nineteenth-century women's travel writing in India has produced, remains linked to the memory of one of the most striking examples of imperialist hubris.

Notes

1 Letter to her friend Theresa Lister, October 1834, *Miss Eden's Letters*, ed. V. Dickinson (London, 1919) 245, quoted in Marian Fowler, *Below the Peacock Fan: First Ladies of the Raj* (London: Viking, 1987) 20.

2 Biographical information given in Fowler; Janet Dunbar, *Golden Interlude: the Edens in India 1836-1842* (London: Allan Sutton, 1955); Pat Barr, *The Memsahibs: The Women of Victorian India* (London: Secker & Warburg, 1976); and Julia Keay, *With Passport and Parasol. The Adventures of Seven Victorian Ladies* (London: BBC, 1989).

3 Quoted in Fowler 19.

4 For a description of British society in India see Dennis Kincaid, *British Social Life in India 1608-1937* (London: Routledge & Kegan Paul, 1938) and Hutchins, *The Illusion of Permanence.*

5 The phrase is V.S. Naipaul's (*The Mimic Men*, 1967) and has been borrowed by Homi Bhabha as a metaphor for the colonial subject: 'not quite/not white'. See Homi Bhabha, 'Of Mimicry and Man' 132.

6 See George Bearce, *British Attitudes Towards India 1784-1858*, chap. 7, 180-212.

7 See also Bernard S. Cohn, 'Representing Authority in Victorian India', Hobsbawm and Ranger 165-209.

8 See Hutchins, especially chap. 8, 153-85.

9 Emily Eden, *Up the Country: Letters written to her Sister from the Upper Provinces of India*, 2 vols. (1866); reprinted in vol. 1 (London: Virago, 1983) 31. All further references to be given in parentheses in the text.

10 By 'Indians' she means, of course, the British in India. The inhabitants of India were, in colonial parlance, 'natives'.

11 See Pratt, *Imperial Eyes.*

12 Janet Dunbar sees a development in Eden's attitude from a casually racist to a more critical position. See Dunbar, *Golden Interlude.*

13 See, especially, Kenneth Ballhatchet, *Race, Sex and Class under the Raj: Imperial Attitudes and Policies and their Critics, 1793-1905* (London: Weidenfeld & Nicolson, 1980) 98.

14 See Peter Mudford, *Birds of a Different Plumage: A Study of British-Indian Relations from Akhbar to Curzon* (London: Collins, 1974) 138-66.

15 To travel by means of relays of coolies.

16 See Hutchins 109.

17 Susan Blake similarly discerns a sense of shared class superiority prevailing over gender or race barriers in the case of Mary Hall, a woman traveller in Africa. See Susan Blake, 'A Woman's Trek: What Difference Does Gender Make?' *Women's Studies International Forum* 13.4 (1990): 347-55.

18 See Ballhatchet 116-22.

19 John F. Riddick, ed., *Glimpses of India: An Annotated Bibliography of Published and Personal Writings by Englishmen, 1583-1947* (New York: Greenwood, 1989) 33.

20 See, for eg., Keay 1-35.
21 Fowler 3.
22 J.K. Stanford, *Ladies in the Sun: The Memsahibs' India 1790-1860* (London: Galley, 1962) 99.
23 Alan Greenberger, *The British Image of India. A Study in the Literature of Imperialism 1880-1960* (London: OUP, 1969) 204.
24 Quoted in the Introduction by Elizabeth Claridge to the 1983 Virago edition of Emily Eden's *Up the Country*, x.
25 See Hutchins chap. 2, 20-52.
26 See Bernard S. Cohn, 'The British in Benares: A Nineteenth-Century Colonial Society', *Comparative Studies in Society and History* 4 (1961-2): 172.
27 Fowler 5.
28 Barr 202.
29 Barr 3.
30 See also Cohn, 'Representing Authority' 176.
31 Flora Annie Steel, *The Garden of Fidelity* (London: Macmillan, 1929) 166.
32 See Bearce 193-5.
33 As Patrick Brantlinger points out, even the most reluctant imperialists were imperialists. See Patrick Brantlinger, *Rule of Darkness: British Literature and Imperialism, 1830-1914* (Ithaca: Cornell University Press, 1988) 7.
34 Reprinted in the 1983 edition.
35 Notes to *Up the Country* (reprinted 1983) by Edward Thompson, 404.

Chapter 5

'Mutiny' Writings by Women

Englishwomen's Mutiny narratives offer a wealth of interesting insights into the role of women in empire. What they enact is the ambivalent position between instrumentalization and collusion that women played out. What is particularly revealing is the intersection of race, class, and gender discourses in the British reconstruction of the events of 1857. In this chapter I will discuss both the construction of women within the web of these discourses, as well as the self-construction of women in their autobiographical texts.

As recent historians have shown, the Indian Mutiny of 1857 was only one of a series of armed revolts against British rule in India: 'Among the myths which became current in the wake of the rebellion of 1857-8 was the idea that it was a unique event . . . In fact armed revolt was endemic in all parts of early colonial India. What distinguished the events of 1857 was their scale and the fact that for a short time they posed a military threat to British dominance in the Ganges Plain.'[1]

In fact, the very term 'Mutiny' insisted on by British historians is an attempt to domesticize the revolt and reduce it to an uprising of discontented sepoys (native mercenaries in the East India Company army). Instead, the Revolt was more in the nature of popular insurgency, a coalition of civilian and military forces — a fact that eyewitness accounts corroborate, but that traditionalist historians tend to gloss over. Other historians, however, see it as the first war of Indian independence.

It all began on 10 May 1857 when three native regiments stationed at Meerut, just north of Delhi, shot their officers, butchered their wives.

and proceeded to march to Delhi. There they proclaimed the old Mughal emperor Bahadur Shah, long reduced to a mere puppet by the British, Emperor of India. The revolt spread all over North India and flared up at a string of British stations, forcing some of them like Agra and Lucknow into a state of siege for long months. The causes for the uprising have been exhaustively discussed. Traditional historians tend to foreground the controversy surrounding the greased Enfield rifle cartridges distributed to the troops — these cartridges were rumoured to be greased with both cow and pig fat, and as the ends had to be bitten off before use, revolted the feelings of both Muslim and Hindu soldiers — in an attempt to stress the forces of irrationality at the root of the entire uprising. Other historians have proved, however, that the cartridge issue only served as a final spark for long pent-up tensions and grievances against British rule. Central among these were the ever-tightening turn of the screw of land revenue on the peasant population and the introduction of land reform leading to the creation of a class of landed magnates, as well as Governor-General Lord Dalhousie's 'doctrine of lapse', by which independent states could be incorporated into the British possessions under the pretext of a sovereign's heir being either illegitimate or unsuitable. As Indian rulers traditionally considered adopted sons equal to natural sons in questions of succession, this policy led to a series of independent states devolving onto the paramount power. The greatest discontent was caused by the seizure of the large state of Oudh, a step against which sagacious British administrators such as William Sleeman had insistently warned. Among the rulers who nursed a grievance against the British was the later rebel leader Nana Sahib, whose pension and title, though guaranteed by treaty, were nonetheless cancelled by the British administration.

As Rudrangshu Mukherjee has pointed out, 'The uprising offered a unique conjuncture when élite disaffection and popular insurgency could come together.'[2] Mukherjee points out that political figures such as Nana Sahib had the role of rebel leader thrust upon them by the militancy of the insurgent population. He probes the question why the rebels of a popular insurrection turned to figureheads such as the Mughal emperor or deposed members of royalty as leaders and comes to the conclusion that '[t]he answer lies in the rebels' quest for legitimacy'.[3] And it is precisely in this conservative element that C.A. Bayly detects one of the main reasons for the ultimate failure of the rebellion: it was from the start intent on turning the clock back to the age of Mughal rule in India before the ascendancy of the British.[4]

Apart from economic and dynastic grievances there were other causes for the revolt, however. Even among farmers and landowners given preferential treatment by the British, dislike of British rule and resentment of the overbearing manner of British officials was widespread.[5] The government remained largely ignorant of the mood of the people. A factor that played a decisive role in the rebellion was a resurgence of religious fervour, fanned by religious leaders of both Hindus and Muslims. The influence of missionaries and the reforming zeal of the government fuelled fears of forced conversion to Christianity and gave rise to suspicion and hatred of everything European.

The Cawnpore Massacre

The episode of the Mutiny that remained seared on British memory was the massacre of women and children by Nana Sahib at Cawnpore (now Kanpur). Entrenched in some miserable barracks, General Wheeler, 'an aged and incompetent general',[6] surrendered on the condition of being granted safe conduct to boats on the river. While they were boarding the boats, however, the tattered remains of the garrison were massacred by the surrounding Indian troops. The women and children were hauled back and interned in a part of Nana Sahib's palace. At the news of the approaching punitive force led by General Havelock, Nana Sahib ordered the prisoners to be butchered and their bodies thrown into a well, where they were later found by British troops.

Mukherjee points to a difference between the massacre of British soldiers at the river and that of the women and children later on. Whereas the first, public massacre served the purpose of a staged ritual — 'The violence embedded in British rule was eradicated through counter-violence'[7] — the slaughter of the women was carried out in secret, by hired murderers (the sepoys refused to fire). The significance of these atrocities, however, lies in the retrospective legitimation they provided for the reign of terror unleashed by British punitive expeditions against the rebels. General Neill, for instance, indiscriminately orderd villagers to be slaughtered and villages to be burned. Even the historian J. W. Kaye, otherwise noted for his eulogizing accounts of British national heroes of the Mutiny,[8] admits in one passage:

> Over the whole of the Sepoy War — there is no darker cloud than that which gathered over Allahabad in this terrible summer . . . It is on the records of our British Parliament, in papers sent home by the Governor-General of India in Council, that 'the aged, women and children, are sacrificed, as well as those guilty of rebellion.' They were not deliberately hanged, but burned to death in their villages. ... Englishmen did not hesitate to boast, or to record their boastings in writing, that they had 'spared no one' and that 'peppering away at niggers' was very pleasant pastime.[9]

It remains one of the best-preserved myths that British excesses were a reaction to the news of the Cawnpore massacre — British soldiers were goaded into a frenzy of righteous fury at the thought of the horrors committed on British women by natives.[10] Yet this myth was countered by contemporary eyewitness accounts, such as that by the war correspondent of the *Times*, William Howard Russell, who earned his spurs in the Crimean War. The image he delineates of the British punitive forces is one of insensible brutality and a burning lust for plunder. Of the excesses he writes, 'These 'severities' could not have been justified by the Cawnpore massacre, because they took place before that diabolical act.'[11] Retributive action by the British was so severe that many parts of Northern India showed a significant drop in population in the following census.[12]

THE RAPE MYTH

However, the news of Cawnpore led to a mass hysteria in Britain and reports were embellished by sensationalist accounts of the rape and mutilation of British women at the hands of the rebels. Nana Sahib, it was rumoured, had tried to force the women into his zenana and had instigated the murder in his rage at their refusal. Salacious 'eyewitness' reports purporting to corroborate the rumours, such as the following letter to the *Times*, are particularly revealing of the fantasies and obsessions projected onto the mutineers — in this case by a clergyman:

> They took 48 females, most of them girls of [sic] from 10 to 14, many delicately nurtured ladies, — violated them and kept for the base purposes of the heads of the insurrection for a whole week. At the end of that time they made them strip themselves, and gave them up to the lowest of the people to abuse in broad

> daylight in the streets of Delhi. They then commenced the work of torturing them to death, cutting off their breasts, fingers, and noses, and leaving them to die.[13]

Subsequent inquiry commissions set up by the British were unable to verify a single case of rape or mutilation. In fact, as Mukherjee has pointed out, the religious fervour of the rebels, their revolt against what they perceived as contamination by the British, would itself foreclose rape as a means of humiliation: 'The preservation of religious and caste purity could thus eliminate rape.'[14] Furthermore, the objective of the rebels was chiefly to annihilate foreign rule and every trace of the British. This is confirmed by an eyewitness account of a captured sepoy questioned as to why he had killed women and children: 'When you kill a serpent, you kill its young', he replied.[15] Instead of rape, women prisoners were often humiliated — they were taken to grind corn or expected to cook for their captors, all activities British ladies in India were certainly not used to performing. The aim of the rebels seems to have been above all to degrade the very people who had humiliated them: in other words, to turn the tables of power in their own favour.

But it was precisely this conclusion that was impossible for the English to accept. Rape myths continued to flourish, and there was even a demand to execute officials who cautiously advised clemency for mutineers.[16] For the first time, a spirit of popular imperialism arose in Britain, where interest in the Indian possessions previous to the Revolt of 1857 had been limited to travel narratives and lurid missionary accounts.[17] In her illuminating analysis of the function of the Mutiny myths, Jenny Sharpe has pointed out that the reality from which they served to deflect was that of colonial power relations reversed.[18] By equating the body politic with the Englishwoman's body, the reality of insurgency was sexualized and contained, to be transmuted into merely a barbaric crime. What is screened is the real casualty of the war — its cost in British men's lives. Most of the British deaths during the Mutiny were, after all, the result of disease or wounds. What she finds significant is that there are no tales of British men dismembered — this would involve endangering the already precarious mystique of British men as the superior, invulnerable race.

A further mechanism is at work in these discourses, too — that of 'blaming the victim'. The violence of the rebels foregrounded in Mutiny accounts serves to obscure the original violence inherent in colonial relations of power. As Patrick Brantlinger points out, 'In the basic fantasy, repeated endlessly in novels, plays, poems, and histories, the imperialist dominators become victims and the dominated, villains. Imagining the Mutiny in this way totally displaced guilt and projected repressed, sadistic impulses onto demonicized Indian characters.'[19]

In his sifting through the enormous outpourings of Mutiny literature, Brantlinger identifies Nana Sahib as the arch-villain of the piece, 'Satanic locus of all oriental treachery, lust, and murder',[20] whose familiarity even in the nurseries of Britain is revealed to us in the remark of the Anglo-Indian novelist Flora Annie Steel, 'Nana Sahib was hung, drawn, and quartered by children hundreds of times'.[21]

There are further aspects of the race, class and gender dimensions of the rape myth that Jenny Sharpe brings to light. The fact that the British woman's body is the site on which racial and colonial battles are fought points up the gender constructions of women prevalent at the time. Women are of value merely as property of their men, and it is over control of this property that the battle is fought. The interest in the signifier 'woman' further lies in its encoding as an icon of empire or the nation. While during the nineteenth century the trope of nation-as-woman is increasingly circulated — the image of woman in question usually marked as chaste or maternal or a mixture of both — women themselves were denied legal rights and marginalized in both politics and society.[22] The concept of nation itself implies a strong element of homo-social bonding — a notion that fitted in well with British society in India, which was organized along the lines of a large gentlemen's club. Women were permitted a space only in the very margins of this world, while simultaneously they were fetishised and idealized as a symbol of all the ideals worth fighting for. Interestingly enough, while for the next hundred years the chivalrous ideal of protecting the ladies[23] remained one of the main articles of faith of the British in India, the women themselves are harshly treated in the outpourings of (often misogynous) colonial writing— and this treatment culminates in the dictum, 'It was the ladies who lost us the Empire'.[24] Of course, the woman in question in this image is the middle-class British woman. As Jenny Sharpe points out, one of the most eloquent silences in Mutiny writings (including the accounts by women) concerns the fate of the lower-class soldiers' wives in India. And, of course, the focus is always on the fate of European women as opposed to native women: in effect, she notes, 'the native woman is not rapable'.[25]

THE TALE OF MISS WHEELER

A case in point for the ideal of woman delineated above is the tale of Miss Wheeler. The daughter of the very same (incompetent) general at Cawnpore mentioned above, she gained legendary fame by defending herself with a pistol against the threat of dishonour by sepoys and after finishing off a number of them, killing herself as well. The picture of the beauteous girl, long hair rippling down her back, defending herself against leering natives, was well-known to Victorian readerships. (It was printed in Charles Ball's *History of the Indian Mutiny*, 1858). In 1865, however, the eminent historian George Trevelyan toppled poor Miss Wheeler from her pedestal in his historical account entitled *Cawnpore* (1865) by claiming that she had merely been abducted by a sowar (native cavalry man), had converted to Islam and was still living with him. He concludes disdainfully that she was 'by no means of pure English blood'.[26] The present-day historian Christopher Hibbert embellishes this tale further with the information that on her death-bed she told a Roman Catholic priest that she had been well-treated by her husband and had no wish to contact the British authorities.[27]

In this tale a further seam of colonial ideology is laid bare: the articulation of sexuality with race and the importance of the control of sexuality in colonial discourse. The purity of the English woman was to be upheld above all because she was the repository of the purity of the race. Her own sexual agency was never at issue — according to nineteenth-century gender constructions she was not granted sexual agency, anyway.[28] If she succumbed to 'dishonour', her claims to racial purity were seen as dubious. Irrespective of her own wishes in the matter, the salient fact remains that once having lived with a native, it was impossible for Miss Wheeler to return to British society. Going native — whether by a man or a woman — threatened the very demarcation between the races colonial rule was grounded on. The analogy between the colonial configuration and the Prospero-Caliban constellation is striking and has been analysed by different critics, as well as poets and writers.[29] Here, too, Prospero seeks to control the sexuality of both Miranda and Caliban. When Caliban seeks to transgress the strict borders Prospero has drawn, his efforts are brandmarked as criminal. Conveniently, Prospero can displace his guilt at usurpation onto the usurped.[30] Miranda herself seems to have no agency. Thus the rape myth functioned to legitimize both colonial rule as well as patriarchal control of women's sexuality. Vron Ware demonstrates a similar mechanism at work in the racial conflicts in America's South.[31] Incidents of lynching were always linked to prior rumours of interracial contact between black men and white women. In a deeply patriarchal society, these cases were invariably construed as rape, women automatically denied sexual agency in the matter.

The suspicion that sexual jealousy might constitute a piece in the puzzle of the colonial constellation has been voiced by several critics.[32] Kenneth Ballhatchet notes the anxiety caused to the Viceroy Lord Curzon and Secretary of State Lord George Hamilton by the visit of some Indian soldiers in Britain at the turn of the century. In their correspondence they detect a 'very unpleasant characteristic' in recent years — 'the craze of white women for running after black men'. Hamilton expands on this theme:

> Apparently it pervades all classes of society: the smartest peeresses were only too ready to make a fuss with Bikaner and other Indian chiefs, and as you go lower in the social scale, so does this tendency manifest itself more strongly and in a way characteristic of the habits and lives of the respective classes of the community. At Hampton Court the great difficulty of the officers was in keeping the white women away from our Native soldiers.[33]

Despite all assertions to the contrary, it seems sexual attraction between the races was not a one-sided affair.

In the meantime, the pathological lust of the native for white women passed into the realm of common sense thinking. At every moment of ideological crisis it would be brandished as a truism. One such moment was the Ilbert Bill controversy of 1883. The law member of Viceroy Lord Ripon's Council wished to extend equal powers to Indian magistrates by enabling them to try Europeans in criminal matters as well — a minor legal point, it seemed. Instead, a cry of outrage welled up in the country, accompanied by the burning of the effigies of Ripon and Ilbert. 'Would you like', the *Friend of India* asked, 'to live in a country where at any moment your wife would be liable to be sentenced on a false charge, the Magistrate being a copper-coloured pagan?'[34] Significantly, the outrage focused on the image of white women being defiled in court by the lascivious gaze of a native judge. In fact, the main forms of protest were staged by women, who took the campaign firmly in hand. The fact that most of the court cases would be concerned with European male planters, notorious for abusing their labour, seemed beside the point. Indians were by no means unaware of their role as Caliban, as the following line from a native paper reveals: the issue at stake, it said, was the refusal of white women 'to submit to the jurisdiction of the Calibans lusting after the Mirandas of Anglo India'.[35] It is against this backdrop that E. M. Forster's subversion of colonial discourse in *A Passage to India* (1924) becomes apparent: by constructing a case of rape of a white woman by a native as hallucinatory Forster undermines one of the main pillars colonial self-legitimacy is built on.

Mutiny Accounts By Women

So far we have looked at the role of 'woman' as an icon of empire. What about the real women who were forced to endure sieges, whose husbands were murdered and whose eyewitness narratives account for no mean portion of Mutiny literature? It is these women that I wish to focus on now. Despite their shortcomings, it is these women to whom our sympathy must accrue. Nevertheless, it would be reductionist to overlook the power relations enacted in their texts and the function their narratives served. Unlike the disembodied traveller produced in most other travel narratives I have looked at, the body of the narrator underpins the narrative in this variant of experiential travel literature — the narrator's suffering reinforces the authenticity of the narrative. By recoding the violence offered to the body politic as a violence focusing on their bodies these women affirm the colonial construction of the Mutiny and help to deflect from the political issues at stake. Their texts support the official rape myth in circulation. However, their texts tell another story than the official story as well. The most striking impression left by these texts is the sense of women's agency pervading them. In contrast to the near-pornographic accounts[36] of many male writers, rape forms the silence around which the women's texts are constructed. This is partly due to the constraints on what could be written as a woman. But instead of spinning lurid yarns of white slavery, they are more concerned with constructing their narrative persona as active in self-survival than as a victim waiting to be sacrificed.[37] By constructing a resourceful and independent female subject they pose a threat to the colonial image of woman as a passive victim. In fact, by writing their experiences the gender role of women as passive is further undermined. Furthermore, what their texts conjure up is the image of a grotesque colonial world— a world 'out of joint' with all the moorings loose. It is the fragility of colonial power to which their writings bear testimony.

I wish to focus on two texts. *A Lady's Escape from Gwalior and Life in the Fort of Agra During the Mutinies of 1857* (1859) by R. M. Coopland is one of the many eyewitness accounts of a siege. The second text is an account by the only officer's wife to accompany a punitive force engaged in fighting the rebels: *Campaigning Experiences in Rajpootana and Central India, during the Suppression of the Mutiny, 1857-1858* (1859) by Frances Isabella Duberly. In reality women played no insignificant role in offering resistance to the rebels. They were often the first to report on the local situation, like Kate Moore, who succeeded in sending a telegram from Meerut on the night of the first rebel attack.[38] Their letters were also often published in the *Times*.

Mrs. Coopland is quite explicit on this count:

> Some men think that women are weak and only fitted to do trivial things, and endure petty troubles; and there are women who deserve no higher opinion: such as faint at the sight of blood, are terrified at a harmless cow, or make themselves miserable by imagining terrors, and unreal sorrows; but there are many who can endure with fortitude and patience what even soldiers shrink from. Men are fitted by education and constitution to dare and to do; yet they have been surpassed, in presence of mind and in the power of endurance, by weak women (116-17).

Not only are women the equal of men in courage and strength of mind — they are frequently *more* courageous than men. In other words, Coopland stakes a claim to an equal share of the cake of glory, for herself and her fellow sufferers — 'hundreds of ladies suffered all over India' (116).

Coopland makes no bones about attacking deficiencies of the government and reveals a number of facts embarrassing to the authorities:

> It seems surpassingly strange that so little notice was taken of the impending danger by those whose duty it was to care for the safety of a mighty empire. We had, at the beginning of the year 1857, three regiments *less* than before the annexation of Oude. There were no European regiments at many of the largest stations: Allahabad, Cawnpore, Benares, and Delhi, were all left to the protection of disaffected regiments. The Government at Calcutta, in serene complacency, was coolly issuing orders for the disbanding of regiments: as though that could in any way stop the evil. (79)

She also gives the government the blame for her husband's death — by not sending off the ladies to safety immediately, the chances of escape for the men, who insisted on staying at their side upto the last moment, were greatly diminished (107).

She quotes a letter of her husband's laying the blame for the revolt on 'weak tampering with idolatry and flattering vile superstitions' (85) — a hardline view that is echoed in many accounts and seeks the blame not in an excess of proselytizing energy but rather in the reverse, in governmental tolerance of Hindu and Muslim customs.

Coopland skillfully builds up suspense in her narrative, which begins innocuously enough like a travel narrative. She describes her arrival in Calcutta as a young bride and her trip to the station of Gwalior, where her husband is chaplain. Her text is strewn with dark hints such as the description of a picturesque town she passes through: 'How little did I then think, that *that* pretty, homelike station, in a few short months, would be a scene of devastation and ruin' (26). 'I have dilated sufficiently on the bright side of war; the dark side has yet to come', she warns (66). A note of foreboding is struck in her description of a dust-storm:

> Suddenly one afternoon a violent wind came on, filling the air to a great height with fine dust, rendering it almost dark, and casting a lurid light over everything. . . . The trees bent and shook, and the storm came on in all its fury. It grew darker and darker, and felt quite suffocating; everything was covered with fine sand, and the doors and windows shook and rattled (72-3).

The Mutiny is naturalized as a natural catastrophe in this passage. The world indeed darkens for Mrs Coopland and the other British in India. After news of the uprisings at other stations, the pressure becomes unbearable: 'I hope few will know how awful it is to wait quietly for death. There was now no escape; and we waited for our death-stroke. The dread calm of apprehension was awful'. (113) Then one night the attack comes—her husband is killed and 'eight miserable women, alone and unprotected' (131) attempt to make their escape to the nearest station (Agra), helped by one faithful servant. What follows is a phantasmagoria of nightmare scenes, populated by insolent servants and leering villagers and rebels:

> The sepoys soon returned, and crowded in to stare at us. They made the most insulting remarks, and then said, 'Let us carry them to our line', whereupon they seized our hands, and dragged us along very fast. . . . It seemed as if God had forsaken us, and that hell reigned on earth. No words can describe the hellish looks of these human fiends, or picture their horrid appearance: they had rifled all the stores, and drank brandy and beer to excess . . . The sensation of horror and helplessness oppressed us like a night-mare ... (127, 132).

In fact, the images conjured up are strongly reminiscent of the French Revolution.[39] Once again class conflict is conflated with colonial conflict. Even after she reaches safety, her respite is only short-lived. Soon the British are assigned quarters in the fort of Agra in preparation for a siege. Around 5,800 people move into the fort, of whom about 2,000 are Europeans and the rest half-castes and native servants. Unlike other besieged women Coopland does not present her experience as an unmitigated nightmare, with shells exploding all around. The besieged fort in Agra was relatively fortunate and the residents were not deserted by all their servants, either. Coopland mentions musical parties and a wedding taking place as well as the birth of her own baby. A remarkable feature of mutiny accounts is how class barriers within the British community remain intact: 'even at the most perilous moment of the siege the etiquette of Anglo-Indian life remained as rigid as in time of peace'.[40] Of the lower orders a Mrs Harris muses, 'It is wonderful how little that class of people seem to feel things that would kill a lady'.[41]

Not surprisingly, the Mutiny accounts of women abound in expressions of antipathy towards natives and calls for bloody retribution. However, the contemporary reader is occasionally taken aback by the violence of the rhetoric. Mrs Harris declares, 'You can only rule Asiatics by fear',[42] and Mrs Coopland is haunted by the thought of servants gloating over her fate, despite the evidence of some faithful retainers. She calls for the Mughal capital Delhi to be razed to the ground:

> I could not but think it was a disgrace to England that this city, instead of being rased to the ground, should be allowed to stand, with its blood-stained walls and streets, — an everlasting memorial of the galling insult offered to England's honour. . . .
>
> Delhi ought to be rased to the ground, and on its ruins a church or monument should be erected, inscribed with a list of all the victims of the mutinies — if it be possible to gather the names of ALL those who were massacred, — and the funds for its erection should be raised by a fine levied on every native implicated in the mutinies, but not openly accused of murder (278-9).

Similarly, Mrs Bartrum hopes, 'Our European regiments . . . will not be slow in avenging the blood of our brothers and sisters; and soon all that remains of this ancient Indian capital will be one vast tomb.'[43]

As the British regain control of the country, it is deemed safe enough for Mrs Coopland to travel to Delhi and thence to Bombay to embark on her journey home. At Delhi she is invited by an officer as an amusement to go and see the captive emperor. She describes how they burst into his room without announcement, and goes on to narrate,

> As we looked at him we thought how strange it was that this frail old man, tottering on the brink of the grave, could harbour such a plot and such deep revengeful feelings against us. His face was pale and wan, and his eyes weak and uncertain, seeming to shun our scrutiny; but an aristocratic expression of face reminded us of his noble descent. He had a venerable-looking white beard, and he swayed about in a frail decrepit way, exciting feelings that were a mixture of contempt, abhorrence, and pity: contempt, for the degraded position to which he had brought himself by his wild scheme of reinstating himself on a throne which he could only hope to enjoy for a passing year or two;

> abhorrence, that he could give up our poor countrymen to be brutally murdered, and even, it is said, feast his eyes and ears on their dying anguish; and pity, that he should have so short a time for repentance, and that the descendant of a line of kings, whose splendour and power were boundless, should be thus degraded (275-6).

A tension is visible in this passage. The key to this lies once again in the analogy to the French Revolution — only this time Coopland is on the wrong side. Despite her protestations of abhorrence — the emperor's brutality is, however, couched in careful terms ('it is said . . .') — the text abounds in reminders of royal pedigree. By contrast, the British right to rule is not legitimized in a single line. Where other texts of this period downplay the legitimacy of Moghul rule and point up the 'unspeakable benefit' of British rule, Coopland's text evinces a confusion as to who the intruders here are.[44] At a moment of British triumph, the narrator's own conservative values, it seems, are thrown into confusion.

In the last line of her book Coopland reminds her readers of the 'privilege of living in a country where freedom reigns' (316). The question, 'Freedom for whom?' never seems to strike her once throughout her narrative.

The Crimean Heroine

Mrs Duberly did not experience the Mutiny as a victim, but as an avenging angel. She is an extraordinary woman who has somehow been overlooked by feminist historiography so far. As the only officer's wife to accompany the British troops during the Crimean War (not counting soldiers' wives, who don't count), she gained notoriety as the 'Crimean heroine'. Her published war diary became a best-seller, though she was also severely criticized for being too unladylike. Queen Victoria declined her dedication and ignored her pointedly when inspecting the troops on their return. E. E. P. Tisdall has taken the trouble to edit Mrs Duberly's private letters and affords us interesting insights into her character. Riding roughshod over gender regulations, she is proud to report, 'Jennings said the other day that he [a mettlesome pony] was the greatest man out here; for Mrs Duberly bullies everybody, and the pony bullies her.'[45] In another letter she justifies herself for her reputation: 'If you couldn't cleave your way with a hatchet out here, I wonder where you'd be — trampled into your grave long enough ago!'[46] Her respect for feminine notions of propriety is accordingly scant: from the Crimea she writes home, 'I have long ago given up all petticoats except a gown tail and wear a pair of man's trousers and thick boots. Petticoats are impossible.'[47]

When her husband's regiment, the 8th Royal Irish Hussars, is ordered to India to help quell the mutiny, she does not hesitate to accompany it. The feeling of battle is exhilarating to her: 'I never, never shall forget the throbbing excitement of that short gallop, when the horse beneath one, raging in his fierce strength, and mad with excitement, scarcely touched the ground'(135). Unfortunately, the Indian campaign was to become a feat of endurance, involving marching incessantly at the heels of a retreating guerilla-like enemy, rarely seeing active service. Nevertheless, Mrs Duberly is proud to conclude her book with the reckoning that,

> I close the record of our first year's Field Service in India, wherein that part of the Brigade, which was accompanied by my husband and myself, passed only one European station, Deesa, and marched in spite of Indian sun and Indian rain, and in the toilsome pursuit of an ever flying foe, a distance of 2,028 miles, more than 1,800 of which I have myself accomplished on horseback. (246)

Perhaps because of the monotony of the experiences recounted, her book about India did not sell as well as the first. Childless, and burdened with a spineless husband (another letter to her sister: 'If I had but a *Master* under whom I could work! Instead of a friend I am obliged to support'[48]), she channels all her energy into constructing her persona. Her cup of happiness is full when she receives the following paean to herself: 'You will eclipse every woman of modern times. You must give an enormous fillip to the men of your regiment when they see a delicate woman beating them clear out of the field.'[49]

Chiefly sustained by a spirit of adventure, Mrs Duberly is not very interested in Indian politics. Still, we get a clarion call for revenge from her:

> When I think upon this terrible insurrection, and recollect how deeply the rebels have stained themselves with English blood, the blood of English women and of little helpless children, I can only look forward with awe to the day of vengeance, when our hands shall be dipped in the blood of our enemies, and the tongues of our dogs shall be red through the same. (26)

She is, however, fascinated by the activities of aristocratic women rebels. When she meets the aging Baiza Bai, another horsewoman and warrior of a bygone era, she immediately strikes up a rapport with her and notes admiringly, 'She is over seventy years of age, but apparently as energetic as in the days of her fiery and intriguing youth. . . .' (154). In the case of the rebel leader, the Queen of Jhansi, her reactions are more ambivalent. When she learns of the legendary death of the Rani (in men's battle attire), she can only wonder at her 'fierce and desperate courage' (145), but is careful to echo the usual platitudes of relief at the death of so disruptive a spirit. Privately she draws another conclusion (and possibly an analogy to herself): in a letter to her sister she notes, 'After all, one determined woman is worth more than half a score of most men; for nothing will turn her from her object.'[50]

Later we come across an extraordinary passage, one that echoes the *Times* correspondent William Russell's scenes of the plundering English army. It works as a mirror passage to the lines quoted above. Mrs Duberly approaches a town that has just been ransacked by her regiment:

> Some circumstances that came under my notice were very distressing. A man shot in the head, and who was bleeding profusely from the wound, was tended by his little daughter, apparently about twelve years old, who held up her hands imploring mercy and pity as we passed. Nor was I the only one who tried to re-assure and comfort her. One of our servants, when he joined us later in the day, brought with him a little boy, about seven years old, who he found standing by his dead father, who had been shot and fallen from his horse. The man, the child and the horse were in a group, and our servant charitably took the other child and placing him before him on his own horse, brought him into camp. I became possessed too of a small white dog, which, together with a baby of six or seven months old, was found lying on a bed when the mother, frenzied, I suppose, by terror, had fled, and *left her child behind*. The little one was sitting up and laughing, pleased at the horses and soldiers as they passed. . . .
>
> It seems to me that all this Indian warfare is unsatisfactory work, and although it may be true that in this rebellion severity is mercy, yet, on the other hand, there have been cases of ruthless slaughter, of which perhaps the less said the better. (231-2)

The narrator is guarded in her critique, and packages her statement in understatement ('it seems to me . . . unsatisfactory . . . there have been cases . . . the less said the better.') It is the scenes of terror and devastation conjured up in the text that leave a deep impression on the reader's mind. Incidently, the text presents a native of humane characteristics. But the most haunting image remains that of a terror-striken mother and a laughing baby. In a rare moment in women's Mutiny writings, the agents of terror evoked by the text are not the rebels, but the British. And in a rare insight the Indian woman is shown to be rapable, too.

Notes

1 C. A. Bayly, *Indian Society and the Making of the British Empire* 169-70.
2 Rudrangshu Mukherjee, ' 'Satan Let Loose Upon Earth': The Kanpur Massacres in India in the Revolt of 1857', *Past and Present* 128 (August 1990) 104.
3 Mukherjee 104.
4 Bayly 188.
5 Bayly 192.
6 Michael Edwardes, 'The Mutiny and Its Consequences', William Howard Russell, *My Indian Mutiny Diary*, ed. Michael Edwardes (London: Cassel, 1970) xiii.
7 Mukherjee 113.
8 See Salahuddin Malik, 'Nineteenth Century Approaches to the Indian 'Mutiny' ', *Journal of Asian History* 7 (1973): 113.
9 J. W. Kaye, *History of the Sepoy War in India, 1857-58*, 3 vols. (London, 1881) 2: 269-70, quoted in Mukherjee 111.
10 The myth is cultivated even today, for instance in celebratory accounts such as Pat Barr's *The Memsahibs*.
11 Russell, *My Indian Mutiny Diary* 282.
12 Bayly 194.
13 *Times* 25 August 1857, quoted in Jenny Sharpe, *Allegories of Empire: The Figure of Woman in the Colonial Text* (Minneapolis: University of Minnesota Press, 1993) 66.
14 Mukherjee 116.
15 R. M. Coopland, *A Lady's Escape from Gwalior and Life in the Fort of Agra During the Mutinies of 1857* (London, 1859) 234. All further references to be given in parentheses in the text.
16 See Dennis Kincaid, *British Social Life in India* 203.
17 See Hutchins, *The Illusion of Permanence* 79-100.
18 See Jenny Sharpe, 'The Unspeakable Limits of Rape: Colonial Violence and Counter-Insurgency', *Colonial Discourse and Post-Colonial Theory: A Reader*, eds. Patrick Williams and Laura Chrisman (Hemel Hempstead: Harvester, 1993) 221-43.

19 Patrick Brantlinger, *Rule of Darkness* 222.

20 Brantlinger 204.

21 Flora Annie Steel, *The Garden of Fidelity* 14.

22 See Andrew Parker, Mary Russo, Doris Sommer, and Patricia Yaeger, eds. *Nationalisms and Sexualities* (New York: Routledge, 1992) Introduction 1-18.

23 On the re-emergence of the cult of chivalry in the Victorian age see Mark Girouard, *The Return to Camelot: Chivalry and the English Gentleman* (New Haven: Yale University Press, 1981).

24 Quoted in Helen Callaway, *Gender, Culture and Empire: European Women in Colonial Nigeria* (Basingstoke: Macmillan, 1978) 5.

25 Sharpe 232.

26 G. O. Trevelyan, *Cawnpore* (London, 1865) 255, quoted in Sharpe, *Allegories of Empire* 73.

27 Christopher Hibbert, *The Great Mutiny: India in 1857* (London: Penguin, 1978) 194-5, quoted in Brantlinger 295.

28 See Nancy F. Cott, 'Passionlessness: An Interpretation of Victorian Sexual Ideology, 1790-1850', *Signs* 4.2 (1978): 219-36.

29 See, for instance, O. Mannoni's *Prospero and Caliban: The Psychology of Colonization* (London: Praeger, 1956).

30 See Paul Brown, ' 'This thing of darkness I acknowledge mine': *The Tempest* and the discourse of colonialism', *Political Shakespeare: New Essays in Cultural Materialism*, eds. Jonathan Dollimore and Alan Sinfield (Manchester: MUP, 1985) 48-71.

31 See Vron Ware, *Beyond the Pale: White Women, Racism and History* (London: Verso, 1992) 167-224.

32 See, for instance, Kenneth Ballhatchet, *Race, Sex and Class under the Raj*; also Margaret Strobel, *European Women in British Africa and Asia* (Bloomington: Indiana University Press, 1991).

33 Quoted in Ballhatchet 119-20.

34 Quoted in Peter Mudford, *Birds of a Different Plumage* 200.

35 Quoted in Mrinalini Sinha, 'Chathams, Pitts, and Gladstones in Petticoats', *Western Women and Imperialism* 99.

36 Benita Parry, *Delusions and Discoveries. Studies on India in the British Imagination 1880-1930* (London: Allen Lane Penguin, 1972) 70.

37 I am particularly indebted to Jenny Sharpe for this insight. See Sharpe, *Allegories of Empire* 69-73.

38 S. B. Chaudhuri, *English Historical Writings on the Indian Mutiny 1857-1859* (Calcutta: World, 1979) 135-54.

39 Some critics claim Dickens' *A Tale of Two Cities* (1859) was influenced by Mutiny accounts. See Brantlinger 208.

40 Kincaid 201.

41 Katherine Harris, *A Lady's Diary of the Siege of Lucknow* (London, 1858) 56.

42 Harris 49.

43 Katherine Mary Bartrum, *A Widow's Reminiscences of the Siege of Lucknow* (London, 1858) 5.
44 Note, for instance, Mrs Mackenzie's invective, 'None of the Musalman Princes ...whom we have dispossessed were hereditary Sovereigns: they were rebellious Viceroys and Governors who had seized the opportunity of confusion to make themselves independent....' See Mrs Colin Mackenzie, *Six Years in India* iii.
45 Letter to her sister Selina, quoted in E. E. P. Tisdall, *Mrs. Duberly's Campaigns: An Englishwoman's Experience in the Crimean War and the Indian Mutiny* (London, 1963) 148.
46 Tisdall 148.
47 Tisdall 116.
48 Tisdall 178.
49 Tisdall 179.
50 Tisdall 200.

Chapter 6

The Philanthropic Traveller

Honoria Lawrence, wife of the legendary administrator Henry Lawrence, laments that life in India meant 'no delightful rambling walks, no visiting the poor, no going out alone unquestioned'.[1] High on the list of leisure activities of middle-class English women in the nineteenth century was visiting the homes of the poor. Unlike Honoria Lawrence, however, many women travellers to India did not see themselves forced to abandon their activity in India. Instead, they transferred their attention from the poor to another object of compassion — the downtrodden Indian woman. In fact, the degraded condition of Indian women is a topos that runs through women's writing on India throughout the century, from the narrative of Maria Graham (1812) to the memoirs of Vicereine Lady Dufferin, who was to found a Trust for medical aid to native women in the 1880s. In this chapter I wish to focus on only one philanthropic traveller — Mary Carpenter — who is, however, an exemplary case as she was a well-known social reformer in Britain, too, and was influential in generating interest in the Indian women's question among feminists. Her text was extremely popular in its day. Before looking at her text I would like briefly to trace the historical roots of women's philanthropy in the nineteenth century.

The Origins of Women's Philanthropy

The roots of women's social reformism lie in the period between 1780 and 1830, the period of accelerated transition of the English society from an aristocratic society to an industrial capitalist society controlled by the bourgeoisie. It was during this period that a new Evangelical ethos of family and domesticity took shape.[2] The Evangelical project involved an ambitious reform of manners and morals, and had as its pivot the family. The home was seen as the centre of religious life. This was linked to a division of public and private spheres. As Catherin Hall remarks, 'The basic split was between the world as hostile and the home as loving — a split that became commonplace in Victorian England'.[3] Thus when he was in London the reformer William Wilberforce wrote to his wife, 'Pray for me . . . It will be a comfort to me to know that you all who are, as it were, on the top of the mountain, withdrawn from and above the storm, are thus interceding for me who am scuffling in the vale below'.[4] The ideology of domesticity reflected material changes in the social and economic world: with the growth of capitalist modes of production the middle-class family home was increasingly separated from the work place. Whereas previously merchants and manufacturers had lived in close proximity to their workshops or warehouses, gradually a move towards suburban family homes was discernible.[5]

Within the ideology of domesticity the role women were to play was clearly defined. Women were firmly relegated to the private sphere and barred entrance into public life. Writers such as Hannah More set up a catalogue of traits that were identified as naturally 'feminine'. A compensation was offered to women in their role as moral guardians of the nation. From the image of women as naturally licentious beings current in the eighteenth century women were now desexualized and became the repository of moral virtues.[6] For women to fulfil their new role they had to be well educated. As Hall explains,

> A clear distinction was made between the education of the daughters of the poor and those of the upper and middle classes. The daughters of the poor should be trained as servants or as good wives; the emphasis in their schooling should be on industry, frugality, diligence and good management. The daughters of the well-to-do, on the other hand, should be educated for moral excellence, and that meant that the traditional girls' training which they had been receiving was quite inadequate. To be able to dress well, to dance and play the piano, was not enough.[7]

Women's philanthropic enterprise was inextricably linked to the ideology of domesticity. As Anne Summers and F. K. Prochaska[8] have shown, increased wealth, leisure and a spirit of religious revival were the main forces behind middle-class women's large-scale engagement in charity work. An increased dependence on servants, as well as the large numbers of poor entering domestic service, were an added inducement for their efforts — improving the quality of domestic servants became a vital concern. Summers has pointed out that these women can be regarded as employers of labour in their own right.[9] As one Reverend J. S. Brewer reminds the ladies, 'you are exercising in your own families a vast social and political power' and goes on to explain,

> The female servants in your household, whom you have taken and instructed in their respective duties — whose manners you have softened — who have learnt from you how to manage a household — who have caught up from you, insensibly, lessons of vast utility, lessons of order, lessons of economy, lessons of cleanliness, lessons of the management of children, of household comfort and tidiness; these women eventually become the wives of small tradesmen and respectable operatives. They carry into a lower and a very extended circle the influence of your teaching and your training. Visit a hamlet of a village where the cottager's wife has been a servant in the squire's mansion, and you shall see the result immediately, in the air of comfort, order, and neatness which reigns around — in the gentle and respectful manner of the woman — in the tidiness and respectability of her children.[10]

In other words, the programme underlying charity work was the wish to transpose middle-class domestic values to the working classes through the strategies of self-control and self-regulation of the poor. Ironically, the effect was often to increase the work-load of the poorer woman. Both Summers and Prochaska argue that a deeply conservative impulse informed women's philanthropy. Working-class women were exhorted to provide a haven of domesticity for their menfolk in order to draw working men off the streets and thus isolate the poor from each other. Solutions on an individual basis were offered for wide-ranging social problems. Charity was a means to contain the contamination of the French Revolution from spreading.[11] Nevertheless, the emancipatory effect of charity work for middle-class women is indisputable. It permitted women to leave the confinement of their homes. It enabled the women to gain in self-confidence, to gather experience and even gain administrative skills. In addition, it 'gave women a taste of power outside their own homes'.[12]

THE DEGRADED INDIAN WOMAN

Particularly in the wake of the Mutiny a new sphere of activity for female reformers emerged: the degraded Indian woman. At a time when British rule in India increasingly legitimized its presence in the name of its mission to bring the light of civilization to the unenlightened masses of the East, women social reformers linked their cause to that of the empire. Philanthropy gained a new impetus in the women's movement in the later part of the century. Antoinette Burton identifies a specific 'white woman's burden' in early feminist attitudes towards their Eastern sisters.[13] The image of Indian women is neatly summed up in the following remark by the social activist Josephine Butler,

> Their helplessness appeals to the heart, in somewhat the same way in which the helplessness and suffering of a dumb animal does, under the knife of a vivisector. Somewhere, halfway between the Martyr Saints and the tortured 'friend of man', the noble dog, stand, it seems to me, these pitiful Indian women, girls, children, as many of them are.[14]

Indian women were above all seen as helpless and childlike, as victims in dire need of Western women's help. While she does not deny their real concern with the condition of Indian women, Burton points out that this concern was linked to a sense of moral superiority, an attitude termed 'maternal imperialism' by historian Barbara Ramusack.[15] One of the earliest women reformers to visit India was Mary Carpenter. The activities of Indian female reformers of this period, on the other hand, left no dent on the image of the Indian woman circulated in the West.

Burton detects other elements in British feminists' attitudes to Indian women: feminists' preoccupation with the condition of women in India and the East 'not only expresses their imperial assumptions but also underscores a militant national and racial pride which characterized the diverse campaigns for female emancipation in Britain'.[16] She uncovers a feminist preoccupation with race preservation, racial purity, and racial motherhood. This is, of course, to be seen in the context of conservative attacks against feminists which played on fears of racial deterioration due to women taking up careers.[17] In fact, a consistent strategy of early feminism has been to deflect conservative criticism by appropriating the very values conservatives espoused and shaping them to their own ends. A case in point is the concept of women's moral superiority, advocated by supporters of women's domestic role, which was brandished by feminist activists as an argument to support the entrance of women into the public sphere, arguably in dire need of this moralizing influence. This brings us to the function the image of Indian womanhood had for British feminism. By demonstrating a commitment to a 'white woman's burden', feminists sought to legitimize their entrance into the field of politics and to claim a share of national and imperial power. As Burton reminds us, 'Historians must not lose sight of the fact that feminism(s) are and always will be as much quests for power as they are battles for rights. Nineteenth-century feminists sought empowerment by a variety of means—education, the vote, welfare legislation — not the least of which was by allying their cause with British imperial rule.'[18]

While it may have been difficult for early feminists to escape a hegemonic discourse such as the imperial discourse, modern Western feminists' sense of superiority towards third-world women is less easy to understand. Women of colour have been 'writing back' for some time and have accused Western feminists of constructing a white middle-class brand of feminism that claims to speak for all women, irrespective of class, colour or sexual preference. The image produced in feminist writings on other women is, they claim, rooted in a reductive and homogeneous notion of womanhood and is always implicitly juxtaposed with an individualistic presentation of Western woman. And the trope of Eastern woman as victim continues to flourish:

> This average third world woman leads an essentially truncated life based on her feminine gender (read: sexually constrained) and her being 'third world' (read: ignorant, poor, uneducated, tradition-bound, domestic, family-oriented, victimized, etc.). This, I suggest, is in contrast to the (implicit) self-representation of Western women as educated, as modern, as having control over their own bodies and sexualities, and the freedom to make their own decisions.[19]

Chandra Talpade Mohanty calls instead for respecting the heterogeneity of women, of restoring agency to them and for a recognition of the social and historical constructedness of the concept of 'woman'. However, the tenacity of the trope Eastern-woman-as-victim is not only a characteristic of feminist discourse, but is discernible in a wide spectrum of writings. Take, for instance, the project of restoring white women's role in empire to its proper place in history. For Joanne Trollope, author of *Britannia's Daughters. Women of the British Empire* (1983), the full horror of the purdah system (seclusion of women) is revealed in childbirth:

> Women brought up to believe that to show themselves to a man not their husband was the most degrading shame upon earth, would frequently die undelivered of a baby rather than summon male medical help. Conservative mothers-in-law frequently strengthened this tragic resolve and sent for a *dai*, a native midwife, who in her ignorance could inflict such horrifying injuries as actually pulling off the limb of a half-born baby in her efforts to induce it to emerge.[20]

The text hints darkly at all the horrors associated with the East: child sacrifice, mutilation, ignorance and superstition. Ironically, the overtly feminist project of the book is belied by a belligerent denial of indigenous traditional female skills — what is truly needed here, it seems, is the strong male hand of Western science.

Colonialism and the Condition of Indian Women

What is regularly ignored by philanthropic-minded women travellers to India is the implication of colonial rule in the oppression of Indian women. As Lata Mani has shown in the case of sati, the colonial rulers' interpretation of a cultural practice as one grounded in scripture and their privileging of religious leaders' interpretations as authoritative had the effect of valorizing sati as a religious practice. In the debate on the abolition of sati, native arguments in favour of sati (by traditionalists) or against it (by social reformers) were based on the assumptions created by colonial discourse (see chapter 1 on women Orientalist travellers). In general, the colonial codification of law tended to privilege high caste Hindu norms over customary law, usually 'to the disadvantage of *all* Hindu women, whether rural or urban'.[21] Further, as is often the case with resistance to foreign rule, a conservative backlash was widespread in

India which emphasized a return to traditional values and constructed a myth of the 'traditional' submissive Indian wife. British colonial rule was anxious to align itself with conservative forces, as these were seen as a stabilizing factor for empire.

In addition, well-intentioned social legislation was often counterproductive. Kumkum Sangari and Sudesh Vaid demonstrate this in the case of the Widow Remarriage Act (1856), intended to ease the oppression of young widows in their in-laws' houses. The main stake high-caste families had in opposing widow remarriage was the property a widow inherited from her husband, which she would take with her into the new marriage. The Act debarred a widow from any right to inheritance from her husband's property on remarriage, thus ceding to pressure from high-class in-law families. But as a widow would have to give up her children on remarriage as well, the burden on widows was not made any lighter. On the other hand, lower-caste women (the majority), for whom widow remarriage had hitherto been customary, were adversely affected by the clauses on property inheritance. Joanna Liddle and Rama Joshi point out that despite the British claim to have improved the condition of women in India, their reforming impetus was highly selective.[22] Thus the British introduced a law for the restitution of conjugal rights, which was rooted in English ecclesiastical law and which allowed a person to sue his spouse for refusing to fulfill her conjugal obligations. In fact, the British image of the Indian woman as downtrodden served a distinct function in colonial discourse, namely to legitimate further British rule and bolster the belief in Western cultural superiority. Philanthropic women travellers to India colluded in this project.

The introduction of capitalism to India in conjunction with British educational policies led to the creation of a class of Western-educated, urbanized bourgeoisie in India. Modelling themselves on English gentlemen and imbued with the ideology of domesticity, this class had a stake in the seclusion of their wives as a means of differentiation from lower classes. As Sangari and Vaid remark, 'This process is not dissimilar to the one which pushed the middle class woman into the seclusion of the private sphere as a mark of class status and superiority (among other things) in Victorian England'.[23] It is from within this class that a call for female education was launched. The gentlemen concerned were anxious to have a wife educated up to their level and endowed with the accomplishments of English ladies. A missionary relates that a Brahmin gentleman was anxious to have her teach his daughters to darn stockings, an article recently adopted by Indian gentlemen which posed immense problems for Indian tailors. In addition to darning, the gentleman wished the missionary to teach his daughters to behave themselves like English ladies.[24] The demand for female education increased particularly in the post-Mutiny period and led to an influx of women missionaries who were willing to teach within the zenanas (thus removing the main obstacle to women's education, the opposition to male teachers). As Geraldine Forbes has discussed, zenana teaching represented a prestigious career for women missionaries, who enjoyed generous conditions and the prestige involved in entering the houses of the elite — in contrast to teaching low-class native converts, as would otherwise fall to their lot. However, once again we find that ironically enough they served to add to the oppression of Indian women, who were now forced to learn additional alien skills to please their husbands.[25]

Mary Carpenter and Female Education

Mary Carpenter's decision to help the cause of women's education in India was also fuelled by the call for help by an Indian gentleman. However, unlike the missionaries, she had no high opinion of zenana teaching with its domestic distractions and emphasized the need for schools for girls run by women teachers. At the time of her trip she was already a well-known social reformer particularly in the field of juvenile delinquency. She is described (rather unkindly) by a contemporary as 'all physics, philanthropy, blankets, and moral pictorial pocket handkerchiefs'.[26]

Mary Carpenter (1807-77) herself was fortunate enough to receive an excellent education, her curriculum including Latin, Greek, mathematics and science.[27] Her education was taken charge of by her father, a prominent Unitarian minister and school instructor and fervent anti-slavery activist, to whom she was bound in an unusually close relationship. After his death from suicide — a shock from which she never recovered — she set out to compile a volume of *Meditations and Prayers*, supported the anti-slavery movement, established two reformatories for juvenile delinquents and engaged in a study of prison conditions. Throughout her life she published a regular flow of writings on questions of social reform with titles such as 'What shall we do with our Pauper Child?' (1861). One of the formative experiences of her youth was meeting the Indian reformer and anti-sati campaigner Rajah Rammohun Roy, who visited Bristol on the invitation of her father. In 1866 she published a review of his career (*The Last Days in England of Rajah Rammohun Roy*) and her travel account is dedicated to him. She embarked for India at the age of fifty-nine and made four trips to India between 1866 and 1876.

One of the most striking things about Mary Carpenter's text is the fact that it is a *public* text, an intervention in public discourse. This is to say that her text practically elides personal statements, but abounds in formal statements of thanks for the hospitality of various high-ranking officials, appeals for donations, exhortations for more commitment on the part of British women, etc. While Vol. 1 loosely traces her itinerary to a few large cities, Vol. 2 focuses almost entirely on 'General Observations' on the state of female education, of prison discipline and a few other circumscribed areas of interest. Lengthy addresses to various societies and letters addressed to various officials containing a catalogue of her recommendations and suggestions, as well as excerpts from reports and speeches of thanks addressed by various societies to herself are submitted for the reader's scrutiny. Even in the descriptions of the cities she visits, the text is impatient to get to the focal points of her interest — the schools, jails and missionary stations in each town. A shrewd sense of diplomacy is discernible — letters harrying local authorities are interspersed with statements such as, 'It is most gratifying to an Englishwoman to find how much had been done, both by our Government and by private individuals, to promote the welfare of this great country', or, more explicitly,

> The enormous press of business which has to be transacted in that vast empire, the comparatively small number of official gentlemen on whom these duties fall, the immense variety of departments requiring attention, each one of which is sufficient to be all-absorbing to those engaged in it, the immense distances which have to be traversed in going from one part of the empire to the other, and the difficulties of communication between the great centres of civilisation, — all these considerations rather lead to astonishment that so much has been done, rather than that some departments lag behind the general progress. (2: 205)

The point she is making is, of course, adroitly kept under wraps until the final phase of the sentence. Balm for the official soul — until she embarks on another round of exhortation.

Her credo is outlined in the following passage:

> The devoted work of multitudes of Englishwomen in that great continent, shows what our sex can do: new light, the rapid progress of civilisation, the wants created by it, reveal increasing need of women's work in India. May many more Englishwomen arise, who shall devote themselves to the glorious and blessed work of raising their Eastern sisters, to fill that place in society for which the Creator has destined them! (2: 83)

Carpenter's rhetoric locates her firmly within the project of the 'white woman's burden', duty-bound to uplift the Indian woman. At the same time she launches an appeal to other women to follow in her footsteps.

Carpenter's commitment to the ideology of domesticity and the concept of two spheres is quite explicit: 'Our Heavenly Father has created the two sexes with different powers, and for different spheres of work, in his world. One cannot take the duties of the other without disturbing the order of His providence' (1: 62).

One of the irritating things about India for many travellers is the inversion of many of the gender norms prevalent in Western society. Thus many of the professions occupied by women in England are in India traditionally in the hands of men — for example, domestic service or tailoring. However, Carpenter hopes to change all that, and is encouraged by a meeting with Indian officials in the education department: 'It was very satisfactory to hear a deputy sub-inspector say with some pride, 'My wife made all the clothes I have on; it was she who made this vest.' The native inspectors seemed all to feel their professional honour concerned in bringing forward their wives as much as possible' (1: 94).

While this example of male smugness might make the modern reader feel heartily sorry for the wife in question, Carpenter seems to approve and continues relentlessly in her description of an orphan school:

> In England, such girls would be generally intended for domestic service, and prepared for its duties while at school. I was informed, however, that such can rarely be the case in India, owing to the universal employment of men in the household occupations, with us exclusively appropriated to women; it would not,

> therefore, be safe for a young girl to be placed as servant in a family. The girls are usually married when about fifteen or sixteen to native converts, and it is of importance that they should be prepared to be good wives and mothers of families. Mrs. Nesbit has them trained, therefore, to do all kinds of housework; this is not only in itself very useful, but is valuable in strengthening the muscles. Laundrywork is at home an excellent occupation in these respects, and is besides very often remunerative; it appears, however, that this is never carried on in schools. Attention is, however, paid to needlework, and some is even taken in for customers. The singing was sweet, and in other respects this school gave me satisfactory proof that, under good female instruction, Hindoo girls are quite equal to their English sisters (1: 106-7).

All three utterances quoted above are classic statements of the ideology of domesticity and philanthropy. First, the emphasis on the two natural (or God-given) spheres for men and women — unfortunately subverted in the Indian context (Carpenter will have been driven to distraction to learn that laundering, too, was an occupation traditionally carried out by men in India.) Next, a vision of ideal womanhood as a repository of domestic virtues. Lastly, a blueprint for the education of the lower orders in the ideals of domesticity and order. As it is their destiny to serve the upper classes — even if this is exasperatingly difficult to implement in India in this case — it is wise to keep their muscles supple.

There is only one dissonance in the domestic rhapsody presented in the text — the role of the narrator. Mary Carpenter is anything but a paragon of domestic virtues. Even if readers are unaware of the very different education she herself enjoyed and her status as a single woman, they can hardly ignore the fact that it is a business trip Carpenter is on, not a pleasure cruise. In fact, Carpenter loses no opportunity of pointing this out: 'I was also obliged to decline a very tempting offer to accompany a party to the much-desired Neilgherries . . . I had no strength or time for anything but the objects of my journey' (1: 289). At another point she is even more explicit: 'The sail from Bombay is very beautiful. It is only necessary to fancy oneself on a pleasure excursion instead of a business voyage, thoroughly to enjoy the glorious harbour. . . .' Her text itself, with its incorporation of public addresses, letters addressed to the government and official documents, constitutes a form of public discourse, as has been argued above. It presents her as a public persona, engaged in tough negotiations with the authorities, not as a private traveller. In fact, Carpenter was the first woman to speak publicly (to the National Reformatory Union in 1856).[28] In addition, to further the cause of female education Carpenter advocates model teachers' training schools, to be run entirely by women with the main responsibility in the hands of a Lady Superintendent. She calls for adequate pay and prestige to be attached to the profession to encourage women to take it up. In effect, what Carpenter is doing is calling for increased career opportunities for women — in modification of Disraeli's dictum, 'the East is a career'. Thus the figure of Mary Carpenter represents a reification of the internal contradictions inherent in the ideology of domesticity.

Mary Carpenter and the Civilising Mission

Carpenter forms a pleasant contrast to most other travellers to India in refusing — for whatever true reason — to satisfy the reader's voyeuristic desire to learn about the zenana: 'I should gladly give some pleasing detail of many of my visits to the zenanas, were I not withheld by feelings of respect to domestic privacy' (1: 213). She is one of the few travellers to evince a feeling of delicacy towards the people whose hospitality she enjoys. In her approach to women's education she displays pragmatic good sense by admitting that attempts at converting the students to Chrisitanity in the schools would be counter-productive. ('It must be an essential condition that no one while in the institution should, under any circumstances, be allowed in *religious interference of any kind.*') (1: 123). There are also very few of the usual racist remarks to be found in her text. In fact, Carpenter numbers numerous Indian gentlemen among her friends. She is willing to accept anglicized, preferably converted Indians as equals. However, her text evinces a deep sense of disturbance at all aspects of Indian life. This is exemplified in her descriptions of the native parts of towns, such as the following:

> Shortly after my arrival, I drove through the busiest part of the native town, Chidpore Road. It was dirty and narrow; indeed, the low shops seemed placed one before another to make the most of the room. The naked salesmen here wear their long black hair instead of the turban. A variety of races may be seen,

> many having come from distant parts to dispose of their produce. The odours arising from this district are indescribable; it would appear that the native gentry who reside in this locality, must have their sense of smell blunted by long habitude, and thus are not aware of the extreme unhealthiness of such a condition. Here, to my surprise, I found that the Brahmo Samaj[29] is situated, and that in a lane turning out of it is the once sumptous mansion which still bears the name of Dwarkanath Tagore. On the occasion above alluded to, there was a stoppage in the way; we soon perceived that this proceeded from an idol procession. A number of trumpery-looking stands were being carried along, on which were hung a great variety of broken flags, or anything that came to hand to make a display — such as one might fancy our ragged-school children might have collected together for a procession; these stands were carried by the most grotesque-looking men and boys, generally in a state of nudity, but in many cases adorned with some one article of clothing, which might have been procured from a rag-shop. One wore a cocked hat, with nothing else upon his body; another, a soldier's jacket; these articles were evidently regarded with considerable pride by the wearers. (1: 182-3)

The text deploys a string of negatively valorized adjectives and nouns to describe this scene ('dirty', 'narrow', 'odours', 'unhealthiness', 'trumpery-looking', 'ragged', 'grotesque', to name but a few). What emerges is a classic example of a representation of the other as a threat. Other travellers (such as Anne Katherine Elwood) have found quite different ways of describing the native part of Calcutta, with its riot of colours, smells and impressions. But for Carpenter clearly the scene exudes a sense of menace, and the threat it poses is to her sense of order. As the anthropologist Mary Douglas points out, '[t]here is no such thing as absolute dirt: it exists in the eye of the beholder'.[30] Carpenter seems to register the other mainly in terms of an offense against order. It offends her sense of order and propriety to find distinguished Indian gentlemen living in this part of town; it offends her sense of order to see so much 'nudity'. (The text's obsession with nakedness will be discussed below.) Not only does the text register a bourgeois anxiety at the disorder of social compartments, however — it also hints at a sense of colonial anxiety. The grotesque native body, after all, does nothing less than perform a parody of the colonizer and his culture — the items of clothing she mentions are all European articles, appropriated and distorted beyond recognition. The civilizing mission seems to have gone wrong badly here.

By contrast a missionary's residence is described in quite different terms:

> At the other side of the town, however, were pleasant English residences and institutions; and I was soon most comfortably installed in one, the residence of the Church missionary, the Rev. Mr. Blumhardt, and his family. . . . Morning revealed fresh sources of pleasure. Around the compound were erected a chaste and simple village church, a school-house for the children, taught by native converts, and superintended by the ladies of the family; also a college for native students, superintended by the worthy pastor himself. Cottages there were besides, neat little Indian dwellings for a few native converts holding some office; one I entered, to give my good wishes to a catechist and his family, as well as the girl's school; the students were absent, enjoying their Christmas holidays. On the other side of the house was a pleasant garden, carefully laid out and attended to with flowers in bloom, or soon to burst from their buds. (1: 259)

A utopian vision of India is evoked here, an India of native converts (Carpenter is very fond of native converts, who she immediately detects by 'a more open and happy expression of countenance') (1: 185) — neat, orderly, 'chaste', and under the firm supervison of the British. What appears before our eye is a microcosm of England with the cottage image that is of such importance in Evangelical discourse.

Carpenter makes no bones about her feelings of repulsion towards the degraded and idolatrous religion of Hinduism. Even a sense of curiosity will barely induce her to enter a temple: 'A heathen temple, however, was no great attraction to me. . . .' (1: 117) When she does pay a visit to the world-famous Elephanta caves, it is with a sense of 'painful awe' (2: 6) that she registers its artistic treasures. She is at pains to point out that the 'grotesque symbolic figures [are] not quite worthy to be compared with the cherubic hosts of many of our ancient paintings' (2: 6) and concludes, 'nothing is to be found anywhere calculated to elevate or purify the mind' (2: 7). With relief she heads for a picnic in front of the caves, 'where it was refreshing again to be in the open air, and a sumptous banquet was laid before us, which inspired us with feelings forming a striking contrast with what we had just experienced' (2: 8). A revealing example for how preconception informs perception is given in the following description of a famous temple: 'An air of dilapidation prevails, as usual in such enclosure. One could not wish it otherwise, in a place devoted to supersition and degrading ceremonies' (1: 285).

An obsession with nakedness runs through the text, hinting at a sense of repressed sensuality so characteristic of Victorian norms if not of Victorian reality. Thus Carpenter loses no opportunity of commenting on the want of decency in both men and women. Clearly this is an important index of civilization (inextricably bound up with Christianity) — things are quite different in the case of native converts:

> . . . a striking difference beween them and the heathen is at once perceptible in the sense of personal decency shown in their clothing and general demeanour. Among the lower orders whom I had hitherto seen, the men and children are usually devoid of any garment, except perhaps a cloth round their loins; at the same time they wear silver ornaments, and pearl or other earrings; the women are bedizened with any ornaments they can get hold of, with very miserable raiment, only partially covering the person. Here everyone was neatly and decently dressed, and I did not notice any ornaments in the place; though these are not forbidden by the missionary, they are not valued as they used to be (1: 79).

The conflation of indecent clothing with a superfluity of ornamentation reveals the deep influence of Puritanism and Evangelicalism pervading this kind of discourse, so common to missionaries and social reformers, and applied to all heathen societies. Signs of human vanity are frowned upon as a distraction from religious thoughts. Understandably, Carpenter is dismayed when she visits a school only to be confronted with an appalling scene at breakfast: 'What was the consternation of us ladies, when the door was thrown open, to behold seventy young men sitting on the floor with their food before them, stripped to the waist! We speedily withdrew' (1. 113). Later she expands on her ideas:

> Little progress has, however, been made in one respect, which appears to me essential to proper self-respect — viz., suitable covering to the person. The native costume is here, simply, a piece of cloth tied round the loins. . . .
>
> My friend now conducted me to the High School, which is a commodious building for 400 scholars, and well provided with teachers; what was my amazement at being introduced to this large body of young gentlemen with only this scanty costume! They were well educated, and polite in their manners, though their appearance was so uncivilised. I could not but think that a little kind influence, on the part of their instructors, might lead them all to take that first step, so necessary to civilised social intercourse, before proceeding to book-learning. Some words, kindly inscribed by some of them in my book, showed that their education had not in other respects been neglected (1: 296-7).

Strangely enough the students seem to be lacking neither in 'self-repect' nor in civilization— but the narrator allows herself no textual leeway to reflect on these contradictions.

Mary Carpenter and the Gaze of Surveillance

As Carpenter's narrative progresses, an increasingly chilling note is struck. What gradually emerges is a master plan for the control and regulation of Indian society, of which the reform of education and morals is only one element. David Arnold puts British measures for improving the condition of women into historical context:

> India's colonial state could never aspire to an absolute and exclusive control over the body of each and every one of its subjects. But there existed a latent claim that became operative in certain administrative, judicial and medical contexts. The early nineteenth-century attempts to abolish *sati* and female infanticide were preliminary demonstrations of this arrogation of corporal power. Colonial penology is rich in other illustrations.[31]

The regulation and control of the colonial body secured the colonial control of society.

Mary Carpenter has also expended some thought on reforms of the penal system. She calls for provision of female supervisors for female convicts and urgently advocates separate sleeping-cells for the prisoners to prevent moral contamination by other prisoners, and also advises the authorities to deploy the fear of isolation as an effective disciplinary measure (2: 205-14). In her discussion of education for working class children she recommends the establishment of factory schools. Approvingly she quotes a 'benevolent and enlightened' (1: 134) mill-owner who writes of his plans of introducing a school at his factory for the children he employs: 'It will be found that, after receiving this elementary instruction, order will prevail in the factory; they will be enabled to distinguish their numbers on the roll-call, which will save time, and avoid confusion on the pay-day; and they will attend to their work much better' (2: 134).

Education thus serves above all to produce a more orderly, disciplined and effective work-force and in this way increase productivity. In fact, the benevolent mill-owner entitles his book *How to Develop Productive Industry in India and the East*. The complicity of social reform with industrial capitalism is neatly encapsulated here.

Another area of concern for Carpenter is the establishment of reformatory schools for criminal youths (or those that might turn criminal — there does not seem to be much of a difference either way). Nonexistent in India so far, Carpenter envisions these institutes as a means to break in 'wild and lawless' (2: 198) youths from vagrant tribes. With approval she describes a social experiment carried out by the government consisting in interning members of these tribes and inducing them to take up agricultural work, thus producing useful members of society. The experiment is successful and Carpenter quotes an official report:

> Of course they were still addicted to begging and other pursuits natural to the gipsy class, but they had made an immense advance in civilisation. They had learnt the rights of property. . . . Clean clothes were to be seen on their leading men, and generally that scarcity of clothes and passionate love for jewellery, so common amongst such people all over the world, was not quite so conspicuous. (2: 196)

By now it will be apparent why this idyllic state of affairs should bring a glow to the hearts of women like Carpenter. In the discourses of social reformism an advance on the scale of civilization was demonstrated by respect for property, authority and morals. However, the grand project of the supervision of society was not restricted to social workers. As Foucault has shown, an increasing concern with the surveillance of society is discernible in European societies since the Enlightenment. One of the first models of this 'new type of gaze'[32] is the 'Panopticon' invented by Jeremy Bentham. This was a type of prison organized around a central tower where an overseer was placed who could watch the prisoners around the clock through the cell windows opening onto the tower. The underlying principle was that of 'the visibility of bodies, individuals and things, under a system of centralised observation.'[33] In other words, what was aimed at was a transparent society with no dark spaces (such as the zenana), where surveillance could not be exercised. But, as Foucault points out, the ultimate goal was not an intervening regulatory mechanism but an interiorization of the gaze, a mode of society where every individual regulated him or herself. This project Foucault defines as characteristic of nineteenth-century societies.

In her conclusion Carpenter sums up the beneficial effect the voyage has had on her:

> Having discovered in myself a power of which I was not before conscious, of giving extemporary addresses in public, whenever I felt a distinct call to do so, in the explanation of my views and objects, an expected means was opened to me of disseminating what appeared to me important truths. Couched in simple language, they appeared to be readily comprehended by the general audience; and being reported in the public papers, frequently by natives themselves, an impulse appeared to be given to the minds of my hearers, and to others in different parts of the country. (2: 218)

As we have seen, social work comprised a distinct emancipatory effect for the philanthropic woman. In the case of Mary Carpenter, her trip to India helped her evolve a more distinctive public personality. The keynote of her persona is given, though inadvertently, in the passage quoted above — a sense of power. Philanthropy gave middle-class women a sense of personal empowerment. It also served the ends of social surveillance, whether at home or in the empire — the gaze of surveillance was, in Foucault's words, the eye of power. Thus the fantasies enacted by the text are the pleasures of surveillance.

Notes

1 Quoted in Barr 37.

2 See, especially, Catherine Hall, 'The Early Formation of Victorian Domestic Ideology', *Fit Work for Women*, ed. Sandra Burman (London: Croom Helm, 1979) 15-39.

3 Hall 24.

4 R. I. and S. Wilberforce, *The Life of William Wilberforce* (London, 1838), 5: 77, quoted in Hall 24.

5 Hall 29; also see Anne Summers, 'A Home From Home — Women's Philanthropic Work in the Nineteenth Century', Burman 36-7.

6 Nancy Cott traces this development in her essay 'Passionlessness'.

7 Hall 28-9.

8 F. K. Prochaska, 'Women in English Philanthropy 1780-1830', *International Review of Social History* 19 (1974): 426-45.

9 Summers 39.

10 Rev. J. S. Brewer, 'Workhouse Visiting', *Lectures to Ladies on Practical Subjects*, ed. Rev. F. D. Maurice (Cambridge, 1855) 273-7, quoted in Summers 40-41.

11 Prochaska concludes, 'There is no doubt a grain of truth in the old cliché that the English became pious when the French became republican.' See Prochaska 438.

12 Summers 45.

13 See particularly Antoinette Burton's 'The White Woman's Burden. British Feminists and 'The Indian Woman', 1865-1915.'

14 Josephine Butler, *The Storm-Bell* (June 1898) 59, quoted in Burton 144.

15 See Barbara N. Ramusack, 'Cultural Missionaries, Maternal Imperialists, Feminist Allies: British Women Activists in India, 1865-1945', *Western Women and Imperialism* 119-36.

16 Burton 149.

17 See also Anne Davin, 'Imperialism and Motherhood', *History Workshop* 5 (Spring 1978): 9-66.

18 Burton, 152.

19 Chandra Talpade Mohanty, 'Under Western Eyes' 56.

20 Joanne Trollope, *Britannia's Daughters. Women of the British Empire* (London: Pimlico, 1983) 87.

21 See Kumkum Sangari and Sudesh Vaid, 'Recasting Women: An Introduction', in *Recasting Women: Essays in Colonial History*, eds Kumkum Sangari and Sudesh Vaid (New Delhi: Kali for Women, 1989) 7.

22 See Joanna Liddle and Rama Joshi, 'Gender and Imperialism in British India', *Economic and Political Weekly* 26 Oct. 1985: 72-78.

23 Sangari and Vaid 11.

24 Geraldine H. Forbes, 'In Search of the 'Pure Heathen'. Missionary Women in Nineteenth Century India', *Economic and Political Weekly* 26 April 1986: 6.

25 Forbes 7.

26 Patrick J. Murray, *Reformatory Schools in England and France* (London, 1854), 58, quoted in Harriet Warm Schupf, 'Single Women and Social Reform in Mid-Nineteenth Century England: The Case of Mary Carpenter', *Victorian Studies* 17.3 (1974): 303.

27 I am indebted to Schupf for all biographical information.

28 See Schupf 311.

29 A reform movement within Hinduism which sought to incorporate Christian ideas and rejected the notion of caste. The Tagore family played a leading role in the movement.

30 Mary Douglas, *Purity and Danger: An analysis of concepts of pollution* (London: Routledge & Kegan Paul, 1966) 2.

31 David Arnold, 'Touching the Body: Perspectives on the Indian Plague, 1896-1900', *Selected Subaltern Studies*, eds, Ranajit Guha and Gayatri Chakravorty Spivak (New York: OUP, 1988) 393.

32 Michel Foucault, 'The Eye of Power. A conversation with Jean-Pierre Barou and Michelle Perrot', *Power/Knowledge. Selected Interviews* 146.

33 Foucault 146.

Chapter 7

Women and Travel

MODES OF TRAVEL

One sometimes wonders whether we are too ready to take the two-spheres ideology for gospel truth.[1] As Sara Mills points out, whatever the Victorian ideal, large numbers of middle-aged and middle-class women seem to have been roaming around the world in the latter half of the nineteenth century.

A rapid change in the mode of transport to India is observable in the course of the nineteenth century. Until the 1830s a voyage to India around the Cape of Good Hope took five to seven months. Later the overland route through Egypt to Suez gained in popularity — Anne Katherine Elwood claims the distinction of being the first woman to travel by this route. Her claim is, however disputed by a Mrs Lushington.[2] The journey to India shortened progressively in the course of the century, and with the advent of steamship lines and the opening of the Suez Canal in 1869 dwindled to a mere fortnight.[3]

Modes of travel within India were much slower in changing. Although by the end of the century a substantial part of India was linked by railway, travel to the interior still usually took the form of relays of bearers, though travel on horseback, by camel, or by bullock-cart are also mentioned.[4] Not everyone travelled in the magnificent style of Emily Eden, with a train of 12,000 attendants, or in the 'Lalla Rookh' style of Anne Katherine Elwood. Nevertheless, even the most modest traveller was accompanied by at least half a dozen servants, comprising the cook, waiter, laundry-man, water-carrier, valet, maid, and groom for the horses, in addition to the coolies bearing the palanquins, the luggage and the tents (and, for big-game hunters, the guns). Camping did not imply the spartan affair it does today, but instead large spacious tents furnished with tables, chairs and rugs. Three-course meals were served at each halt. Generally the coolies carrying the tents as well as the cook, scullery boy and other kitchen staff were sent on a day in advance of the travellers themselves, so that the pitched tents and a steaming meal awaited the travellers when they arrived. An early woman traveller travelling only in the company of another woman has only words of praise for the natives she encounters:

> During the whole of this journey, we were strongly impressed with a feeling of gratitude and good-will towards the natives of India, who, upon all occasions, manifested an anxious desire to assure us of their respect and attachment. The highly civilized state of the country, and the courteous manners of all classes of the people, render travelling both easy and agreeable to those persons who are contented with the performance of possibilities, and who are not inclined to purchase an ill name by acts of tyranny and oppression (Roberts 1: 163).

What she hints at is that travellers of less exemplary behaviour meet with a less pleasant reception, as we shall see.

Travellers, Tourists and Philistines

In his study of tourism James Buzard points to the function travel fulfills for the traveller's self-definition.[5] This is no less true of an age prior to the large-scale influx of tourists into India. Emma Roberts, the devotee of the picturesque East, writing in 1835, defines herself in radical opposition to the philistines of Anglo-Indian society, who are wholly uninterested in the marvels of the country they reside in. She remarks acidly:

> In this age of tourists, it is rather extraordinary that the travelling mania should not extend to the possessions of the British Government in India; and that so few persons are induced to visit scenes and countries in the East, embellished with the most gorgeous productions of nature and of art. . . . The Smelfungus tribe is very numerous in India; necessity, and not 'a truant disposition', has occasioned the greater portion of the servants of the Company to traverse foreign lands; and the sole remark

> frequently made by persons who have sojourned amid the temples and citron groves of Agra, consists of a simple statement, that 'it is exceedingly hot' (2: 289-90).

Smelfungus was Laurence Sterne's nickname for his disgruntled traveller in *A Sentimental Journey through France and Italy* (1768) — a clear allusion to his contemporary Smollett. This, according to Jonathan Culler, is 'what travellers always do: feel superior to other travellers.'[6] As is apparent in similar passages by travellers anxious to distance themselves from other travellers, the reader is privy to the elitist assumptions of the narrator.

Emma Roberts has a crusade: to popularize the Oriental magnificence of India that so strikes her. In one of her most eloquent passages, clearly influenced by Romantic writing, she writes herself as a female Lord Byron, the Romantic poet who was another famous traveller, uncovering the wonders of the East:

> Perhaps Lord Byron himself, when he stood upon the Bridge of Sighs, his heart filling with reminiscenes of Othello, Shylock, and Pierre, scarcely experienced more overwhelming sensations than the humble writer of this paper, when gazing, for the first time, upon the golden crescent of the Moslems, blazing high in the fair blue heavens, from the topmost pinnacle of this splendid relique of their power and pride. The delights of my childhood rushed to my soul; those magic tales, from which, rather than from the veritable pages of history, I had gathered my knowledge of eastern arts and arms, arose in all their original vividness. I felt that I was indeed in the land of the genii . . . (2: 300-1).

All the markers in the text produce her as cultivated, well-read and sensitive. 'Intellectual pilgrims' like herself are appalled at the almost sacrilegious behaviour of the philistines:

> . . . the few intellectual pilgrims, who wander amidst the wrecks of bygone splendour, must make up their minds to endure sights and scenes of the most incongruous nature: pic-nic parties bivouacking in the tombs, and being entertained at their repasts by the performances of a set of nautch girls[7]; young men amusing themselves with a game of qoits; and groups of flirting unimaginative women, speculating on the probabilities of getting up a quadrille (3: 198-9).

The same self-righteous anger is displayed by Fanny Parks towards Anglo-Indians disporting themselves in front of the Taj Mahal: 'Can you imagine any thing so detestable? European ladies and gentlemen have the band to play on the marble terrace, and dance quadrilles in front of the tomb!' (1: 355) By contrast, she produces herself as a traveller of deep sensibility and tact:

> I cannot enter the Taj without feelings of deep devotion: the sacredness of the place, the remembrance of the fallen grandeur of the family of the Emperor, and that of Asaf Jah, the father of Arzumund Banoo, the solemn echoes, the dim light, the beautiful architecture, the exquisite finish and delicacy of the whole, the deep devotion with which the natives prostrate at the tomb, all produce deep and sacred feelings; and I could no more jest or indulge in levity beneath the dome of the Taj, than I could in my prayers (1: 356).

The phenomenon is one with which we are familiar in later travel accounts. The traveller displays her aesthetic sensibilities and erudition to rhetorically align herself with the native population, firmly drawing a boundary between herself and other travellers.

For later travellers, like Constance Gordon Cumming, the creation of a unique travelling self is more fraught with danger of encroachment. Cumming needs not only to differentiate herself from the philistines of Anglo-Indian society, but also from the tourists who are beginning to arrive on the Indian scene. Cumming, too, is anxious to distance herself from the average Anglo-Indian with their apathy and disdain for anything Indian: 'this is only the work of 'those wretched niggers', so most resident Britons scarcely give it a thought' (152). She laments, 'One of the perpetually recurring aggravations of travelling in India, is the impossibility of getting definite information as to what things and places are really best worth seeing. It is so very exceptional to find any one, who takes the smallest interest in anything native, unless it has reference to coining rupees' (54).

She boasts of having seen more places of interest during her year of travel than most Anglo-Indians during a lifetime's residence in India (55). By the end of the century Cook's was organizing travel between India and England, conducting globe-trotters through India and even taking charge of arrangements for Indian pilgrims visiting Mecca.[8] Isabel

Savory gives voice to the malaise of travellers in the age of tourism when she writes, 'It would be absurd to describe the journey out to India; as well might one launch forth into impressions of Piccadilly from a hansom, since half society has already been bored by the voyage to the East, and the remaining half still more bored by reading accounts of it.'[9] (3)

By the time Savory travels the store of untouched spots off the beaten track is dwindling fast. Cumming makes a point of seeking out the path 'wholely untrodden by white feet' and asserts that 'the chief delight was to leave the beaten track, and find out all manners of delightful nooks almost unexplored, and for that reason all the more enjoyable' (132). The greater the number of travellers prowling about the earth, the more urgent the project of self-constitution and differentiation through travel. And the elitist overtones of the traveller's text always draws the reader into complicity with the traveller.

The traveller's trauma is neatly encapsulated in the following incident related by Cumming:

> While we were basking on our pleasant island like a pair of turtles, or crocodiles, . . . suddenly we beheld a most startling apparition! Something rustled in the tall grass, and brushed aside the wild plum-trees, and stalked curiously onward. We could scarcely believe our eyes. Just imagine Robinson Crusoe's feelings on seeing Friday, and then imagine ours on beholding a brace of white men taking a day's shooting on our beloved desert isle! Its romance was gone. In another second they were also gone, but we were conscious of no longer being the sole pale-faces in the district, and as we sat next morning on the Yogis' pillars beneath the great sacred banyans, we could see civilised creatures clad in common domestic broadcloth, busy photographing! (538)

The invaders of the traveller's idyll are no longer dangerous natives, but other travellers. Paradoxically, these are registered not with a feeling of solidarity, but as a threat. The traveller prefers to fantasize him/herself as unique and autonomous (a Robinson Crusoe) rather than a social being. The colonial, acquisitive connotations of the Robinson Crusoe image have been too often pointed out to bear repeating.[10] Interestingly enough, the narrator adopts the Robinson image as a metaphor for the traveller in general ('our' island).

Finally, it might be interesting to take a look at the reactions of the Anglo-Indian philistines to travellers from England. Anglo-Indians are often praised for their hospitality — hotels being virtually unknown in India for most of the century, travellers were dependent on the hospitality of Anglo-Indians, to whom they were either related, or furnished with a letter of introduction. However, their hosts were notoriously suspicious of busybody travellers from home, especially influential persons. A type of traveller who is often held up as figure of ridicule is the official traveller — usually a Liberal M. P. on a flying visit to India to criticize Indian conditions. This type of travelling bogey was best exemplified in Kipling's poem *Pagett, M. P.* Anglo-Indian residents of India were suspicious of government policy in general and that of the home government in particular as being far too liberal. An obscure memsahib, Mrs King, sums up the Anglo-Indian attitude to critical travellers in the following passage:

> It is said that a good deal of mischief is being done by the fashionable visitors who now flock to India in the cold season, are delighted and flattered by the novelty of native hospitality, courtesy, and often servility, and to whom the English officials are of course in no way either novel or interesting, and who then return home and spread the idea that the English in India require snubbing and the trusty natives exalting. It may be so, but these passing visitors are not in a position to be good judges. A visitor can only see things very superficially, he is wholly irresponsible, and he finds it pleasant to pose as a kind of champion, and be lavishly gracious to the natives and studiously cold to his fellow-countrymen. If his life were cast, as theirs is, among these same natives, he would find this enthusiasm and novelty wear off. He would find that a gulf was fixed between him and men who, however long their acquaintance, would never admit him into their home life, would consider their wives and daughters insulted if he so much as alluded to them, would sooner die than eat at his table, and who in their inmost heart would not sorrow if every Christian were driven into the sea. (1: 47)

This classic piece of colonial paranoia need not interest us further.[11] More interesting is the fact that conservative-minded travellers such as

Mary Billington aligned themselves with this position toward visitors from England, warning that the present harmonious state of affairs in India was unlikely to last 'if every officious busybody who scampers across in three weeks from Bombay to Calcutta is permitted to dictate what he (or worse, she) thinks should be done' (268). One wonders whether Billington, a journalist, scampering across India on an extensive tour, includes herself in this category.

GENDER AND TRAVEL

Travel did not only provide women with an opportunity for self-definition (with distinctly elitist overtones) but also enabled them to transgress the gender norms of their times. By entering the public sphere and thus defying the separate spheres ideology which relegated women to a life of domesticity, they gained control of their own lives and negotiated a form of gender power. Women travellers — especially those travelling alone — found themselves the focus of curious and not always sympathetic gazes. In fact, they often interiorized this form of social surveillance by emphasizing their adherence to 'feminine' propriety, particularly in the matter of clothing — that often, as in the case of corsets or voluminous skirts, were a real hindrance to mobility. Marianne North, the well-known naturalist and traveller, attributes the scepticism she encounters in society to the fact that 'they were so accustomed to feminine helplessness' (2: 11). Often the subject of unkind caricatures and satires, the most blatant piece of male hostility they encountered was, of course, the refusal of the Royal Geographic Society to admit women until 1913.[12]

Women travellers frequently give eloquent voice to the sense of freedom and independence travel entails. Fanny Parks enthuses:

> How much there is to delight the eye in this bright, beautiful world! Roaming about with a good tent and a good Arab, one might be happy for ever in India: a man might possibly enjoy this sort of life more than a woman; he has his dog, his gun, and his beaters, with an open country to shoot over, and is not annoyed with — 'I'll thank you for your name, Sir.' I have a pencil instead of a gun, and believe it affords me satisfaction equal, if not greater than the sportsman derives from his Manton (2: 191).

Constance Gordon Cumming is no less exuberant about travel as a means of escape from conventions:

> We had by this time become thoroughly enamoured of our gipsy life, and were daily more and more enchanted with its freedom. The escape from every phrase of civilised formality, from all fixed laws of action, from regular hours, each meal being henceforth a movable feast, no wearisome seven or eight o'clock dinner to waste two precious hours, but a merry supper by our camp-fire whenever we were ready for it; and then 'early to bed and early to rise' — in short, it was an escape from the old stereotyped existence whose comfortable, commonplace round we had run, till it had become altogether monotonous and humdrum . . . (336-7).

In other words, travel acted as a spur to fantasy, permitting women to imagine other, freer, selves. One form of travel for which this was particularly true was the hunting expedition. Despite Parks' protestations in the passage quoted above, the text cannot repress a sense of envy at her male contemporaries on their hunting trips — at another point she laments that a contemporary travel account, Captain Mundy's *Sketches in India*, is 'a much more amusing journal than I can write. I have no tigers to kill. . . .' (1: 268) Her experience of big game hunting can only be vicarious, and she incorporates accounts of sporting by male friends into her text, one of whom pays her the following tribute (which she does not fail to pass on to her readers): 'You have at heart a large share of the hunting principle, supposed to characterize mankind in a wild state.' (2: 125). While women are reported participating in hunting trips as early as the 1830s by Emma Roberts ('ladies delight in such expeditions') (2: 233), serious sport is rigorously restricted to men: 'To ladies, hog-hunting is of course quite out of the question, and there are very few whose nerves could stand against the terror and carnage of an expedition against tigers, to say nothing of the fatigue to be encountered in a chase which frequently lasts for hours under a burning sun' (Roberts 2: 280).

Women hunters had to contend with disapproval well into the twentieth century, as exemplified in Queen Victoria's dictum that 'only fast women shot' and in the following statement by Lord Warwick, 'I have met ladies who shoot and I have come to the conclusion, being no longer young and a staunch Conservative, that I would prefer them not to.'[13]

Hunting by women was thus emphatically poaching on a male preserve, a world suffused with myths of masculinity. John MacKenzie has pointed to the 'sexual sublimation of the hunt', 'the tensions induced by the great risk and the ecstasy of release when the hunter prevails and stands over his kill.'[14] In addition to its overtones of virility and elitism, hunting served as a field of practice for war. In combating guerilla campaigns stalking natives took the place of animal hunting and demanded the same skills.[15] Further, as MacKenzie has pointed out, the hunting ethos was imbricated with the ideology of imperialism. In fact, the world of hunting seems to embody an imperial world in microcosm, an elite ritual with its insistence on similar virtues of manliness, courage, endurance and fortitude. The flood of sporting literature to appear around the turn of the century was no doubt informed by the discourse of imperial adventure literature. At a time when the realistic novel was suffused with a sense of bourgeois disillusionment, the imperial novel still offered one of the last sites for fantasies of adventure and escape.[16]

By the end of the century more and more women had joined the ranks of the big-game hunters and produced a stream of sporting accounts with titles such as *How I Shot My Bears* by Mrs R. H. Tyacke (1893). Isabel Savory waxes eloquent about the freedom and escape from conventionalities hunting implies, as in the following passage: 'There is no feeling like it! To be in your oldest of old clothes, to feel you are going out of the reach of letters, telegrams, and the faces of the civilised world; free to go and to do exactly as the spirit of the moment moves you; only yourself to answer to: time is of no object; you may wait or hurry, eat where you like, sleep where you like. It is the *only* life . . . '(113).

Nevertheless, the narrator evinces a sense of unease at the transgressive gender behaviour displayed by women hunters, selfconscious about a hunting incident to a fellow huntress that 'unnecessarily ventilated M.'s skirt and exposed a large amount of boot!' (21) She is at pains to justify hunting for women in terms of the loftiness of philosophical thoughts (about life and death) it calls forth, and exclaims:

> Are these the feelings, aroused in all thinking minds by the nobility of creation, which we have often heard censured and mis-called *unwomanly* and *hard*? The staid matron and the Society butterfly may through a touch of jealousy, or by reason of their narrow prejudices condemn women whom happy

> occasion has enabled to call into play those latent forces and capabilities with which they have been endowed; but the trophies which decorate the walls of their *sanctum sanctorum* call forth admiration and reverence, rather than constitute mute witnesses of outraged womanhood (28-9).

While Savory celebrates the freedom hunting offers women, she remains defensive about its implications for gender norms.

It is not only by travelling that women rebel against the constraints of these norms and the constructions of feminine space. Writing accounts of their experiences is a form of public utterance that is premised on an autonomous and articulate narrative persona and thus also constitutes a form of gender empowerment. As we have seen throughout, women's autobiographical writings provide a site for the production of a gendered form of subjectivity and identity. These writings enable women to produce a mythology of self as independent and in control. Since, as Foucault has argued, subjectivity is not a given but is discursively produced — 'the individual is an effect of power'[17]— notions of what subject positions are open to women are determined by the range of discourses in circulation. Like other forms of autobiographical writing, travel writing produces a public self that transgresses the ideology of domesticity. But travel writing provides women with a twofold access to the public sphere: by giving women a public voice *and* by locating them in that highly public sphere, the world of travel. Though they might stress femininity in their accounts of travel, by the very act of travel (as well as by writing about their travels) they implicitly reject gender norms. This empowerment also functioned vicariously for women readers of these narratives, who were provided with alternative gender role models as well as an opening for pleasurable fantasies of adventure and escape from conventional norms.

Travel and Colonialism

Given that the individual subject is a constructed and not a natural category, the question that remains to be probed is its ideological implications. As Marxist critics such as Felicity Nussbaum have shown, the concept of the autonomous self is closely bound up with bourgeois capitalist societies. A market economy requires the idea of a free and coherent subjectivity to sustain the idea of the individual's free choice, both of goods and the conditions of labour. But the concept of a sovereign subject is also bound up with imperialism. Spivak points out that 'the consolidation of Europe as sovereign subject, indeed sovereign and subject', is based on defining its colonies as 'Others'.[18] The production of the autonomous, individualistic female heroine of travel is, of course, always also predicated on a construction of the other as more backward in every respect. In fact, the very notion of travel serves to confirm Western self-definition as superior. Savory exhorts the reader: 'If the Chinese had travelled as did the old Venetians, China might have produced a Bellini, a Titian, a Tintoretto, or a Paul Veronese, instead of stagnating in pigtails and grinning idols' (405).

For her, as for many travellers, colonized countries represent a vast playing-field, where natives form either a picturesque appendage or fulfill useful functions as carriers, servants, etc. When they presume to trespass on the traveller's world, they are seen as poachers on private territory. In fact, Savory calls for stricter game laws as native hunters 'who shoot simply for food' are ruining the country (279). With deep regret she notes that the tourists' paradise of Kashmir has been returned to a native ruler. Had the region been kept in British hands, she fantasizes, 'the country, properly cultivated, would be a great source of revenue, instead of its fertile valleys being wasted on a degraded, lazy, good-for-nothing people' (250). As so often, denigration of native inefficiency serves as justification for British rule.

Hunting trips are probably the closest women get to a taste of the Great Game of imperial politics. But women travellers are implicated in the politics of imperialism in other ways, too. As James Clifford has pointed out, 'independence was, in varying degrees, a myth': travellers were dependent on a well-developed imperial infrastructure of carriers, guides, etc.[19] Especially women travelling alone were aware of the protection afforded them by the power of British rule. They enact the paradox of gender powerlessness and racial power. Honoria Lawrence boasted, 'An unprotected woman can travel safely thus from one end of India to the other thanks to the spell of the English name'[20], and Christine Bremner conceded, somewhat more graciously, that 'the safety of a single traveller depends on the goodwill of the villagers and on the length of England's right arm.'[21] The fact that the efficiency of this infrastructure was ensured by the iron grip of colonial rule is openly admitted by many travellers (though conveniently overlooked by celebratory critics today). Marianne Postans, for example, writes:

> Travellers complain of their inability to procure guides from the native villages — undoubtedly a very common evil; but it is scarcely surprising, that poor men should object to be seized on their fields, or dragged from their homes, to walk ten or sixteen miles before a stranger's horse, often at night, and through dense jungles, for a few pice;[22] sometimes receiving only abuse or illtreatment for the services they render. (1: 218-19)

It is not only the material realities of travel that are bound up with colonial power — it is the knowledge produced by travel writing which itself constitutes a form of power. Talal Asad's findings regarding the implication of anthropology in power relations has a direct bearing on travel writing.[23] Asad argues that even the 'disinterested' production of knowledge is affected by preconditions in the field which are structured by power relations. Further, he points to the uses to which this knowledge was put as determined by the power constellation in place. In our case this means that the knowledge collected and disseminated by women travellers in India served to bolster the colonial project of 'knowing' the other to facilitate control. Asad's last point refers to the epistemological assumptions about the production of knowledge referred to in the Introduction. The anthropologist/traveller's claim to neutrality is itself a reflection of a mode of perception that posits a transcendent observing ego. What it elides is not only the concrete relations of power at work in the situation of the viewer, but also the very politics of representation. Colonial discourses were predicated upon their monopoly of the power of representation. These travellers' texts did not merely 'depict' reality, they created it.In this way they 'helped in the ideological reproduction of the empire.'[24]

To return to the concept of gender power: what I am arguing for, in fact, is a more complex model of power. It is imperative for feminist critics to avoid the reduction of power relations to gender relations, still prevalent in the works of many critics. Power is not inherently male — nor is feminism, as we might remind ourselves, about rejecting power! It is only when we admit subjectivity to be the site of different, even contradictory identifications (such as class and race) that we can deal productively with the issue of women travellers and power. By analogy with the case of women philanthropists, it becomes clear that transgressive does not necessarily mean progressive. To put it differently: the transgression of gender norms does not necessarily lead to a progressive politics — as is exemplified in the wide-scale refusal of women travellers to support the suffragette movement.[25]

Women's travel was, after all, an individualistic strategy of escape that reflected the values of the bourgeois construction of self and not a politics of gender solidarity. Their writings — through the emphasis on propriety and feminine decorum—help to reaffirm dominant gender norms as a regulative 'technology of the self' at the same time as they implicitly transgress these norms. In addition, in the case of women travellers to India, very rarely do we find in their texts a challenge to colonial inequality. In fact, Dea Birkett makes the point that women travellers actually exploited racial inequality in order to realize their own personal project of freedeom. They slipped, as it were, into the role of 'honorary males' to enjoy the privileges of race in colonialism.[26] A passage by Fanny Parks epitomizes this (apparent) paradox: 'This wandering life is very delightful; I shall never again be content 'to sit in a parlour sewing a seam,' which the old song gives forth as the height of felicity! Much sooner would I grope through a dark alley idol hunting —' (2: 452). What we find here is a classic conjunction of gender rebellion and colonial rapaciousness.

Nevertheless, women's travel in India did contain subversive implications for colonial ideology — simply by undermining the very gender constructions built into this ideology. An important aspect of colonial rule was its justification on the grounds of the dangers accruing to white women from ever-lascivious natives. This idea served both to marginalize women in the running of empire and relegate them to a purely domestic role and to control their sexuality *vis-à-vis* Indian men. Independent women wandering all over the empire proved that British women were quite capable of managing their own affairs and exposed the hypocrisies inherent in colonial ideology — its inconsistencies in notions of race and gender.

It remains a moot point whether the subversive implications of women travellers were contained by colonial ideology and their texts in effect served to further colonialism's ends. Certainly their texts helped to disseminate the colonial construction of India and reaffirm colonial ideology. Their travels were dependent on colonial infrastructure and the very fact that they travelled alone in safety could be used to further the rulers' claims of a Pax Britannica. Still, both the personae of the travellers and their texts appear more complex. Thus women travellers often displayed a partial adaptation to hegemonic norms (including dominant political discourses) precisely to enable them to escape these norms in other ways. This strategy seems to me evocative of what I would term the Thatcher-syndrome. In a perceptive article Maureen McNeil has looked at the implications of the persona of Margaret Thatcher for feminism.[27] In an analysis of the image of Thatcher, she argues that Thatcher draws on feminine roles such as that of the housewife while undermining their usual connotations of powerlessness. At the same time, she taps traditional, culturally sanctioned sources of female authority such as the stern nanny image. Thus she simultaneously draws on and disavows discourses of femininity. By analogy, women travellers often play up their femininity (stressing their feminine clothing, etc.) while transgressing gender norms. And, they too draw on traditional forms of female authority: we must not forget that middle-class women, whether in England or in the colonies, were mistresses of servants in their own right and thus have always had access to certain forms of power. The significance of the Thatcher paradigm as well as of the woman traveller lies in their undermining of the conventional implications of travel and power — hitherto coded as implicitly male, their appropriation by women is no longer seen as an inherent contradiction. For readers, too, women travellers opened up realms of fantasy that — and herein lies the point — were not (or no longer) registered as transgressive. To sum up: as in the case of women's autobiographical writings and the ideology of the bourgeois self, women travellers simultaneously colluded with colonial ideology and subverted it by undermining the gender premises it was grounded on.

Finally, it remains to be noted that women travellers did exert pressure on colonial ideology to adapt its ideal of women and incorporate the image of the active, adventurous woman. Savory exultantly notes the change in women travellers to India over the century — while originally the only motivation imputed to women travelling out to India was that of husband-hunting,

> . . . suffice it to say that there are, every year, women who come out, and who travel over the globe, with the object of seeing other sides of that interesting individual, man, other corners of the world, other occupations and other sports — women, in short, who will enjoy a little discomfort for the sake of experience.
>
> To rove about in gipsy fashion, meeting with trifling adventures from time to time, is a complete change for an ordinary English girl; and it is very easy to find every scope for developing self-control and energy in many a 'tight corner' if such occasions are sought for (201-2).

The ideals she names are the attributes of the New Woman, not the domestic female subject of the Victorian Age. The passage is, of course, a hymn directed at herself and her own self-construction as a 'sportswoman' in India.

Power and Resistance

Finally, I wish to look at women travellers' implications not only in colonial power structures but in concrete inter-personal relations of power. What is striking is the traces of native resistance to colonial power inscribed in these texts. This is not an attempt either to prove Foucault's dictum that power always entails resistance, nor to demonstrate that there was resistance to colonial rule in India — too blatant a point to need making.[28] Instead, what I am interested in is those forms of resistance that have left their traces within these colonial texts.

With a few exceptions — Flora Annie Steel horse-whipping her servant, Fanny Bullock Workman chastizing her mutinous coolies on one of her mountaineering trips — most women travellers leave no record of physically exerting power over their native attendants.[29] What we do get a glimpse of, however, is the organized coercion of colonialism. Constance Gordon Cumming describes the system of forced labour made available for travellers (a pre-colonial coercive technique adopted by the British) as follows:

> The notion of paying a man sixpence for his day's labour strikes the new-comer as being decidedly mean, as, of course, he has to feed himself and his family. It is, however, the regular wage of the country, and the poor creatures not only contrive to exist on it, but even lay aside a fraction as an offering for their gods. The

> only objection of the hill-men to act as coolies is that they are often obliged to neglect their own fields just when their presence is most required. Their attendance is, however, compulsory; that is to say, the headman of each village is obliged to furnish any reasonable number required by travellers. Our regiment of thirty was about the minimum with which it is possible for a party to travel (324).

The travellers have few qualms in taking advantage of this situation. Christine Bremner, one of the few travellers vocal in her critique of empire, when faced with the reluctance of villagers to act as coolies during rice-planting time, decides: 'Whatever theories may obtain as to the substantial equality of our Aryan brother, there are many occasions when, and individuals to whom, it would be unwise to concede such a principle. I therefore replied in an authoritative tone that unless at least three more coolies were quickly brought round, a report of his neglect should reach the Rajah-Saheb.'[30] (155)

The form of power usually exerted by women travellers consists of the threat of violence from other sources, as in the passage by Bremner quoted above. Sometimes, however, the villagers' cunning knows no bounds. In addition to labour, villagers were expected to supply visitors with provisions — at fair prices, of course. Certain recalcitrant villagers — 'being determined, if possible, to keep away all mutton and flour-consuming sahibs' (Cumming 451) — tried to dissuade the travelling party by directing them to a dilapidated rope bridge. However, they 'little knew what it was to have to do with 'the dominant race' ' and did not succeed in turning the travellers back. Next,

> The villagers, finding that their little strategem had failed, tried a new plan, and when we reached the village we found it deserted; every soul had vanished with their flocks and their herds, nor did they return for some days after the departure of their unwelcome visitors. We wandered in and out of their vineyards; among their fields and picturesque carved houses, overgrown with rich tangles of gourds and divers fruits, in every corner of their sacred enclosures and temples. We might even, had we been so inclined, have taken Durga's[31] sacred fish from their tanks — for there remained literally no one to say us nay. (451)

In incidents such as these the material realities of colonial travel emerge. This time, however, the last laugh seems to be on the side of the villagers. The colonizers take possession of a ghost town. Their sense of frustration at this piece of passive resistance prefigures the impotence of the entire empire some decades later in the face of the games played by another sly native, Mahatma Gandhi. All that remains for 'the dominant race' is the childish fantasy of revenge by desecrating religious sites — not exactly satisfying when there are no witnesses.

The most telling example of native voices having the last say *within* (and against) the text of a woman traveller is presented in the hunting account of Isabel Savory. Savory is full of praise for India — if it were not for the natives. Her text is obsessed with examples of native depravity and she strings anecdote after anecdote of hearsay to bolster her point. In fact, an awareness of this obsessiveness appears briefly in the following apology: 'The following is a last example connected with a subject which must begin to pall upon my readers' (382) — before launching into another lengthy tale of native stupidity.

In addition to the usual string of attendants, hunting parties also required large numbers of beaters, who were responsible for making the quarry break cover. Often wild animals like tigers or boars would turn to attack the unarmed beaters, and Savory's text is littered with references to casualties. These are usually attributable — once again — to native stupidity. Of her beaters she remarks: 'The whole hundred and fifty were arrant cowards, and nothing but the lure of annas[32] (for which a native would sell his soul) would have induced one of them to come with us. Certainly the roll of natives, who have been injured and killed when beating is a long one; but as a rule they suffer entirely from their own want of proper caution and lack of common sense' (209).

It is against this backdrop that at least one example of native devilishness in her text backfires. She relates:

> Natives are exceedingly practical. A sahib accidently shot a boy one day when he was out in the jungle. The next morning he received a deputation from the man's relatives, who handed him a written document in the form of a valuation of the deceased's life, soliciting payment for the same, to which was appended a receipt for the amount demanded. It ran in this form:

To CAPTAIN F.
To one bloody murder committed. Five Rupees.
Contents received on the —day of—, 18—.

I will leave it to the murdered boys' relatives to have the last word.

Notes

1 Sara Mills voices this suspicion in *Discourses* 27.
2 Mrs. Charles Lushington, *Narrative of a Journey from Calcutta to Europe, by Way of Egypt, in the years 1827 and 1828* (London, 1829).
3 See Riddick, *Glimpses of India* xi.
4 Hutchins hints that Macaulay's first taste of India—a trip of 400 miles 'on the shoulders of natives' — might have left its mark on his later policies. See Hutchins 104.
5 See James Buzard, *The Beaten Track*.
6 Jonathan Culler, 'The Semiotics of Tourism', *Framing the Sign: Criticism and its Institutions* (Norman, Okla: University of Oklahoma Press, 1989) 157.
7 Dancing girls.
8 See Simon Gartrell, 'Introduction: Travel and Travel Writing', in *The Ends of the Earth 1876-1918*, ed. Gatrell (London: Ashfield, 1992) 11.
9 Isabel Savory, *A Sportswoman in India: Personal Adventures and Experiences in Known and Unknown India* (London, 1900) 3. All further references to given in parentheses in the text.
10 See particularly Peter Hulme, *Colonial Encounters: Europe and the Native Caribbean 1492-1797* (London: Routledge, 1986) 175-224.
11 In this connection see Bhabha's essay 'Sly Civility', *October* 34 (1985) 71-80, where he argues that the colonial subject desires the native to hate him in order not to have to face the vertiginous possibility that the native is simply indifferent to him.
12 On the debate surrounding this issue see Dea Birkett, *Spinsters Abroad: Victorian Lady Explorers* (Oxford: Blackwell, 1989) 214-29.
13 I am indebted for both quotations to Maria Aitken, *A Girdle Around the Earth: Adventuresses Abroad* (London: Constable, 1987) 85.
14 John M. MacKenzie, 'The Imperial Pioneer and Hunter and the British Masculine Stereotype in Late Victorian and Edwardian Times', *Manliness and Morality: Middle-Class Masculinity in Britian and America 1800-1940*, eds J. A. Mangan and James Walvin (Manchester: MUP, 1987) 180.
15 See MacKenzie 188.
16 See Edward Said, *Culture and Imperialism* (London: Chatto & Windus, 1993) 226.
17 Michel Foucault, 'Truth and Power', *Power/Knowledge* 98. For 'power' Althusserian critics tend to substitute 'ideology'.

18 Spivak, 'The Rani of Sirmur', *Europe and Its Others*, ed. Francis Barker *et al.* (Colchester: University of Essex, 1985) 1: 128.

19 Clifford, 'Travelling Cultures', *Cultural Studies*, eds Lawrence Grossberg, Cary Nelson and Paula Treichler (London: Routledge, 1992) 106.

20 Quoted in Barr 75.

21 Christina S. Bremner, *A Month in a Dandi: A Woman's Wanderings in Northern India* (London, 1891) 101. All further references to be given in parentheses in the text.

22 Indian coin.

23 See Tala Asad, 'Anthropology and the Colonial Encounter', *The Politics of Anthropology: From Colonialism and Sexism Toward a View from Below*, eds Gerrit Huizer and Bruce Mannheim (The Hague: Mouton, 1979) 85-94.

24 Margaret Strobel, *European Women and the Second British Empire* 46.

25 This fact seems hard for many critics to grasp. At a recent conference on women travellers (at Oxford on 12 November 1994), a speaker expressed her surprise at the fact that so many of the travellers vehemently opposed the vote for women. Surprising, that is, only if we are engaged in a quest for role models with coherent, unfragmented subjectivites.

26 See Birkett, *Spinsters Abroad.*

27 Maureen McNeil, 'Making and not making the difference: the gender politics of Thatcherism', *Off-Centre: Feminism and Cultural Studies*, eds Sarah Franklin, Celia Lury, and Jackie Stacey (London: Harper Collins, 1991) 221-40.

28 See Robert Young's objection to Homi Bhabha's scrutiny of hidden forms of native resistance in colonial texts. However, Bhabha's point is not overt but covert forms of resistance. See Young 149-50.

29 We do have Isabel Burton bounding out of her carriage to chastize a 'black' abusing his cow, but her zeal is more appropriately subsumed under her own brand of the civilizing mission, namely campaigning to eradicate cruelty to animals among the natives. See Isabel Burton, *A. E. I. Arabia Egypt India: A Narrative of Travel* (London, 1892) 231.

30 Ruler.

31 A Hindu goddess.

32 Indian coins.

Chapter 8

Coda: Gazing Back

It is not my intention to simply reverse the binarism of self and other by attempting to retrieve the lost voices of the other. As Gayatri Spivak warns, such a project would merely reflect the narcissistic desire of the Western self to set up an autonomous, individuated other formed in its own image. If subjectivity is accepted to be the site of different, contradictory identifications, however, there can be no coherent, authentic other but only a plurality of voices. Indeed, attempts to produce a counter-narrative voiced by an authentic other tend to fetishize an ahistorical, essentialist other while marginalizing certain voices, leading inescapably to the question, 'whose authentic voice?' (This dilemma is familiar to feminist critics in search of women's voices.) The identity of the other is no more secure than that of gender—the other is as little a unified subject position as is the self. As I have pointed out in the case of women, essentialist notions invariably entail the exclusion of some. For Spivak, within colonial discourse 'there is no space from where the subaltern (sexed) subject can speak.'[1] When excavating the traces of an Indian Rani[2] in colonial correspondence she concludes, 'Caught in the cracks between the production of the archives and indigenous patriarchy . . . there is no 'real Rani' to be found.'[3] Attempting to speak *for* the other once again objectifies him or her by constituting the other into an object of knowledge.[4] Instead, she calls for a focus on how the subaltern subject has been constructed within discourse—both colonial and indigenous.

Spivak's reticence has often been the focus of attacks by various critics[5] who accuse her (as well as Homi Bhabha) of occluding the native's voice. In their hunt for the authentic native voice, however, critics often fail to avoid the pitfalls of essentialism.[6] It seems to me more productive to analyze the very constructedness of categories like the 'other' and to point up the fact that these are relational terms whose function is to enable the self-definition of the sovereign self. What is also overlooked in critiques of Spivak and Bhabha is that all Spivak disavows is the possibility of salvaging authentic voices of the other, not the possibility of *resistance*. Even the subaltern woman, permitted no subject position within either colonial or patriarchal discourses from which she can speak, is neverthless left with the option of resistance[7] and is not denied agency.[8] In fact Spivak's and Bhabha's approach seem to me to elicit a far greater sense of respect for the difference of the other than rigorous efforts to unearth heroic naive voices.

What interests me here is the subaltern's voices as inscribed into the text of the colonial self — native gazes that exert a pressure on travellers' texts. What they reveal is the ambivalence at work (at play) in all texts. To repeat: I am not hunting for the authentic native, but for the other as a trace in these texts. What I would like to look at is the crevices and crises in these women travellers' own narratives. In his critique of Said's *Orientalism*, Homi Bhabha points out that the colonizer does not have a monopoly of power but that power works far more ambivalently and productively, as Foucault has shown.[9] An example for the dispersal of power is provided in Bhabha's concept of colonial mimicry, which he defines as 'the desire for a reformed, recognizable other, as *a subject of a difference that is almost the same, but not quite*'.[10] A goal of the civilizing mission was to reform native populations into mimic Englishmen, a strategy that served the function of colonial regulation and discipline. However, the very product of this strategy posed a threat to colonial authority by exposing the contradictions and hypocrisies it was grounded on: while endowing the colonial subject with the Enlightenment ideas of liberty, for instance, the structure of colonial rule was based on a denial of these very liberties to the colonized other. Thus the mimic native only serves to parody colonial rule: 'the look of surveillance returns as the displacing gaze of the disciplined, where the observer becomes the observed'[11] and thus constituted a mode of resistance. In addition, mimicry subverts colonial strategies of knowledge by presenting a native other that is emptied of its signification — there is no essential native to be observed, catalogued and categorized. Mimicry thus threatens the self/other dichotomy.

COLONIAL MIMICRY

A classic example of colonial mimicry is provided by the community of Eurasians in India. Originally the product of liaisons between East India Company officials and Indian women, they were at first patronized and supported by the British, who perceived them to be a prop of British rule. A policy reversal took place at the end of the eighteenth century, when Eurasians were forbidden from holding senior administrative or army posts. The historian Kenneth Ballhatchet traces several reasons for this development. The Evangelical revival in Britain condemned the immoral liaisons that were a feature of British Indian life in the eighteenth century. Further, a young generation of Eurasians were seen as a threat to a British monopoly of posts, admirably suited as they were through their cross-cultural background for positions of responsibility in India. The revolution in Haiti in 1791 led by Toussaint L'Ouverture, which sent a profound shock through the societies of the colonial powers, were thought to be largely the work of the educated classes of mixed descent. With a jolt colonial authorities realized the potential of these classes not only for collaboration, but for subversion. The increased racialization of colonial relations, with the Eurasians seen as a threat to racial borders, was also a reaction against moral and ethical attacks on colonialism in Britain.

By the nineteenth century the Eurasian community had become the laughing stock of British society and Eurasians are almost always vilified and derided in British texts.[12] Even Mary Carpenter, with her bias towards Christian natives, admits she is led 'fully to believe in the correctness of the general impression, that they inherit many of the faults of the two races from which they spring, and that they have the sympathy of neither' (1: 223). Emma Roberts, writing at a time when inter-cultural marriages were still common and admitting that 'connexions between Indian women and English gentlemen of rank and education [were] often of the tenderest and most enduring description' (2: 56), nevertheless pours scorn on the vulgarity of Eurasian women:

> At native festivals, the wives of Portuguese drummers, and other functionaries of equal rank, are to be seen amid the crowd, arrayed in gowns of blue satin, or pink crape, fantastically trimmed; with satin slippers on their feet, their hair full-dressed, and an umbrella carried over their heads by some ragged servant, making altogether an appearance not very unlike that of Maid Marian on May-day (3: 20).

Writing in the 1830s, Roberts differentiates scrupulously between liaisons between Indian princesses and English gentlemen — such as that of Colonel Gardner of legendary fame, to whose zenana Fanny Parks gains access — and the Eurasian community, usually the product of liaisons between lower class Indian mistresses and British men. She is careful to lay the blame for prejudice towards Eurasians at the door of the Indians, however: 'It cannot be too strongly impressed upon the reader's mind, that these exclusions orginated in the prejudices of the natives, who, while professing their willingness to be governed by Europeans, absolutely refused to submit to persons springing from outcast females' (3: 98).

It might appear, however, that the lady is protesting too much. Anne Wilson, far more sympathetic to Indians than most of her peers, makes the same careful distinction along class lines. When a high-ranking Indian educated at Oxford admits his love for an English girl to her, she muses 'in a sentimental hour . . . if such a marriage would be quite an impossible experiment for this particular woman to try, if her heart was in it, and if the two were, as he said, essentially kindred spirits.'[13] By the time Wilson is writing, however, her opinions are a radical deviation from received opinion, and even she admits that the couple will have to be prepared to face social ostracism. Racial distinctions had gained precedence over class boundaries in the later period of British rule, as is exemplified in the government's vehement opposition to cross-cultural marriages even of Maharajahs.[14] The bugbear of miscegenation had swollen to enormous proportions, and Kipling voiced a general sentiment when he calls for East and West to remain in their separate worlds in his famous words of warning: 'A Man should, whatever happens, keep to his own caste, race and breed. Let the White go to the White and the Black to the Black. Then, whatever trouble falls is in the ordinary course of things — neither sudden, alien nor unexpected.'[15]

Wilson, who is full of sympathy for 'one of the most unfortunate races in the empire' (295), goes on to describe the look on their faces in the following manner: 'It was so helpless, as if, with their childish self-complacence in abeyance, they acknowledged their inborn weakness and waited for succour' (296). The text fleetingly admits that this community 'owe their existence to our presence in India' (295), but resists the political implications of this statement, taking refuge instead in the concept of a tragic ineradicable racial flaw, conflated with the construction of the infantile native.

The most revealing example of a disruption of the smooth surface of the colonial textualization of the Eurasian is to be found in Amelia Falkland's text. As wife of the governor of Bombay, one of her duties involves visiting a school for half-caste orphans and foundlings, accompanied by other officials. The incident bears citing in full:

> As we descended into the hall, a ridiculous incident occurred, and one of the gentlemen of the party, who had just arrived from England, found himself in a very unforeseen position. A very little child, an inmate of the institution, with large black eyes, a flattish nose, and a complexion shading off from bistre into yellow ochre clung round his legs; and looking up most imploringly into his face, cried out, 'Pa-pa! Pa-pa!' All the efforts of our friend to disentangle himself from the affectionate embraces of the poor little innocent were useless. It only clung closer, and cried 'pa-pa! pa-pa!' more vehemently. How long the struggle lasted I know not, for I hastened to escape from a scene which was much too laughable (1: 26).

Does the symbolism of the scene, this transposition of sexual/racial guilt into a farce, require any further comment? And is it overstretching a point to read the Englishwoman's escape from colonial realities as emblematic of Western woman's self-construction as a spectator of, and not an actor in, empire?

Collecting Cultures

Peter Stallybrass and Allon White note a correlation between a nineteenth-century bourgeois regulatory effort directed at rural forms of tradition in Britain and the compensatory mania for collecting native artifacts in the colonies.[16] The acquisitive connotations of collecting native culture have been commented on. A travesty of this phenomenon is enacted in the Westernized Indian's grotesque collection of European artifacts, which are crowded into native rooms in a medley of the valuable and the trivial. This is the subject of much derisive comment by British authors. In Cumming's text, however, an awareness of colonial mimicry at work is discernible:

> The same incongruities are remarkable in the internal arrangements of a native house, of which the family rooms are furnished only with carpets and cushions, but the show room in which they receive Europeans is generally crammed with heterogeneous foreign articles — perhaps a dozen English clocks of divers pattern, all going; priceless vases and the most trumpery English toys; the cheapest framed prints of French damsels, and of sacred subjects (not cheap to their purchaser, you may be very sure!) Perhaps as a treasure beyond price, an old barrel organ, and some of the commonest statuettes side by side with exquisite jewelled cups.
>
> I am not sure however that a Hindoo gentlemen might not be equally astonished to find *our* rooms decorated with the brooches and anklets of the poorest Indian women, betal plates, brass ink-horns, and beautiful metal plates and bowls — nay, even funny little gods and goddesses surrounded by brazen lamps and bells, and sacrificial vessels intended for use in their temples; rosaries also and prayer-wheels, and hubble-bubble vases — no longer used for smoking, but filled with roses! — nay, even bathing-slippers of inlaid wood, and ridiculous Indian playthings (112).

This is a rare moment of insight in a traveller's text — when the traveller plays along with the native gaze at the travelling eye/I and reveals a perception of the relativeness of the norms of the traveller's own culture. It is not the native, as so often, who is held up to ridicule here; the text's last laugh is on the traveller.

Colonial Mockery

A further example of a native chuckle at the expense of the traveller is presented in Marianne Postans' text. Postans describes a tourist attraction in Bombay, a hospital for animals run by the religious community of

Jains, a Hindu off-shoot remarkable for their enormous respect for all living creatures.[17] She writes:

> The hospital for aged and diseased animals at Surat, is very similar to that of the 'Pingera Pool,' in Bombay; and like that merciful institution, is a richly endowed Jain establishment, containing every comfortable and necessary arrangement for the protection and good treatment of the animals received. Travellers of the olden time, have described the means of gratifying insect appetite in the entymological departments of this vast boarding house, as those most loathsome and disgusting; but as no customs of the kind exist at present, I am induced to believe that persons may have been misled by false representations; in short, that the quizzing servitors of the animal hospital, amused themselves by testing the credulity of the traveller 'Logue'.[18]

The veracity of this traveller's tale is not at issue here. Instead, it presents us with an example of native mockery of the Western traveller's gullibility and lust for sensationalism. At a deeper level the other refuses to play along with the role assigned to him/her as object of the knowledge-production of the traveller. While the narrator draws on a rhetoric of superiority by relegating the hoax to the past, it is the very indeterminacy of the other (is it or is it not a hoax?) that causes the greatest irritation to the colonial traveller's text.

The Other's Voice

A stock joke in British texts on India is the comic mistakes Indians make when using the English language. Isabel Savory, for example, presents the reader with reams of samples of Indian English, including the example of a cook who misspelt the entire French menu of his master (One wonders how many English cooks were perfect in their French spelling, let alone people like the Savories.) One of the most open-minded of travellers, Anne Wilson is one of the few British in India to point to the large-scale mutilation of Indian languages by the British, most of whom flaunt Hindustani phrases in execrable grammar in their texts. After relating an amusing interview with an Indian youth in quaint English, she reminds her readers of 'the marvellous manners of Indians, who never betray by a shade that one has probably tampered as much with their language as the scion of the 'Bhera old family best' did with ours' (45), thus revealing an awareness of the contingency of one's own norms. It is in Wilson's text that we find an educated native speaking back, and that too most emphatically.

Wilson is taken by a friend to meet an Indian playwright, allegedly one of the best-known dramatists of Bengal. (She however omits to give his name.) The description of the encounter is suffused with repressed excitement:

> . . . my little friend exclaimed, 'Ah, here he comes,' and I heard swift steps traversing the corridor, which ran round the central courtyard of the house. Even the steps would have arrested my attention, because an Indian's step is usually noiseless, as if he did not lift his foot from the ground. These were rapid, impetuous, resolute. Then our host entered, and I saw he was quite unlike any type of Indian I had ever met. He was tall and slight, with silvery, straight hair, which fell back from his lofty, narrow forehead to his neck. He had a hooked nose, a sensitive, mobile mouth, and piercing, dark eyes, intent and mournful in their expression. He might have been a lawyer-poet. . . . I felt as if I had known him always, and as if we began as old friends. We sat down opposite to each other, and talked for an hour! (317)

In this context it is necessary to recall that at this period racial segregation was at its height. Wilson herself admits at an earlier point in the text that 'some Europeans of the old school would not allow a lady to accept an Indian gentleman's proffered hospitality . . . or receive an Indian as visitor, far less dine with him' (33-4). Despite her husband's greater tolerance, the extravagance of meeting an Indian gentleman in his house merely in the company of another lady is palpable in the text. What follows is even more of a scandal: 'We are a conquered race', (317) the poet tells her. He adds: 'Memsahib, may I say something? Do you know what we call your race? We call you the Vaishyas[19], the merchant class. You are interested in our fields and canals, in material improvements, but in us, in ourselves, in our homes, you are not interested.' (318)

The narrator attempts to mould the interview into a triumph for the British/Christianity but making the poet cede that he has no objections to the country becoming Christian, if this meant 'not that we should dress like monkeys in the hope of becoming Englishmen, but that we should worship Christ' (319). On this note the encounter ends (in the text). The narrator incorporates several strategies of containment into the narrative, such as omitting the name of the poet (he remains a picturesque sample of a native for us, instead of a concrete person) and stressing that he is very different from the usual run of native (his appearance; his step — the silent footfalls Wilson seems to be used to reveal that her main contact with natives is with servants). In spite of possible authorial editing, however, the voice of the other — authentic or not — escapes complete narrative control and remains etched on a text that otherwise is a paean to benevolent paternalistic rule.

OTHER GAZES

The construction of the travelling subject as being in sole possession of the gaze is, as has been argued, closely bound up with the post-Enlightenment epistemic divide between subject and object of observation and is premised on a disembodied, transcendent observing subject. Occasionally, however, the traveller is aware of being the focus of the other's returning gaze. Only very rarely does this awareness lead to a realization of the traveller's own involvement in the viewing process and the dialectic of gazes, neither of which has a privileged access to a transcendent truth. In our assortment of women travellers this type of knowledge is only articulated in specific moments within Emily Eden's text. More common is the traveller's perception of other gazes as a threat, as in the following hysterical passage by Isabel Savory: 'One realises at once what it is to be the only Englishwoman among thousands of natives. Every eye is on you — not rude or staring, but you feel *eyes* everywhere; and you begin to realise that were there no cantonments outside, you would probably have one of the many knives in your back, — which reflection puts you on your mettle' (56).

While Savory represents a classic example of colonial paranoia, the text cannily sets up an equation between the traveller's gaze and power. By admitting that her own freedom to gaze at the other is enabled and backed by colonial power, Savory indirectly articulates the implication of the traveller in colonial structures of power as well as the intersection of knowledge-production with relations of power.

My last example of the gaze of the other is that of a barrage of critical gazes directed at the British. No inarticulate subaltern here, the gazes at issue are those of a highly sophisticated and articulate other. They hint at an entire world of subversive discourse with the colonizing subject as object of their critical and mocking gazes.[20] This is Roberts reporting:

> In Delhi, the opinions entertained upon the subject are widely, though secretly, circulated through the medium of the native *ukhbars*, scandalous chronicles, very much resembling a few of our English newspapers, except that they are in manuscript: the language is Persian, and the editors do not scruple to write at full length the names of those who are the subjects of the most atrocious libels. It is not very easy for an European to procure a sight of the animadversions passed upon the conduct of himself or his friends; some artifice is requisite to obtain samples of the method employed to amuse the reading portion of the native community at the expense of persons differing so widely in the habits of their public and private life. . . . The following description of a European entertainment will convey some idea of the estimation in which such promiscuous meetings are held.
>
> 'The gentlemen of exalted dignity had a great feast last night, to which all military chiefs and lieutenants were invited. There was a little hog on the table, before Mr.—, who cut it in small pieces, and sent some to each of the party; even the women ate of it. In their language, a pig is called ham. Having stuffed themselves with the unclean food, and many sorts of flesh, taking plenty of wine, they made for some time a great noise, which doubtless arose from drunkenness. They all stood up two or four times, crying 'hip! hip!' and roared before they drank more wine. After dinner, they danced in their licentious manner, pulling about each other's wives.' (3: 187-8)

What is presented here is not a parody but an alternative manners-and-customs account. It is incorporated into a traveller's text that seeks to bend it to its own ends — Roberts is highly critical of the arrogance of the British in India. The narrator produces herself as privy to secret discourses of the other and in this capacity serves the function of a private eye. Despite the careful staging of native voices here, the excess of the other's gaze eludes the narrator's attempt at containment and leaves a trail of unease in its wake. And this unease stems not from the critique of the colonial rulers but from the realization of being the object of observation. By exposing the type of English she disapproves of as the focus of native gazes, the narrator simultaneously exposes the traveller's position of authority, predicated on a panoramic viewing point, as illusory. If certain rambunctious members of the English community are the object of the other's mocking gaze, what is to prevent this gaze being trained on the traveller-narrator herself?

Notes

1 Spivak, 'Can the Subaltern Speak?' 129.

2 Queen.

3 Spivak, 'Rani of Sirmur' 146-47.

4 In the field of ethnography James Clifford comes to a similar conclusion: even a dialogic field-work situation is ultimately reproduced and thus arranged and constructed within the ethnographer's text. See 'On Ethnographic Auhority', *Representations* 2.2 (1983): 118-46.

5 See Benita Parry, 'Problems in the Current Theories of Colonial Discourse', *Oxford Literary Review* 9.1-2 (1987): 27-58, and Nicholas Thomas, *Colonialism's Culture.*

6 In his book Thomas argues convincingly against constituting an authentic other, but in his critique of postcolonial critics he falls into the same trap by calling for more agency for the native.

7 Focus of Spivak's interest is the Indian woman's appropriation of sati as a means of asserting a will of her own.

8 On a definition of agency which is not automatically bound up with humanist definitions of subjectivity, see Mohanty, 'Us and Them.'

9 Bhabha, 'The Other Question' 157.

10 Bhabha, 'Of Mimicry and Man' 126. Emphasis in the original.

11 Bhabha, 'Of Mimicry and Man' 129.

12 Once again, Emily Eden forms an exception to the rule, as shown above.

13 Lady Anne Campbell Wilson, *Letters from India* (1911; London: Century, 1984) 116. All further references to be given in parentheses in the text.

14 See Ballhatchet, 116-22. Also see Parry on colonial literature, where mixed marriages are consistently doomed — as in Kipling's 'Beyond the Pale'. See Parry, *Delusions and Discoveries.*

15 Rudyard Kipling. 'Beyond the Pale', *Plain Tales from the Hills* (Leipzig: Tauchnitz, n.d.) 166.

16 Peter Stallybrass and Allon White, *The Politics and Poetics of Transgression* (London: Methuen, 1986) 172.

17 Orthodox Jains wear face-masks to avoid inhaling insects and thus killing them.

18 A suffix denoting plurality.

19 The third large subsection in the hierarchy of the Hindu caste system. They are superseded by Brahmins and the caste of warriors and rulers. Surely this is not where the British would position themselves on the Hindu scale!

20 Of course we know that there was a great deal of parody, farces, skits, etc. critical of the British at this time. The interest lies in its having made its way into a colonial text. See Partha Chatterjee, 'Colonialism, Nationalism, and Colonized Women: The Context in India', *American Ethnologist* 16 (1989) 622-33.

Conclusion

> This pose of 'seeing India' which had seduced him to Miss Quested in Chandrapore was only a form of ruling India . . .
>
> — E.M. Forster, *A Passage to India*

Do women travellers perceive India differently than male travellers? Is there, in fact, a female gaze? This much-vexed question in feminist criticism appears to me rooted in a dream of replacing dominant discourses with marginalized discourses, alternative voices from the borders of society. Sadly, the truth is less glamorous. There is no specifically female gaze. Instead, there is a wide spectrum of gazes by women travellers. These travelogues certainly deserve to be salvaged from the dust-heap of memory — not as alternative voices, but as a rich contribution to the literature of the Raj.

I argue that there is no female traveller's gaze — for the simple reason that gender is only one of a mulitplicity of factors that determine identity (salient among which are ethnicity and class). These determinants are frequently mutually contradictory and shifting — not essences frozen in time, but historically variable categories. It is the site of power where subjects are located at a given moment that needs to be scrutinized. While the dominant gender ideology in this period was the ideology of domesticity that implied a subordinate and passive position for women in the public sphere, racial assumptions that gained ever greater importance in the course of the century defined the British woman traveller as superior to Indians — irrespective of their class or gender. While there are exceptions to this constellation — Emily Eden, for instance, demonstrates an upper-class sense of class solidarity with Indians of equal rank that contradicts norms of racial solidarity — the broad outlines of this matrix determined the writings of most nineteenth- century travellers.

This is not to fall back on claims that reject gender as a salient category of analysis, however. The truth, as so often, seems to lie somewhere in the middle: there are both differences and similarities between texts written by women travellers and those written by men. A concept of subjectivity as fractured and unstable would negotiate both the critical pitfalls of a denial of the significance of gender and, conversely, an obsession with gender to the exclusion of all other relations of power. A vertiginous concept of identity poses a threat to cosy essentialist myths of the inherent difference of women's relation to the other. Perhaps we finally need to relinquish the notion of a unified and coherent subject and face the often troubling reality of the fragmentation and volatileness of identity.

It seems far more fruitful to take the historical tapestry into which the texts are woven into account — the material conditions of their production. As we have seen, women travellers remained on the sidelines in most areas of interest for travellers in India — they remained amateurs, whether in the field of Orientalist research or big game hunting. They had no access to the great world of politics that absorbed so many of their male compatriots at this time and provides the colourful backdrop for so many narratives of India written by male travellers — who very often travelled in an official capacity. By contrast, the zenana offered women travellers an opportunity for exploring a terrain closed to British men — and accordingly the source of accounts eagerly received by both publishers and readers at home. These are some of the factors that played a vital role in shaping the views of India produced in the texts of the women travellers.

As I hope to have shown in this study, the spectrum of gazes to be found inscribed into nineteenth-century women travellers' writings leads inevitably to a scrutiny of the different discourses in circulation that construct perception. In other words: the observer is always rooted in the situation of perception and does not transcend it — what we see is a result of our location in the reality of viewing, not the reflection of a given reality. The detached observer is a myth. A myth, however, that is of such pervasive ideological power that it demands a conscious effort to expose its implications. As I have argued, it is the assumptions of the detached viewer paradigm that shape our notion of the other as a separate category and an object of knowledge. Conversely, it is the detached viewer stance that constitutes the individual self as an essentialist phenomenon. Lastly, it is this very concept of transcendent self that creates distance to material relations of power and, in our case, enables the self-constitution of English women as spectators of empire.

There is, however, no simple equation between discourses in circulation at a given point and a certain text: there is always a space for fantasy which inflects the discourses at work. Thus we can observe Fanny Parks' voyeuristic fantasy in the zenana or Mary Carpenter's fantasies of social control informing their texts. These fantasies can also be collective affairs, of course, dreamt by entire generations of travellers.

The notion of observing without involvement in the situation of viewing, for instance, is nothing but the dream of mastery without any implication in the messy realities of power — a colonial fantasy that S.P. Mohanty pins down even in children's narratives of colonialism such as Kipling's *Kim* or *The Jungle Book*.[1] This dream seems to be collectively dreamt by colonial travellers.[2] It functions vicariously for the large audience of armchair travellers as well, who are offered a correlative subject position as readers of these texts. For both traveller and reader this stance manages 'the threat of any real encounter'[3] with the other and the precarious and mutually interactive relation that this implies. The threat that is managed is a fear of loss of control. Thus the concept of the transcendent traveller's gaze is intrinsically linked to questions of power — and its corollary, anxiety about the instability of power.

An analysis of nineteenth-century women's travel writing inevitably involves an engagement with the issue of women's relation to power. What we need to remind ourselves of is the fact that power is not gender-specific but that women, too, have had access to power. A further pitfall to avoid is the notion that all relations of power are gender relations. This leads the way to accept the inescapability of colonial entanglement for English women travelling abroad in the nineteenth century. In fact, the pleasures of travel are often predicated on the pleasures of imperialism — the privileges offered to English women in regions under the control of colonial rule. What also becomes apparent is the fact that the mechanics of women's relation to power was complex and contradictory: negotiating a certain space for freedom and adventure through travel involved a collusion with oppressive norms in matters of decorum, for example.

What most travellers share in common is their collusion in colonialist structures of power. However, the knowledge produced in women travellers' texts was enmeshed in regimes of power as well. This is succinctly if inadvertently revealed in the comment of a celebratory critic of women travellers: 'Touring or residing in foreign lands, women learned history, geography, languages, and politics. They also learned about 'strange' customs. . . . Very simply said, they brought back a powerful commodity — knowledge.'[4] Women travellers were instrumental in shaping a certain image of India and circulating this image in their widely-read texts at the time. Future generations of travellers to India as well as shiploads of memsahibs bound for life in the colonies were influenced by the vision of India disseminated in these texts. Thus certain stereotypes — the devious native, the insidious climate, for example — tended to gain the authority of common sense knowledge. This store of knowledge often had a direct impact on colonial policy — the received wisdom that warned of the detrimental effects of bringing up British children in India is one example of the force of colonial stereotypes.

This is not to imply that women travellers consciously fashioned or circulated colonial myths. An insight into the constitution of knowledge that is linked to vision as the paradigmatic hermeneutic act has already revealed that it was not the reality of India that was at stake. All narrative makes sense of experience through the means of selection and arrangement. And this process of selection is grounded in a web of discourses that shape perception. Thus texts constitute reality and do not reflect a given world. Further, these autobiographical writings are always determined by the project of self-fashioning. It is the constitution of the self that determines how the other is produced textually — all definitions of the reality of the other world are contingent on a definition of the self. Thus the India in the texts of these women travellers is traversed by their writers' own obsessions and desires. And these texts are always directed at a home audience of shared collective assumptions and opinions.

As we have seen throughout, a reading of these colonialist texts exposes contradictions and ambivalences in the colonial narrative itself. In other words, what these writings reveal are the anxieties woven into the very fabric of colonial ideology. For power is inextricably coupled with a sense of its precariousness.

This is not to imply, however, that voices critical of colonial policies were not raised. In fact, by attempting to uncover the crises and cracks in these narratives the contradictions within the subjectivity of these women are revealed. Gazing back at my own 'objects of knowledge', what is most striking is the ambivalence within the different women themselves. Thus Constance Gordon Cumming, vocal in her criticism of British racism against Indians, never once describes an encounter with the educated natives she so endorses — the only natives to find a place in her text are the exasperating class of porters. Christine Bremner, a bluestocking if ever there was one (her text was written for literary societies in London), is probably the most vociferous of this handful of travellers in decrying colonial abuses. The last few chapters of her book drop all illusion of narrating a journey and expound her remarkably astute theories on the economics of colonialism. She states quite clearly:

> . . . though English rule in India is one of the noblest things in the world today, though its subversion would be a heavy blow to civilisation, yet it is impoverishing the country. Britain has secured peace for India, but compels her to pay a price so heavy for the service as to make the invasions and pillaging of all previous conquerors insignificant by comparison (191).

No nationalist politician could produce an analysis more scathing and more to the point. With great perspicacity she concludes that 'the foundation [of British rule in India] is laid on expediency' (214); 'the main motor is self-interest' (213). However, her own conduct while travelling alone through North India is marked by the acquisitiveness of a souvenir-hunter and a disdain for the people surrounding her, whom she presents mainly in the colonial stereotype of the childlike if cunning native. She can only react to their transparent attempts to hoodwink her with a mixture of exasperation and humour. Only one native provokes her ire: a Hindu beggar who avoids her touch for fear of defilement. Here is Bremner describing the scene:

> At Amritsar I well remember a dirty old beggar importuning me for alms when I came down from a many-storied tower I had climbed to view the city. I still feel indignant when I recollect how he dodged so that he might get the silver and yet not touch my hand by the slightest chance. Had I shown the same insulting eagerness to avoid his black, withered, prehensile, ending in white nails, the chief difference between his hand and a parrot's claw, it would have been far more excusable (115).

What we have here is, of course, a classic colonial conjunction: little aggravated the British more than the feeling that the colonized were viewing them with contempt. This was, however, often the case in encounters with religious Hindus, who considered the foreigners polluting. Bremner's wrath is poured out in the string of descriptions she deploys for the beggar's claw-like hand — which, ironically, avoids all contact with her. Colonial certainties such as the hierarchy between colonizer and colonized, between haves and have-nots, are all thrown into confusion by the impertinence of the other — and this disturbance is articulated in a sense of menace.

Another example that explains the fragmentation within the subjectivity of these travellers is provided by the text of Anne Wilson. Even texts such as these imbued with a benevolent and at times reciprocal relationship to the other are affected by these disturbances. As wife of a senior civil servant, Anne Wilson is remarkable for her interest in Indian religion and culture and is one of the very few travellers who shows a keen interest in Indian music, the essential structures of which she grasps after intensive study. She also has a frank encounter with an Indian poet. At one point towards the end of her narrative she describes a train journey that gradually turns into a nightmare. First a waiter announces that there was no more food nor ice in the restaurant-car and that the car itself would be cut off that evening. Later she notices that the train is deserted by foreigners and Eurasians, while the stations it passes are swarming with belligerent Indians. At one point she manages to buttonhole one of the few Eurasian waiters in sight and demand an explanation for the menacing atmosphere at the station. 'It was the day the Mutiny broke out, fifty years ago,' he replies. Nationalist sentiments were seething at the memory of the crushing defeat of the mutiny by the British fifty years ago. He explains to her that all Eurasians had returned to their homes to protect their wives and families. The apolitical Wilson is confounded:

> All this was practically Greek and Latin to me. I had read about the riots in Lahore and Rawal Pindi in the Bombay newspaper. I knew they had followed on the conviction of a newspaper editor. I remembered he had tried to rouse disaffection in the Indian Army. But what had all this to do with the Indian Mutiny?

When her husband fails to pick her up, she passes a night of fear in the dark. However, nothing untoward occurs. But Wilson concludes her tale with: 'A serpent had entered that Garden of Eden and threatened Adam and Eve with eviction, with the most woful results and a hubbub which has barely subsided' (352-5).

In Anne Wilson's world of benevolent paternalism, the serpent, no doubt, symbolizes the educated native who has invaded the paradise of the colonial family. By the time she is writing the rumbles of native discontent are evident and a nationalist movement is rapidly gaining in force. Her reaction of pain and bewilderment was characteristic of a large number of well-meaning colonial administrators who toiled for the improvement of the simple Indian peasants' lot and felt a sense of betrayal at the ingratitude of their flock. Their lives contain other, forgotten, tragic tales of the death of empires. There are so many stories left to be told.

And lastly, there is the irrepressible Fanny Parks, who is so keen to advertise her first-hand knowledge of life in the zenana. Her text produces an image of languid Oriental beauties who only occasionally provoke her resentment when they do not live up to her standards of beauty. In fact, as she admits, 'For a woman not to be pretty when she is shut up in a zenana appears almost a sin, so much are we ruled in our ideas by what we read in childhood of the hooris of the East' (2: 40). But there is another side to Fanny Parks. An enthusiastic horsewoman, she strikes up a friendship with the deposed Mahratta Queen of Gwalior, the Baiza Bai, and spends happy hours prancing about comparing horses and riding styles with the royal train of Amazon-like women. In fact, one cannot repress the feeling that Parks feels far more at home among these practical women than among the idealized houris she foregrounds in her book. At one point she makes the remarkable confession: 'Were I an Asiatic, I would be a Mahratta' (2: 38).

In fact, at rare moments Fanny Parks departs from her voyeuristic stance to show a remarkable sense of cross-cultural empathy with other women. When surveying a mound sprinkled with monuments commemorating women who had committed sati, she exclaims: 'The laws of England relative to married women, and the state of slavery to which those laws degrade them, render the lives of some few in the higher, and of thousands in the lower ranks of life, one perpetual sati, or burning of the heart, from which they have no refuge but the grave, or the cap of liberty, — i.e., the widow's, and either is a sad consolation' (2: 420). She turns the tables on the sensationalism surrounding the social abuse of widow-burning in India and draws a provocative analogy between the condition of women in India and England to point up the oppression of women in both cultures.

If I would like to draw attention to the ambivalence within the subjectivities of these women travellers, I am not by any means attempting to recuperate the cracks in their texts for the space of a unified other, a subaltern voice granted a site for articulation by liberal-minded travellers. The other is no more unified than is the self — no authentic native voice is to be heard. India itself consists of a spectrum of differing realities.

'I want to see the real India,' the traveller Adela Quested in E. M. Forster's *A Passage To India* announces.[5] What emerges from her tragic tale of failure is that there is no 'real' India to be had. The other eludes the grasp of the traveller's transcendent gaze. The desire to *see* and *know* founders on the limits of the epistemic project. For the reality of India is a discursive reality — a palimpsest inscribed upon by generations of travellers. Anne Wilson gives voice to the desire and anxiety of the traveller when she writes,

> How strange these people are! What would I not give to be inside their heads for an hour, to look out at life with their eyes! What do they think about, what do they love, what do they hate, what pains them or gives them pleasure? Are we really like each other fundamentally, or have we not a thought or a feeling in common? Oh the pathos and the loneliness of separate existence![6]

How then, she asks, do we read the other? The project of epistemic mastery is always haunted by the fear of the elusiveness of its goal. If we see self and other only as unstable, relational terms without any essence, however — as a trace, not a presence — we admit the impossibility of ever entirely reading the other.[7]

Notes

1 See S. P. Mohanty, 'Kipling's Children and the Colour Line,' *Race & Class* 31.1 (1989): 21-40.

2 See Mary Louise Pratt's perceptive *Imperial Eyes.*

3 Mohanty 35.

4 Leo Hamalian, ed., Introduction, *Ladies On The Loose: Women Travellers of the Eighteenth and Nineteenth Centuries* (New York: Dodd, 1981) xv.
5 E. M. Forster, *A Passage to India* (1924; Harmondsworth: Penguin, 1979) 46.
6 Wilson 23.
7 See Bhabha's interpretation of what really happened in the caves in terms of a refusal of colonial knowability, in 'Articulating the Archaic: Notes on Colonial Nonsense', *Literary Theory Today*, eds Peter Collier and Helga Geyer-Ryan (Cambridge: Polity, 1990) 203-18. Also see Mason, to whose insights in connection with early travelogues on America I am greatly indebted.

Bibliography

Primary Sources

Bartrum, Katherine Mary. *A Widow's Reminiscences of the Siege of Lucknow.* London: Nisbet, 1858

Billington, Mary Frances. *Woman in India.* 1894; New Delhi: Amarko Book Agency, 1973.

Bremner, Christina Sinclair. *A Month in a Dandi: A Woman's Wanderings in Northern India.* London: Simpkin, Marshall & Co., 1891.

Burton, Lady Isabel. *A.E.I. Arabia Egypt India: A Narrative of Travel.* London: W. Mullan, 1879.

Carpenter, Mary. *Six Months in India.* 2 vols. London: Longmans, 1868.

Coopland, R. M. *A Lady's Escape from Gwalior, and Life in the Fort of Agra during the Mutinies of 1857.* London: Smith, Elder, & Co., 1859.

Cumming, Constance Frederica Gordon. *In the Himalayas and On the Indian Plains.* 1884; London: Chatto & Windus, 1901.

Duberly, Frances Isabella. *Campaigning Experiences in Rajpootana and Central India, during the Suppression of the Mutiny, 1857-1858.* London: Smith, Elder, & Co., 1859.

Dufferin, Lady Harriot Blackwood. *Our Viceregal Life in India: Selections from my Journal 1884-1888.* 2 vols. London: John Murray, 1889.

Eden, The Honorable Emily. *Up the Country: Letters written to her Sister from The Upper Provinces of India.* 2 vols. 1866; London: Virago, 1983.

Elwood, Anne Katherine. *Narrative of a Journey Overland from England, by the Continent of Europe, Egypt, and the Red Sea, to India; including A Residence there, and Voyage Home, in the years 1825, 26, 27, and 28.* 2 vols. London: Colburn and Bentley, 1830.

Falkland, Amelia Cary, Viscountess. *Chow-Chow; Being Selections from a Journal kept in India, Egypt, and Syria.* 2 vols. London: Hurst and Blackett, 1857.

Graham, Maria. *Journal of a Residence in India.* Edinburgh: Archibald Constable, 1812.

Harris, Katherine. *A Lady's Diary of the Siege of Lucknow.* London: John Murray, 1858.

Inglis, Lady Julia Selina. *The Siege of Lucknow, a Diary.* London: James R. Osgood, 1892.

King, E. Augusta. *The Diary of a Civilian's Wife in India 1877-1882.* 2 vols. London: Richard Bentley, 1884.

Leonowens, Anna Harriette Crawford. *Life and Travel in India: Being Recollections of a Journey Before the Days of Railroads.* Philadelphia: Porter and Coates, 1884.

MacKenzie, Helen. *Six Years in India.* London: Richard Bentley, 1857.

Maitland, Julia Charlotte. *Letters from Madras, during the years 1836-39, by a Lady.* London: John Murray, 1843.

Marryat, Florence. *'Gup': Sketches of Anglo-Indian Life and Character.* London: Richard Bentley, 1868.

North, Marianne. *Recollections of a Happy Life: Being the Autobiography of Marianne North.* Edited by her sister Mrs John Addington Symonds. 2 vols. London: Macmillan, 1892.

Parks, Fanny. *Wanderings of a Pilgrim in Search of the Picturesque, during four-and twenty years in the East; with Revelations of Life in the Zenana.* 2 vols. 1850; Karachi: Oxford University Press, 1975.

Postans, Marianne. *Western India in 1838.* 2 vols. London: Saunders and Otley, 1839.

Roberts, Emma. *Scenes and Characteristics of Hindostan, with Sketches of Anglo-Indian Society.* 3 vols. London: Wm. H. Allen, 1835.

Savory, Isabel. *A Sportswoman in India: Personal Adventures and Experiences in Known and Unknown India.* London: Hutchinson, 1900.

Sherwood, Mary Martha. *The Life and Times of Mrs. Sherwood (1775-1851) from the Diaries of Captain and Mrs. Sherwood.* Edited by F. J. Harvey Darton. London: Wells Gardner & Co., 1910.

Steel, Flora Annie. *The Garden of Fidelity.* London: Macmillan, 1929.

Wilson, Lady Anne Campbell. *Letters from India.* 1911; London: Century, 1984

Workman, Fanny Bullock, and William Hunter Workman. *Through Town and Jungle: Fourteen Thousand Miles A-Wheel Among the Temples and People of the Indian Plain.* London: T. Fisher Unwin, 1904.

SECONDARY SOURCES

Adams, Percy G. *Traveler and Travel Liar: 1660-1800.* Berkeley: University of California Press, 1962.

—— *Travel Literature and the Evolution of the Novel.* Lexington: University Press of Kentucky, 1983.

Ahmed, Leila. 'Western Ethnocentrism and Perceptions of the Harem'. *Feminist Studies* 8.3 (1982): pp. 521-34.

Aitken, Maria. *A Girdle Around the Earth: Adventuresses Abroad.* London: Constable, 1987.

Alexander, Joan. *Voices and Echoes: Tales from Colonial Women.* London: Quartet, 1983.

Andrews, Malcolm. *The Search for the Picturesque: Landscape Aesthetics and Tourism in Britain, 1760-1800.* Aldershot: Scolar, 1989.

Archer, Mildred, and Ronald Lightbrown. *India Observed: India as viewed by British Artists 1760-1860.* London: Victoria and Albert Museum, 1982.

Arnold, David. 'Touching the Body: Perspectives on the Indian Plague, 1896-1900'. In Guha and Spivak, pp. 391-426.

Asad, Talal. 'Anthropology and the Colonial Encounter'. In *The Politics of Anthropology: From Colonialism and Sexism Toward a View from Below.* Edited by Gerrit Huizer and Bruce Mannheim. The Hague: Mouton, 1979. pp. 85-94.

Atkinson, George F. *Curry and Rice or the Ingredients of Social Life at 'Our' Station in India.* London, 1859.

Ballhatchet, Kenneth. *Race, Sex and Class under the Raj: Imperial Attitudes and Policies and their Critics, 1793-1905.* London: Weidenfeld & Nicolson, 1980.

Barker, Francis *et al.*, eds. *Europe and Its Others.* Proceedings of the Essex Conference on the Sociology of Literature. July 1984. 2 vols. Colchester: University of Essex, 1985.

Barker, Francis *et al.*, eds. *Literature, Society and the Sociology of Literature*. Proceedings of the Conference at the University of Essex. July 1976. Colchester: University of Essex, 1977.

Barr, Pat. *The Memsahibs: The Women of Victorian India*. London: Secker & Warburg, 1976.

Barrell, John. *The Idea of Landscape and the Sense of Place, 1730-1840*. Cambridge: Cambridge University Press, 1972.

Barthes, Roland. *Mythologies*. Translated by Annette Lavers. 1957. New York: Hill & Wang, 1981.

Basch, Francoise. *Relative Creatures: Victorian Women in Society and the Novel 1837-67*. London: Lane, 1974.

Bassnett, Susan. 'Constructing Cultures: the Politics of Travellers' Tales'. In *Comparative Literature: A Critical Introduction*. Edited by Bassnett, Susan, Oxford: Blackwell, 1993. pp. 92-114.

Batten, Charles. *Pleasurable Instruction: Form and Convention in Eighteenth-Century Travel Literature*. Berkeley: University of California Press, 1978.

Baudet, Henri. *Paradise on Earth: Some Thoughts on European Images of Non-European Man*. New Haven: Yale University Press, 1965.

Bayly, C. A. *Indian Society and the Making of the British Empire*. Cambridge: Cambridge University Press, 1988. Vol. 2, 1 of *The New Cambridge History of India*.

Bayly, C. A., *et al.*, eds. *The Raj: India and the British, 1600-1947*. London: National Portrait Gallery, 1990.

Bearce, George D. *British Attitudes towards India 1784-1858*. London: Oxford University Press, 1961.

Berger, Mark T. 'Imperialism and Sexual Exploitation: A Response to Ronald Hyam's 'Empire and Sexual Opportunity'.' *Journal of Imperial and Commonwealth History* 17.1 (1988): pp. 83-9.

Bermingham, Ann. *Landscape and Ideology: The English Rustic Tradition, 1740-1860*. Berkeley: University of California Press, 1986.

Betterton, Rosemary. 'How Do Women Look? The Female Nude in the Work of Suzanne Valadon'. In *Looking On: Images of Femininity in the Visual Arts and Media*. Edited by Betterton. London: Pandora, 1987. pp. 217-34.

Bhabha, Homi K. 'Articulating the Archaic: Notes on Colonial Nonsense'. In *Literary Theory Today*. Edited by Peter Collier and Helga Geyer-Ryan. Cambridge: Polity, 1990. pp. 203-18.

—— ed. *Nations and Narrations*. London: Routledge, 1991.

—— 'Of Mimicry and Man: The Ambivalence of Colonial Discourse'. *October* 28 (1984): pp. 125-33.

—— 'The Other Question'. *Screen* 24.6 (1983): pp. 18-36.

—— 'The Other Question: Difference, Discrimination, and the Discourse of Colonialism'. In *The Politics of Theory*. Edited by Francis Barker *et al.* Colchester: University of Essex, 1983. pp. 148-72.

—— 'Representation and the Colonial Text: A Critical Exploration of Some Forms of Mimeticism'. In *The Theory of Reading*. Edited by Frank Gloversmith. Brighton: Harvester, 1984. pp. 93-122.

—— 'Signs Taken for Wonders: Questions of Ambivalence and Authority under a Tree Outside Delhi, May 181'. In Gates, pp. 163-84.

—— 'Sly Civility'. *October* 34 (1985): pp. 71-80.

Birkett, Dea. *Spinsters Abroad: Victorian Lady Explorers*. Oxford: Blackwell, 1989.

Bivona, Daniel. *Desire and Contradiction: Imperial Visions and Domestic Debates in Victorian Literature*. Manchester: Manchester University Press, 1990.

Blake, Susan. 'A Woman's Trek: What Difference Does Gender Make?'. *Women's Studies International Forum* 13.4 (1990): pp. 347-55.

Blanch, Lesley. *The Wilder Shores of Love*. London: John Murray, 1954.

Bleicher, Thomas. 'Literarisches Reisen als literaturwissenschaftliches Ziel'. *Komparatistische Hefte* 3 (1981): pp. 3-10.

Blunt, Alison. *Travel, Gender, and Imperialism. Mary Kingsley and West Africa*. New York: Guildford, 1994.

Bode, Christoph. 'Beyond / Around / Into One's Own: Reiseliteratur als Paradigma von Welt-Erfahrung'. *Poetica* 26.1-2 (1994): pp. 70-87.

Bolt, Christine. *Victorian Attitudes to Race*. London: Routledge & Kegan Paul, 1971.

Brantlinger, Patrick. *Rule of Darkness: British Literature and Imperialism, 1830-1914*. Ithaca: Cornell University Press, 1988.

Brenner, Peter, ed. *Der Reisebericht. Die Entwicklung einer Gattung in der deutschen Literatur*. Frankfurt/M.: Suhrkamp, 1989.

—— *Der Reisebericht in der deutschen Literatur. Ein Forschungsüberblick als Vorstudie zu einer Gattungsgeschichte*. Tübingen: Niemeyer, 1990.

Bristow, Joseph. *Empire Boys: Adventures in a Man's World*. London: Harper Collins Academic, 1991.

Brown, Charles Hilton, ed. *The Sahibs: The Life and Ways of the British in India as Recorded by Themselves*. London: William Hodge, 1948.

Brown, Paul. "This thing of darkness I acknowledge mine': *The Tempest* and the discourse of colonialism'. In *Political Shakespeare: New Essays in Cultural Materialism*. Edited by Jonathan Dollimore and Alan Sinfield. Manchester: Manchester University Press, 1985. pp. 72-87.

Burman, Sandra, ed. *Fit Work for Women*. London, 1979.

Burton, Antoinette. 'The White Woman's Burden: British Feminists and 'The Indian Woman', 1865-1915'. In Chaudhuri and Strobel, pp. 137-57.

Butler, Judith. *Gender Trouble: Feminism and the Subversion of Identity*. New York: Routledge, 1990.

Buzard, James. *The Beaten Track: European Tourism, Literature, and the Ways to 'Culture' 1800-1918*. Oxford: Clarendon, 1993.

Callan, Hilary, and Shirley Ardener, eds. *The Incorporated Wife*. London: Croom Helm, 1984.

Callaway, Helen. *Gender, Culture and Empire: European Women in Colonial Nigeria*. Basingstoke: Macmillan, 1987.

Campbell, Mary B. *The Witness and the Other World: Exotic European Travel Writing, 400-1600*. Ithaca: Cornell University Press, 1988.

Carrington, Dorothy, ed. *The Traveller's Eye*. London: Pilot, 1949.

Certeau, Michel de. *Heterologies: Discourse on the Other*. Translated by Brian Massumi. Foreword by Wlad Godzich. Minneapolis: University of Minnesota Press, 1988.

Césaire, Aimé. *Discourse on Colonialism*. Translated by Joan Pinkham. New York: Monthly Review 1972.

Chatterjee, Partha. 'Colonialism, Nationalism, and Colonized Women: The Contest in India'. *American Ethnologist* 16 (1989): pp. 622-33.

Chaudhuri, Nirad. 'On Understanding the Hindus'. *Encounter* (June 1965): pp. 20-33.

Chaudhuri, Nupur. 'Memsahibs and Motherhood in Nineteenth-Century Colonial India'. *Victorian Studies* 31.4 (1988): pp. 517-35.

Chaudhuri, Nupur, and Margaret Strobel, eds. *Western Women and Imperialism: Complicity and Resistance.* Bloomington: Indiana University Press, 1992.

Chaudhuri, S. B. *English Historical Writings on the Indian Mutiny 1857-1859.* Calcutta: World, 1979.

Clifford, James. 'On Ethnographic Authority'. *Representations* 2.2 (1983): pp. 118-46.

—— 'Traveling Cultures'. In Grossberg, Nelson, and Treicher, 1992, pp. 96-116.

—— *The Predicament of Culture, Twentieth-Century Ethnography, Literature and Art.* Cambridge, Mass.: Harvard University Press, 1988.

Clifford, James, and George E. Marcus, eds, *Writing Culture: The Poetics and Politics of Ethnography.* Berkeley: University of California Press, 1986.

Cohn, Bernard S. 'The British in Benares: A Nineteenth Century Colonial Society'. *Comparative Studies in Society and History* 4 (1961-2): pp. 169-99.

—— 'Representing Authority in Victorian India'. In Hobsbawm and Ranger, pp. 165-209.

Copley, Stephen, and Peter Garside, eds. *The Politics of the Picturesque: Literature, landscape and aesthetics since 1770.* Cambridge: Cambridge University Press, 1994.

Cott, Nancy. 'Passionlessness: An Interpretation of Victorian Sexual Ideology, 1790-1850'. *Signs* 4.2 (1978): pp. 219-36.

Cox, Edward Godfrey. 'The Old World'. In *A Reference Guide to the Literature of Travel. Including Voyages, Geographical Descriptions, Adventures, Shipwrecks and Expeditions.* Vol. 1. Seattle: University of Washington Press, 1935. 3 vols. pp. 1935-49.

Cronin, Richard. *Imagining India.* Basingstoke: Macmillan, 1989.

Culler, Jonathan. 'The Semiotics of Tourism'. In *Framing the Sign: Criticism and its Institutions.* Norman, Okla.: University of Oklahoma Press, 1989. pp. 153-67.

Davidoff, Leonore. *The Best Circles: Society Etiquette and the Season.* London: Croom Helm, 1973.

Davidoff, Leonore. 'Class and Gender in Victorian England: The Diaries of Arthur J. Munby and Hannah Cullwick'. *Feminist Studies* 5.1 (1979): pp. 87-141.

Davidson, Lilias Campbell. *Hints to Lady Travellers at Home and Abroad.* London, 1889.

Davin, Anna. 'Imperialism and Motherhood'. *History Workshop* 5 (1978): pp. 9-66.

Diver, Maud. *The Englishwoman in India.* Edinburgh: Blackwood, 1909.

Donaldson, Laura E. *Decolonizing Feminisms: Race, Gender and Empire-Building.* London: Routledge, 1992.

Douglas, Mary. *Purity and Danger: An Analysis of Concepts of Pollution and Taboo.* London: Routledge & Kegan Paul, 1966.

Driver, Felix, and Gillian Rose, eds. *Nature and Science: Essays in the History of Geographical Knowledge.* London: Historical Geographical Research Group, 1992.

Dunbar, Janet. *Golden Interlude: The Edens in India 1836-1842.* London: Allan Sutton, 1955.

Dyson, K.K. *A Various Universe: A Study of the Journals and Memoirs of British Men and Women in the Indian Subcontinent, 1765-1856.* New Delhi: OUP, 1978.

Eagleton, Mary, ed. *Feminist Literary Theory: A Reader.* Oxford: Blackwell, 1986.

Ecker, Gisela. *Differenzen: Essays zur Weiblichkeit und Kultur.* Dünen-Hiddingsel: Tende, 1994.

—— ed. *Feminist Aesthetics.* Boston: Beacon, 1986.

Enzensberger, Hans Magnus. 'Eine Theorie des Tourismus'. *Einzelheiten I: Bewusstseins-Industrie.* Frankfurt/M.: Suhrkamp, 1962. pp. 179-205.

Fabian, Johannes. *Time and the Other: How Anthropology Makes Its Object.* New York: Columbia University Press, 1983.

Fanon, Frantz. *Black Skin White Masks.* Translated by Charles Lam Markmann. 1952. London: Pluto, 1967.

—— *The Wretched of the Earth.* Translated by Constance Farrington. 1961. Harmondsworth: Penguin, 1967.

Ferguson, Frances. 'The Sublime of Edmund Burke, or the Bathos of Experience'. *Glyph* 8 (1981): pp. 62-78.

Forbes, Geraldine H. 'In Search of the 'Pure Heathen': Missionary

Women in Nineteenth Century India'. *Economic and Political Weekly* 26 Apr. 1986: pp. 2-8.

Foster, Shirley. *Across New Worlds: Nineteenth-Century Women Travellers and their Writings*. Hemel Hempstead: Harvester, 1990.

Foucault, Michel. *Power/Knowledge: Selected Interviews and Other Writings 1972-1977*. Edited by Colin Gordon. Translated by Colin Gordon, Leo Marshall, John Mepham, Kate Soper. Brighton: Harvester, 1980.

Fowler, Marian. *Below the Peacock Fan: First Ladies of the Raj*. London: Viking, 1987.

Fox-Genovese, Elizabeth. 'Placing Women's History in History'. *New Left Review* 133 (1982): pp. 5-29.

Frankenberg, Ruth, and Lata Mani. 'Crosscurrents, Crosstalk: Race, 'Postcoloniality' and the Politics of Location'. *Cultural Studies* 7.2 (1993): pp. 292-310.

Franklin, Sarah, Celia Lury, and Jackie Stacey, eds. *Off-Centre: Feminism and Cultural Studies*. London: Harper Collins, 1991.

Gamman, Lorraine, and Margaret Marshment, eds. *The Female Gaze: Women as Viewers of Popular Culture*. London: Women's Press, 1988.

Gates, Henry Louis, Jr, ed. *'Race', Writing, and Difference*. Chicago: University of Chicago Press, 1985.

Geertz, Clifford. 'Thick Description: Toward an Interpretive Theory of Culture'. *The Interpretation of Cultures: Selected Essays*. New York: Basic, 1973. pp. 3-30.

—— *Works and Lives: The Anthropologist as Author*. Oxford: Polity, 1988.

George, Rosemary. 'Homes in the Empire, Empires in the Home'. *Cultural Critique* 26 (1993-94): pp. 95-127.

Ghose, Indira. 'Frauen und Imperialismus: Reiseberichte von viktorianischen Frauen in Indien', 1994. In Nestvogel, pp. 70-85.

—— 'Der Memsahib-Mythos: Frauen und Kolonialism in Indien'. *Feministische Studien* 2 (1995): pp. 34-45.

—— 'Miranda and Caliban in India: The Politics of 'Race' and Gender under the Raj'. *Gulliver* 37 (1995): pp. 149-61.

Girouard, Mark. *The Return to Camelot: Chivalry and the English Gentleman*. New Haven: Yale University Press, 1981.

Gordon, Deborah. 'Writing Culture, Writing Feminism: The Poetics and Politics of Experimental Ethnography'. *Inscriptions* 3/4 (1988): pp. 7-26.

Greenberger, Allen J. *The British Image of India: A Study in the Literature of Imperialism 1880-1960*. London: OUP, 1969.

Greenblatt, Stephen J. *Marvellous Possessions: The Wonder of the New World*. Chicago: University of Chicago Press, 1991.

Groot, Joana de. ' 'Sex' and 'Race': The Construction of Language and Image in the Nineteenth Century'. In *Sexuality and Subordination: Interdisciplinary Studies of Gender in the Nineteenth Century*. Edited by Susan Mendus and Jane Rendall. London: Routledge, 1989. pp. 89-128.

Grossberg, Lawrence, Cary Nelson, and Paula Treichler, eds. *Cultural Studies*. London: Routledge, 1992.

Guha, Ranajit, and Gayatri Chakravorty Spivak, eds. *Selected Subaltern Studies*. New York: OUP, 1988.

Haggis, J. 'Gendering Colonialism or Colonising Gender? Recent Women's Studies Approaches to White Women and the History of British Colonialsim'. *Women's Studies International Forum* 13.1/2 (1990): pp. 105-15.

Hall, Catherine. 'The Early Formation of Victorian Domestic Ideology'. In Burman, pp. 15-32.

Hall, Stuart. 'Signification, Representation, Ideology: Althusser and the Post-Structuralist Debates'. *Critical Studies in Mass Communication* 2.2 (1985): pp. 91-114.

Hamalian, Leo. ed. *Ladies on the Loose: Women Travellers of the Eighteenth and Nineteenth Centuries*. New York: Dodd, 1981.

Haraway, Donna. 'A Manifesto for Cyborgs: Science, Technology, and Socialist Feminism in the 1980s'. In Nicholson, 1990, pp. 190-233.

Harbsmeier, Michael. 'Early Travels to Europe: Some Remarks on the Magic of Writing'. In Barker *et al.*, 1985, 1: pp. 72-88.

Hennessey, Rosemary, and Rajeswari Mohan. 'The Construction of Woman in Three Popular Texts of Empire: Towards a Critique of Materialist Feminism'. *Textual Practice* 3.3 (1989): pp. 323-59.

Hibbert, Christopher. *The Great Mutiny: India 1857*. London: Penguin, 1978.

Hipple, Walter John, Jr. *The Beautiful, the Sublime, and the Picturesque in Eighteenth-Century British Aesthetic Theory*. Carbondale: Southern Illinois University Press, 1957.

Hobsbawm, Eric J. *The Age of Empire 1875-1914*. London: Cardinal, 1987.

Hobsbawm, Eric J., and Terence Ranger, eds. *The Invention of Tradition*. Cambridge: Cambridge University Press, 1984.

Hulme, Peter. *Colonial Encounters: Europe and the Native Caribbean 1492-1797*. London: Routledge, 1986.

Hussey, Christopher. *The Picturesque: Studies in a Point of View*. London: Putnam, 1927.

Hutchins, F.G. *The Illusion of Permanence: British Imperialism in India*. Princeton: Princeton University Press, 1967.

Hyam, Ronald. *Empire and Sexuality: The British Experience*. Manchester: Manchester University Press, 1990.

Inden, Ronald. 'Orientalist Constructions of India'. *Modern Asian Studies* 20.3 (1986): pp. 401-46.

Jan Mohamed, Abdul R. 'The Economy of Manichean Allegory: The Function of Racial Difference in Colonialist Literature'. In Gates, 1988, pp. 78-107.

Jedamski, Doris, Hiltgrund Jehle, and Ulla Siebert, eds. *'Und taet das Reisen waehlen! Frauenreisen - Reisefrauen*. Zurich: eFeF, 1994.

Jones, Vivien, ' 'The Coquetry of Nature': Politics and the Picturesque in Women's Fiction'. In Copley and Garside, pp. 120-44.

Kabbani, Rana, *Europe's Myths of Orient*. London: Pandora, 1986.

Kaplan, Ann E. 'Is the Gaze Male?' In *Power of Desire: The Politics of Sexuality*. Edited by Ann Snitow, Christine Stansell and Sharon Thompson. London: Virago, 1984. pp. 309-27.

Kaul, H.K. *Travels in South Asia: A Selected and Annotated Bibliography of Guide-Books and Travel-Books on South Asia*. New Delhi: Arnold-Heinemann, 1979.

Keay, Julia. *With Passport and Parasol: The Adventures of Seven Victorian Ladies*. London: BBC, 1989.

Kiernan, V.G. *The Lords of Human Kind: European Attitudes Towards the Outside World in the Imperial Age*. Harmondsworth: Penguin, 1972.

Kincaid, Dennis. *British Social Life in India 1608-1937*. London: Routledge & Kegan Paul, 1938.

Kohl, Stephan. 'Reiseromane/Travelogues: Möglichkeiten einer 'hybriden' Gattung'. In *Radikalität und Mässigung: Der englische Roman seit 1560.* Edited by Annegret Maack and Rüdiger Imhof. Darmstadt: Wiss. Buchgesellschaft, 1993. pp. 149-68.

Koselleck, Reinhart. 'Zur historisch-politischen Semantik asymmetrischer Gegenbegriffe'. *Vergangene Zukunft: Zur Semantik geschichtlicher Zeiten.* Frankfurt/M.: Suhrkamp, 1979. pp. 211-59.

Kröller, Eva-Marie. 'First Impressions: Rhetorical Strategies in Travel Writing by Victorian Women'. *Ariel: A Review of International English Literature* 21.4 (1990): pp. 87-99.

Kuczynski, Ingrid. 'Reisende Viktorianishce Frauen und der koloniale Diskurs'. *Gulliver* 34.2 (1993): pp. 10-26.

Kuhn, Annette. *Women's Pictures: Feminism and Cinema.* London: Routledge & Kegan Paul, 1982.

Lauretis, Teresa de. 'Displacing Hegemonic Discourses: Reflections on Feminist Theory in the 1980s'. *Inscriptions* 3/4 (1988): pp. 127-43.

Leask, Nigel. *British Romantic Writers and the East: Anxieties of Empire.* Cambridge: Cambridge University Press, 1992.

—— 'Francis Wilford and the Colonial Construction of Hindu Geography 1799-1822'. Paper given at Romantic Geographies Conference at Glasglow. 27 Sept. 1994.

Levy, Anita. *Other Women: The Writing of Class, Race, and Gender, 1832-1898.* Princeton: Princeton University Press, 1991.

Lewis, Reina. ' 'Only Women should go to Turkey': Henriette Browne and Women's Orientalism'. *Third Text* 22 (1993): pp. 53-64.

Liddle, Joanna, and Rama Joshi. 'Gender and Colonialism: Women's Organisation under the Raj'. *Women's Studies International Forum* 8.5 (1985) pp. 521-29.

—— 'Gender and Imperialism in British India'. *Economic and Political Weekly*, 26 Oct. 1985: pp. 72-8.

Lind, Mary Ann. *The Compassionate Memsahib: Welfare Activities of British Women in India, 1900-1947.* New York: Greenwood, 1988.

Low, Gail Ching-Liang. 'White Skins/Black Masks: The Pleasures and Politics of Imperialism'. *New Formations* 9 (1989): pp. 83-104.

Lowe, Lisa. *Critical Terrains: French and British Orientalisms.* Ithaca: Cornell University Press, 1991.

Macaulay, Thomas Babington. 'On Education for India'. In *Imperialism.* Edited by Philip D. Curtin. London: Macmillan, 1971. pp. 178-91.

MacKenzie, John M. *Propaganda and Empire: The Manipulation of British Public Opinion 1880-1960.* Manchester: Manchester University Press, 1984.

—— ed. *Imperialism and Popular Culture.* Manchester: Manchester University Press, 1986.

—— 'The Imperial Pioneer and Hunter in the British Masculine Stereotype in Late Victorian and Edwardian Times'. In *Manliness and Morality: Middle-Class Masculinity in Britain and America 1800-1940.* Edited by J.A. Mangan and James Walvin. Manchester: Manchester University Press, 1987. pp. 176-98.

—— 'Geography and Imperialism: British Provincial Geographical Societies'. In *Nature and Science: Essays in the History of Geographical Knowledge.* Edited by Felix Driver and Gillian Rose. London: Historical Geographical Research Group, 1992. pp. 49-62.

—— 'Edward Said and the Historians'. *Nineteenth-Century Contexts* 18 (1994): pp. 9-25.

MacMillan, Margaret. *Women of the Raj.* London: Thames & Hudson, 1988.

Majeed, Javed. *Ungoverned Imaginings: James Mill's* The History of British India *and Orientalism.* Oxford: Clarendon, 1992.

Malik, Salahuddin. 'Nineteenth-Century Approaches to the Indian 'Mutiny' '. *Journal of Asian History* 7 (1973): pp. 95-127.

Mamozai, Martha. *Herrenmenschen: Frauen im deutschen Kolonialismus.* Reinbek: Rowohlt, 1982.

—— *Komplizinnen.* Reinbek: Rowohlt, 1990.

Mani, Lata. 'Cultural Theory, Colonial Texts: Reading Eyewitness Accounts of Widow Burning'. In Grossberg, Nelson, and Treichler, pp. 392-408.

—— 'The Production of an Official Discourse on Sati in Early Nineteenth-Century Bengal'. In Barker *et al.* 1: pp. 107-27.

Mannoni, O. *Prospero and Caliban: The Psychology of Colonization.* Translated by Pamela Powesland. 1956. New York: Praeger, 1964.

Mannsaker, Frances M. 'East and West: Anglo Indian Social Attitudes as Reflected in Popular Fiction, 1890-1914'. *Victorian Studies* 24 (1980): pp. 33-51.

Masani, Zareer. *Indian Tales of the Raj.* London: BBC, 1987.

Mason, Peter. *The Deconstruction of America.* Dissertation. University of Utrecht, 1990.

Mason, Philip. *Prospero's Magic: Some Thoughts on Class and Race.* London: OUP, 1962.

McBratney, John. 'Images of Indian Women in Rudyard Kipling: A Case of Doubling Discourse'. *Inscriptions* 3/4 (1988): pp. 47-57.

Melman, Billie. *Women's Orients: English women and the Middle East, 1718-1918; sexuality, religion and work.* Basingstoke: Macmillan, 1992.

Memmi, Albert. *The Colonizer and the Colonized.* Boston: Beacon, 1965.

Middleton, Dorothy. *Victorian Lady Travellers.* London: Routledge & Kegan Paul, 1965.

Miles, Robert. *Racism.* London: Routledge, 1989.

Mills, Sara. 'British Women Travel Writers in India: Discourses of Colonialism and Femininity'. Paper to the ACLALS Conference, Kent. 1988.

—— *Discourses of Difference: An Analysis of Women's Travel Writing and Colonialism.* London: Routledge, 1991.

—— 'Gender and Colonialism: Discourses of Difference'. Paper to the Gender and Colonialism Conference, UCG, Galway, Ireland, 1992.

—— 'Knowledge, Gender and Empire'. In *Writing, Women and Space: Women's Colonial and Postcolonial Geographies.* Edited by Alison Blunt and Gillian Rose. New York: Guildford, 1994. pp. 29-51.

Mitter, Partha. *Much Maligned Monsters: History of European Reactions to Indian Art.* Oxford: OUP, 1977.

Mohanty, Chandra Talpade, Ann Russo, and Lourdes Torres, eds. *Third World Women and the Politics of Feminism.* Bloomington: Indiana University Press, 1991.

Mohanty, Chandra Talpade. 'Under Western Eyes: Feminist Scholarship and Colonial Discourses'. *Boundary* 2.3 (1984): pp. 333-58. Reprinted in Mohanty, Russo, and Torres, pp. 51-80.

Mohanty, S.P. 'Kipling's Children and the Colour Line'. *Race & Class* 31.1 (1989): pp. 21-40.

—— 'Us and Them: On the Philosophical Bases of Political Criticism'. *New Formations* 8 (1989): pp. 55-80.

Montagu, Lady Mary Wortley. *Letters.* 1763. Reprinted in *Embassy to Constantinople: The Travels of Lady Mary Wortley Montagu.* Edited by Christopher Pick. London: Century, 1988.

Moore-Gilbert, B.J. *Kipling and 'Orientalism'.* London: Croom Helm, 1986.

Morgan, Susan. 'An Introduction to Victorian Women's Travel Writings about South-East Asia'. *Genre* 20 (1987): pp. 189-208.

Mudford, Peter. *Birds of a Different Plumage: A Study of British-Indian Relations from Akbar to Curzon*. London: Collins, 1974.

Mukherjee, Rudrangshu. ' 'Satan Let Loose Upon Earth': The Kanpur Massacres in India in the Revolt of 1857'. *Past and Present* 128 (1990): pp. 92-116.

Mulvey, Christopher. *Anglo-American Landscapes: A Study of Nineteenth-Century Anglo-American Travel Literature*. Cambridge: Cambridge University Press, 1983.

Mulvey, Laura. 'Visual Pleasure and Narrative Cinema'. *Screen* 16.3 (1975): pp. 6-18.

—— 'Afterthoughts on 'Visual Pleasure and Narrative Cinema' inspired by Duel in the Sun'. *Framework* 15/16/17 (1981): pp. 12-15. Reprinted in *Feminism and Film Theory*. Edited by Constance Penley. New York: Routledge, 1988. pp. 69-79.

Nair, Janaki. 'Uncovering the Zenana: Visions of Indian Womanhood in Englishwomen's Writings, 1813-1940'. *Journal of Women's History* 2.1 (1990): pp. 8-34.

Nandy, Ashis. 'Sati: A Nineteenth-Century Tale of Women, Violence and Protest'. *At the Edge of Psychology: Essays in Politics and Culture*. New Delhi: OUP, 1980. pp. 1-31.

—— *The Intimate Enemy: Loss and Recovery of Self Under Colonialism*. 1983. New Delhi: OUP, 1988.

Nestvogel, Renate, ed. *'Fremdes' oder 'Eigenes'? Rassismus, Antisemitismus, Kolonialismus, Rechtsextremismus aus Frauensicht*. Frankfurt/M.: IKO, 1994.

Nicholson, Linda J., ed. *Feminism/Postmodernism*. London: Routledge, 1990.

Nochlin, Linda. 'The Imaginary Orient'. *Art in America* (May 1983): pp. 119-90.

Nussbaum, Felicity A. *The Autobiographical Subject: Gender and Ideology in Eighteenth-Century England*. Baltimore: Johns Hopkins University Press, 1989.

Oaten, Edward Farley. *A Sketch of Anglo-Indian Literature*. London: Kegan Paul, 1908.

Ong, Aihwa. 'Colonialism and Modernity: Feminist Re-Presentations of

Women in Non-Western Societies'. *Inscriptions* 3/4 (1988): pp. 79-93.

Parker, Andrew, Mary Russo, Doris Sommer, and Patrick Yaeger. 'Introduction'. *Nationalisms and Sexualities*. Edited by Parker *et al.* London: Routledge, 1992. pp. 1-18.

Parry, Benita. 'Problems in the Current Theories of Colonial Discourse'. *Oxford Literary Review* 9.1-2 (1987): pp. 27-58.

—— *Delusions and Discoveries: Studies on India in the British Imagination 1880-1930*. London: Allen Lane Penguin, 1972.

Paxton, Nancy L. 'Disembodied Subjects: English Women's Autobiography under the Raj'. In *De/Colonizing the Subject: The Politics of Gender in Women's Autobiography*. Edited by Sidonie Smith and Julia Watson. Minneapolis: University of Minnesota Press, 1992. pp. 387-409.

—— 'Feminism Under the Raj: Complicity and Resistance in the Writings of Flora Annie Steel and Annie Besant'. *Women's Studies International Forum* 13.4 (1990): pp. 333-46.

Pease, Donald E. 'Sublime Politics'. *Boundary* 2 (Spring/Fall 1984): pp. 259-79.

Pelz, Annegret. *Reisen durch die eigene Fremde: Reiseliteratur von Frauen als autogeographische Schriften*. Cologne: Böhlau, 1993.

Pfister, Manfred. 'Bruce Chatwin and the Postmodernization of the Travelogue'. *Literature Interpretation Theory* 7 (1996): pp. 253-67.

—— ed. *The Fatal Gift of Beauty: The Italies of British Travellers. An Annotated Anthology*. Rodopi: Amsterdam, 1996.

—— 'Still Going Strong: The Loneliness of the Long-Distance Traveller'. With Indira Ghose. *Journal for the Study of British Cultures* 3 (1996): pp. 149-64.

Pinney, Christopher. 'Colonial Anthropology in the 'Laboratory of Mankind' '. In Bayly *et al.*, pp. 252-63.

—— 'Representations of India: Normalisation and the 'Other' '. *Pacific Viewpoint* 29.2 (1988): pp. 144-62.

Porter, Dennis. *Haunted Journeys: Desire and Transgression in European Travel Writing*. Princeton: Princeton University Press, 1991.

Pratt, Mary Louise. *Imperial Eyes: Travel Writing and Transculturation*. London: Routledge, 1992.

—— 'Scratches on the Face of the Country; or, What Mr. Barrow Saw in the Land of the Bushmen'. In Gates, 1988, pp. 138-62.

Price, Martin. 'The Picturesque Moment'. In *From Sensibility to Romanticism: Essays Presented to Frederick A. Pottle*. Edited by Frederick W. Hilles and Harold Bloom. New York: OUP, 1965. pp. 259-92.

Prochaska, F.K. 'Women in English Philanthropy 1790-1830'. *International Review of Social History* 19 (1974): pp. 426-45.

Punter, David. 'The Picturesque and the Sublime: Two Worldscapes'. In Copley and Garside, pp. 220-39.

Ramusack, Barbara N. 'Cultural Missionaries, Maternal Imperialists, Feminist Allies: British Women Activists in India, 1865-1945'. In Chaudhuri and Strobel, pp. 119-36.

Riddick, John F., ed. *Glimpses of India: An Annotated Bibliography of Published Personal Writings by Englishmen, 1583-1947*. New York: Greenwood, 1989.

Robinson, Jane. *Wayward Women: A Guide to Women Travellers*. Oxford: OUP, 1990.

Rosaldo, M.Z. 'The Use and Abuse of Anthropology: Reflections on Feminism and Cross-cultural Understanding'. *Signs* 5 (1980): pp. 389-417.

Rose, Gillian. 'Geography as a Science of Observation: The Landscape, the Gaze and Masculinity'. In Driver and Rose, pp. 8-18.

Russell, Mary. *The Blessings of a Good Thick Skirt: Women Travellers and their World*. London: Collins, 1986.

Russell, William Howard. *My India Mutiny Diary*. Edited by Michael Edwardes. London: Cassel, 1957.

Said, Edward W. *Orientalism*. London: Routledge & Kegan Paul, 1978.

—— *Culture and Imperialism*. London: Chatto & Windus, 1993.

Sandison, Alan. *The Wheel of Empire: A Study of the Imperial Idea in Some Late Nineteenth and Early Twentieth-Century Fiction*. London: Macmillan, 1967.

Sangari, Kumkum and Sudesh Vaid, eds. *Recasting Women: Essays in Colonial History*. New Delhi: Kali for Women, 1989.

Schäffter, Ortfried. 'Modi des Fremderlebens. Deutungsmuster im Umgang mit Fremdheit'. In *Das Fremde: Erfahrungsmöglichkeiten zwischen Faszination und Bedrohung*. Edited by Schäffter. Opladen: Westdt. Verlag, 1991. pp. 11-42.

Schupf, Harriet Warm. 'Single Women and Social Reform in Mid-Nineteenth Century England: The Case of Mary Carpenter'. *Victorian Studies* 17.3 (1974): pp. 301-17.

Scott, Joan Wallach. *Gender and the Politics of History*. New York: Columbia University Press, 1988.

Sharpe, Jenny. *Allegories of Empire: The Figure of Woman in the Colonial Text*. Minneapolis: University of Minnesota Press, 1993.

—— 'The Unspeakable Limits of Rape: Colonial Violence and Counter-Insurgency'. In Williams and Chrisman, pp. 221-43.

Shattock, Joanne. 'Travel Writing Victorian and Modern; A Review of Recent Research'. In *The Art of Travel: Essays on Travel Writing*. Edited by Philip Dodd. London: Cass, 1982. pp. 151-64.

Simons, Margaret A. 'Racism and Feminism: A Schism in the Sisterhood'. *Feminist Studies* 5.2 (1979): pp. 384-401.

Sinha, Mrinalini. ' 'Chathams, Pitts, and Gladstones in Petticoats': The Politics of Gender and Race in the Ilbert Bill Controversy, 1883-1884'. In Chaudhuri and Strobel eds. pp. 98-116.

—— 'Colonial Policy and the Ideology of Moral Imperialism in Late Nineteenth-Century Bengal'. In *Changing Men: New Directions in Research on Men and Masculinity*. Edited by Michael S. Kimmel. London: Sage, 1987. pp. 217-31.

Sleeman, William. 'The Story of Bysa Bae'. Unpublished ms, India Office Library and Records.

Smith, Sidonie. *A Poetics of Women's Autobiography: Marginality and the Fictions of Self-Representation*. Bloomington: Indiana University Press, 1987.

Spear, Percival, and Romila Thapar. *A History of India*. 2 vols. London: Penguin, 1966.

Spivak, Gayatri Chakravorty. 'Can the Subaltern Speak? Speculations on Widow Sacrifice'. *Wedge* 7/8 (1985): 120-30. Reprinted in *Marxism and the Interpretation of Culture*. Edited by Cary Nelson and Lawrence Grossberg. Urbana: University of Illinois Press, 1988. pp. 271-313.

—— 'Imperialism and Sexual Difference'. *Oxford Literary Review* 8.1-2 (1986): pp. 225-40.

—— *In Other Worlds: Essays in Cultural Studies*. New York: Methuen, 1987.

—— 'The Rani of Sirmur'. In Barker *et al.* 1: pp. 128-51.

—— 'Three Women's Texts and a Critique of Imperialism'. *Critical Inquiry* 12.1 (1985): pp. 243-61. Reprinted in Gates, pp. 262-80.

Spurr, David. *The Rhetoric of Empire: Colonial Discourse in Journalism,*

Travel Writing, and Imperial Administration. Durham: Duke University Press, 1993.

Stacey, Jackie. 'Desperately Seeking Difference'. In Gamman and Marshment, pp. 112-29.

Stafford, Barbara Maria. 'Toward Romantic Landscape Perception: Illustrated Travels and the Rise of 'Singularity' as an Aesthetic Category'. *Studies in Eighteenth Century Culture* 10 (1981): pp. 17-75.

Stallybrass, Peter, and Allon White. *The Politics and Poetics of Transgression*. London: Methuen, 1986.

Stanford, J.K., ed. *Ladies in the Sun: The Memsahibs' India, 1760-1860*. London: Galley, 1962.

Stevenson, Catherine Barnes. *Victorian Women Travel Writers in Africa*. Boston: Twayne, 1982.

Stokes, Eric. *The English Utilitarians and India*. Oxford: Clarendon, 1959.

Stoler, Ann L. 'Making Empire Respectable: The Politics of Race and Sexual Morality in 20th-Century Colonial Cultures'. *American Ethnologist* 16 (1989): pp. 634-60.

Strelka, Joseph. 'Der literarische Reisebericht'. *Jahrbuch für internationale Germanistik* 3 (1971): pp. 63-75.

Strobel, Margaret. *European Women and the Second British Empire*. Bloomington: Indiana University Press, 1991.

Suleri, Sara. *The Rhetoric of English India*. Chicago: University of Chicago Press, 1992.

Summers, Anne. 'A Home from Home — Women's Philanthropic Work in the Nineteenth Century'. In Burman, pp. 33-63.

The Marxist-Feminist Literature Collective. 'Women's Writing: Jane Eyre, Shirley, Villette, Aurora Leigh'. *Ideology and Consciousness* 3 (1978): pp. 27-48.

Thomas, Nicholas. *Colonialism's Culture: Anthropology, Travel and Government*. Oxford: Polity, 1994.

Thompson, Edward. Introduction. *Up the Country: Letters written to her Sister from The Upper Provinces of India*, By Emily Eden. London: OUP, 1930. pp. ix-xiv.

Thürmer-Rohr, Christine. 'Wir sind nicht Reisende ohne Gepaeck: Fragen der letzten zwei Jahre an die weisse westliche Frauenbewegung'. In *Entfernte Verbindungen: Rassismus, Antisemitismus,*

Klassenunterdrückung. Edited by Ilka Hügel *et al.* Berlin: Orlando, 1993: pp. 188-204.

Tisdall, E.E.P. *Mrs. Duberly's Campaigns: An Englishwoman's Experiences in the Crimean War and the Indian Mutiny*. London: Jarrolds, 1963.

Trollope, Joanna. *Britannica's Daughters: Women of the British Empire.* London: Pimlico, 1983.

Vicinus, Martha, ed. *A Widening Sphere: Changing Roles of Victorian Women*. Bloomington: Indiana University Press, 1977.

Visweswaran, Kamala. 'Defining Feminist Ethnography'. *Inscriptions* 3/4 (1988): pp. 27-46.

Waal, E.de. 'Travel'. *The New Cambridge Bibliography of English Literature.* Edited by George Watson. Vol. 3. Cambridge: Cambridge University Press, 1969: pp. 1669-84. 4 vols. 1969-77.

Ware, Vron. *Beyond the Pale: White Women, Racism and History*. London: Verso, 1992.

Weigel, Sigrid. 'Der schielende Blick. Thesen zur Geschichte weiblicher Schreibpraxis'. In *Die verborgene Frau: Sechs Beiträge zu einer feministischen Literaturwissenschaft*. Edited by Sigrid Weigel and Inge Stephan. Berlin: Argument, 1983: pp. 83-137.

White, Hayden. *Metahistory: The Historical Imagination in Nineteenth-Century Europe*. Baltimore: Johns Hopkins University Press, 1973.

—— 'The Historical Text as Literary Artifact'. *Clio* 3.3 (1974): pp. 277-303.

—— 'The Politics of Historical Interpretation: Discipline and De-Sublimation'. *Critical Inquiry* 9.1 (1982): pp. 113-37.

Williams, Patrick, and Laura Chrisman, eds. *Colonial Discourse and Post-Colonial Theory: A Reader*. Hemel Hempstead: Harvester, 1993.

Williams, Patrick. 'Colonial Literature and the Notion of Britishness'. *Literature Teaching Politics* 5 (1986): pp. 92-107.

Winks, Robin W. and James R. Rush, eds. *Asia in Western Fiction*. Manchester: Manchester University Press, 1990.

Wittig, Monique. 'One is Not Born A Woman'. *Feminist Issues* 1.2 (1981): pp. 47-54.

Wolff, Janet. 'On the Road Again: Metaphors of Travel in Cultural Criticism'. *Cultural Studies* 7.2 (1993): pp. 224-39.

Yang, Anand A. 'Whose Sati? Widow Burning in Early 19th Century India'. *Journal of Women's History* 1.2 (1989): pp. 8-33.

Yegenoglu, Meyda. 'Supplementing the Orientalist Lack: European Ladies in the Harem'. *Inscriptions* 6 (1992): pp. 45-80.

Young, Robert. *White Mythologies: Writing History and the West.* London: Routledge, 1990.

Young, Shelagh. 'Feminism and the Politics of Power: Whose Gaze is it Anyway?' In Gamman and Marshment, pp. 173-88.

Youngs, Tim. *Travellers in Africa: British Travelogues 1850-1900.* Manchester: Manchester University Press, 1994.

Index